CARRIE CAROLYN COCO

Also by Sarah Gerard

True Love

Recycle

Sunshine State

Binary Star

CARRIE CAROLYN COCO

My Friend, Her Murder,

and an Obsession with

the Unthinkable

SARAH GERARD

zando

NEW YORK

zandoprojects.com

First Edition: July 2024

Text design by Aubrey Khan
Cover design by Tyler Comrie

The publisher does not have control over and is not responsible for author or other third-party websites (or their content).

Library of Congress Control Number: 2023949184

978-1-63893-046-4 (Hardcover)
978-1-63893-047-1 (ebook)

10 9 8 7 6 5 4 3 2 1
Manufactured in the United States of America

For Carolyn

Contents

List of Characters

CAROLYN'S FAMILY

Susan Balfe
her mother

James "Jim" Bush
her father

Cynthia "Cindy" Marden Bush
her stepmother

Jennifer "Jenny" Schatz
her sister

Michael "Mike" Schatz
her brother-in-law

Ann Caywood
her maternal aunt

Carol Balfe Heidausen
her maternal aunt

Edith "Edie" Balfe
her maternal grandmother

John McKinstry "Mac" Balfe
her maternal grandfather

Carolyn Bush Adams
her paternal aunt

Robin Vance
her paternal aunt

Ruth McKinstry Balfe
her maternal great-grandmother

John Hilton "Grandjohngee" Balfe
her maternal great-grandfather

CAROLYN'S CIRCLE (IN ORDER OF APPEARANCE)

Gabriel "Gabe" Kruis
her colleague at Wendy's Subway

Emily Reilly
her friend, Gabe's partner

Pamela Tinnen
her friend since childhood

Ally
her cat

Cameron Seglias
her friend from Bard

Alexis Graman
her friend from Bard

Moira Donegan
her friend from Bard

Maximus "Max" Agrio
her friend from Bard

Matthew "Matt" Ossias
her paramour

Christine Pfister
her friend from Bard

Danielle Sinay
her friend from Bard

Elizabeth "Lizzy" Crawford
her friend from Bard

Kevin Cassem
her friend from Bard and
Wendy's Subway colleague

Christopher "Chris" Prioleau
her paramour and Wendy's
Subway colleague

Adjua Greaves
her colleague at Wendy's Subway

Rachel Valinsky
her colleague at Wendy's
Subway

Matthew "Matt" Longabucco
her colleague at Wendy's
Subway

Macgregor "Mac" Card
her colleague at Wendy's
Subway

Emily Toder
her colleague at Wendy's
Subway

Michael Assiff
her paramour

Casey Romaine
her friend from Bard

Allison "Ally" Davis
her friend from Bard

Taylor "Iggy" Isaacson
her freshman roommate
at Bard

Masha Mitkov
her friend from Bard

Amanda Roper
her friend since high school

Alexis Novak
her high school teacher

Paula de la Puente
her friend since third grade

Samantha "Sam" Mancino
her friend since middle school

Callie Kocemba
her friend since middle school

Taylor Lambert
her friend since high school

Allyson Erwin
her friend since middle school

Adrienne Tish
her friend since high school

Wolf Willette
her friend since high school

Devon Lopez
her friend since high school

Ian Taylor
her friend since high school

Erin Hart-Parke
her friend since high school

Amalia "Mali" Scott
her roommate on Stanhope Street

Francesca Capone
an early supporter of Wendy's
Subway

Simon Critchley
a philosopher and her professor at
The New School

Rachel Hurn
her former coworker at McNally
Jackson Books

Rachel Levitsky
her writing workshop teacher

RENDER'S FAMILY

Janet Stetson
his mother

Daniel "Danny" Shanahan
his father

Finnegan "Finn" Shanahan
his brother

Betty Jean Stetson
his maternal grandmother

Chandler Alton Stetson
his maternal grandfather

Bonnie Stetson
his maternal aunt

Diana Stetson
his maternal aunt

RENDER'S CIRCLE (IN ORDER OF APPEARANCE)

Sofia Bonami
his on-again, off-again
girlfriend since college

Arun Saxena
his friend since kindergarten

Gregg Haefelin
his former employer in
Rhinebeck

Tamas "Tommi" Panitz
his friend from Bard

Leon Botstein
the president of Bard

Dylan Mattingly
a friend of Finn's from Bard

Thomas Bartscherer
his professor at Bard and
collaborator with Dylan
Mattingly

David Shein
his advisor, associate VP for
academic affairs and dean of
studies at Bard

Gennady Shkliarevsky
his history professor and
academic advisor at Bard

Seth Oclatis
his friend since kindergarten

Jane Smith
his professor, asst. dir.
Bard Learning Commons,
visiting instructor of
writing

Ira Gutner
his former employer at
Samuel's Sweet Shop

John Traver
his former coworker and
the current manager-
partner of Samuel's
Sweet Shop

Patrick Mangan
his coworker at Atelier 4

Sean Rucewicz
his friend from Bard

NEIGHBORS OF CAROLYN AND RENDER (IN ORDER OF APPEARANCE)

Joshua Cruz
their neighbor in the basement
on Stanhope Street

Pat Castellar
their building manager and
neighbor on the ground floor
on Stanhope Street

Rachel Cavell
his neighbor in Rhinebeck
and Janet's colleague
at Bard

Norton Batkin
his neighbor in Rhinebeck
and Janet's colleague at Bard,
Cavell's husband

Lisa Ilene Cahn
his neighbor in Rhinebeck

Mark Lytle
his neighbor in Rhinebeck and
senior thesis advisor at Bard

WITNESSES (IN ORDER OF APPEARANCE)

Officer Onur Cumur
a responding officer

Sergeant Charles Choi
a responding officer

Officer Vahan Bayizian
the officer who rode with Render
in the ambulance

Dr. David Cherkas
Render's ER doctor

Dr. Alexander Sasha Bardey
the defense's expert forensic
psychiatrist

Officer Gregory Teti
a responding officer

Dr. Sean Kelly
the autopsy surgeon

Dr. Kostas Katsavdakis
the prosecution's expert forensic
psychologist

LAWYERS (IN ORDER OF APPEARANCE)

Philip Middler
Render's attorney at the arraignment

ADA Jack Warsawsky
the original prosecutor

ADA Brian Hughes
the trial prosecutor

Justice Richard Buchter
the judge

Zachary Margulis-Ohnuma
Render's cocounsel

Philip Smallman
Render's cocounsel

OTHER BARD STUDENTS, FACULTY, AND ADMINISTRATORS (IN ORDER OF APPEARANCE)

Erin Cannan
the vice president for civic engagement at Bard

Katherine "Kate" Blake
a Bard student and victim of stabbing

Henry Pfeffer
a Bard student and Blake's boyfriend

Jane Brien
the director of Alumni/ae Affairs at Bard

Martha Tepepa
a former recruiter for the Levy Economics Institute at Bard

Jan Kregel
the former director of the Levy Economics Institute, Tepepa's husband

Sara Davis
a Bard alum

Wayne Lo
a student at Bard College at Simon's Rock who perpetrated a deadly mass shooting

Bernard "Bernie" Rodgers
the former vice president and dean of students of Simon's Rock

Ba Win
the former provost of Simon's Rock

Amanda Harris
a Bard alum

Ken Cooper
the former director of security at Bard

Eric Holzman
a former professor of drawing and painting at Bard

Anna Jones
a Bard student and victim of murder

Tor Loney
a Bard alum and Jones's boyfriend

Mark Primoff
Bard's director of
communications

Allannah Capwell
the former director of the
Institute for Writing &
Thinking at Bard

"Penelope"
a Bard alum

Nicola Maye Goldberg
a Bard alum

Robert Kelly
a poet and the former
director of the Written
Arts division at Bard

Christopher Qualiano
a Bard alum

**OTHERS (IN ORDER OF
APPEARANCE)**

Melkorka Licea
a *New York Post* reporter

Patrick Cottrell
author's husband

Officer James Knight
a police officer from Florida

TyRon Lewis
a victim of shooting death
by Knight

Eugene Young
Lewis's friend, a witness to
his shooting

Officer Sandra Minor
Knight's partner

Robert Hutchins
the former president of the
University of Chicago

Leo Strauss
a political philosopher and
former professor at the
University of Chicago

Gregory Gibson
an author and the father of
one of Wayne Lo's victims

Marcus Molinaro
the former mayor of Tivoli,
New York

"Isaac"
a man stalking Carolyn

Commissioner Davis
a parole commissioner

Commissioner Drake
a parole commissioner

Commissioner Segarra
a parole commissioner

Author's Note

Directly quoted writing has retained original spelling and punctuation. To reconstruct Carolyn's story in her own voice, I have gathered her language from text messages, emails, blog posts, poems, essays, social media, and interviews with many of her loved ones in which they recollected their experiences and correspondences with her. Many scenes in this book appear as dramatizations of people's interactions with Carolyn over text and social media. Some have been reconstructed from people's memories and do not represent verbatim conversations.

1.

Stanhope

/'stanhōp, ˌstanəp/
1. a light open horse-drawn carriage for one person
2. an optical device that enables the viewing of a
   microphotograph without a microscope

In September 2016, my friend Carolyn Bush's older sister, Jennifer Schatz, came to visit her in New York City. At twenty-five, "Carrie" was nearly seven years younger than Jenny but, with the same alabaster skin and deep-brown hair, could have been mistaken for her sister's twin. The two had always been best friends, inseparable from the day Carolyn was born.

Jenny's employer rewards those who have been with the company for five years with a five-week paid sabbatical and a thousand-dollar grant, which she had used to book a four-day journey by train from Portland, Oregon, to see her sister. It followed the one-year anniversary of her wedding, at which Carolyn had been maid of honor. Jenny and her husband, Mike, had celebrated their anniversary with a road trip to San Francisco and through the redwood forests. "Then I came home and got on a train, took the train alone in a sleeper cabin, out to New York City to be with Carrie," Jenny says. She stayed a week in Carolyn's second-floor apartment at 1861 Stanhope Street in Ridgewood, Queens.

That year, Carolyn had told their mother that she probably wouldn't have children and possibly wouldn't even marry. Jenny says now that she told her sister she supported her: "Maybe she wasn't going to have a wedding"—or even finish college—but "I was going to be there to celebrate her choices the way that she had come out and celebrated mine, my boring, boring choices."

During Jenny's stay, she and Carolyn went to the Wendy's Subway Next Wave Art Reading Room installed at the Brooklyn Academy of Music, in Fort Greene. As a founding board member of the nonprofit reading room and library, Carolyn was responsible for running a poetry reading for Wendy's Subway that night. Dia Felix, Ricardo Maldonado, and Dorothea Lasky were the readers. Afterward, the sisters went out for drinks at a restaurant called No. 7, nearby. Carolyn's friend Gabriel Kruis, also a poet and founding board member of Wendy's, and his new partner, Emily Reilly, accompanied them.

Gabe has a warm and patient demeanor, and he and Carolyn had grown to be good friends in the years since Wendy's Subway's founding. They exchanged poetry and enjoyed debating philosophy and turning over metaphysical and religious topics together. Sometimes they playfully butted heads. "Scorpio season was upon us," says Gabe, who calls Carolyn "Coco." "Emily, Coco, and I, all being Scorpios, struck up a conversation with our waiter, who was also a Scorpio." The waiter told them about the "three phases" of their sign: Scorpion, Eagle, and Phoenix.

"Everyone was in very high spirits and Coco seemed very happy to have her sister in town," says Gabe. It was funny seeing them together. He had always thought of Carolyn's mannerisms as so distinct. Now he could see they were family traits. *Oh wow, the way you shake my hand*, he thought, upon meeting Jenny. *This bright and steely apprehension of things, still somehow warm.* The Bush sisters had a unique intensity. "Her gestures had a profound effect on my ability to process certain emotions that I might've had a difficult time venting in the past," Gabe says of Carolyn. She and Jenny embodied the world similarly. "They seemed really close."

Aside from the reading, most of that week was spent at 1861 Stanhope, where the sisters cooked together, listened to music, and generally "holed up." "I don't care for New York," says Jenny. She'd visited enough in her twenties, when her best friend, Pamela Tinnen, was still earning her master's in curatorial studies at NYU, where she now works as a curator. Pamela had known the sisters since she and Jenny were in sixth grade, and she describes her relationship with them as familial. Jenny agrees. As much as Pamela was best friends with Carolyn, too, she was perhaps even more like another big sister. People had actually assumed she was Carolyn's sister, especially after Jenny left for college. Carolyn had basically replaced Jenny as Pamela's roommate in Saint Petersburg, Florida. Now Pamela had moved around the corner from Carolyn in Ridgewood, and they had keys to each other's apartments.

"That whole trip was about trying to get to know Carrie's life in New York and understanding Wendy's Subway," says Pamela. Jenny wanted to understand why Carolyn loved New York so much, but she told Carolyn that she didn't want to go into Manhattan. "Carrie never really went into Manhattan anyway, except for school," says Jenny. But upon arriving, Jenny had discovered that Carolyn was not enrolled in classes at The New School that semester. It was a point of contention. She had enrolled there part-time in a program for self-directed study, to finish the bachelor's degree she began at Bard College in 2009. After finishing, she intended to pursue a PhD in literature, or medieval studies, or poetry, or something in between.

"She had decided to delay for another semester, and was working her ass off independently, but wasn't actively in school," Jenny says. They'd had a little argument about it. "She told me she was going to be in school and I wanted to be very respectful of that, and when I arrived, I realized she wasn't." Jenny was afraid that Carolyn had delayed enrolling in classes because of her visit, but she did not want to get in the way of her sister's academic pursuits. "She got kicked out of Bard College," Jenny says, four years earlier. "She flunked out."

Instead of doing touristy things, they went to the farmers market and Jenny put together a big cheese plate with tomatoes. Tomatoes were their thing. Then she made soup and helped Carolyn clean out her closet. Meaning, Jenny sat atop Carolyn's fluffy white comforter, on her wide comfy bed, while her sister took out every piece of clothing she owned and modeled it for Jenny for three or four hours, while Jenny drank wine and said, "Not that, get rid of that. Oh, I love that." They had always helped each other make these decisions, and historically their style had been similar: feminine vintage pieces, in Carolyn's case, with a bit of edge. That day, they took three trash bags of clothes to sell at Beacon's Closet, then came back and spent the night talking.

Carolyn's name was the only one on unit 2A's lease. She had moved into 1861 Stanhope Street in February 2014, after several years of short-term living arrangements, the same year the *New York Times* profiled Ridgewood as "the latest up-and-coming neighborhood." Artists priced out of the increasingly trendy Williamsburg and Bushwick neighborhoods had crept east with the L subway line in recent years. Now Ridgewood was filled with "Broke millennials, underemployed artists, craven property speculators, fearful natives and first-time homeowners," the *Times* described. "Cafés with vegan muffins, yoga studios and destination pizzerias have (naturally) sprouted. Bars with names like Milo's Yard and Bierleichen are slated to open. Guitar cases, tote bags and shearling coats are increasingly frequent accessories on pedestrians."

Carolyn's apartment was an eight-minute walk from the L train on a mostly treeless residential block near a small park and a cemetery. Built in 1905, it was a pale two-story brick row house converted into upper and lower apartments, with roof access, a wraparound gate in front, stone archways over the windows, and a molded plaster overhang decorated in faux garlands. Next door was a moving company, and on the other side was a neighborhood pharmacy.

The small vestibule of the building's front entrance opened onto a stairwell leading up into her unit. Apartment 2A occupied the entire second story and had wood floors, decorative ceiling tiles painted white, crown molding, and some greenery beyond the many windows, a rarity in this neighborhood.

Carolyn's roommate, Render Stetson-Shanahan, had moved in a year after her, relocating to the city from Rhinebeck, New York (his hometown ninety-eight miles north, where he'd lived with his parents), with a six-month stop in between, at the apartment of family friends on the Upper East Side. His bedroom was bigger than hers, and the stairs outside his door led down into the building's vestibule. They shared a bathroom. The living room was furnished with a leather couch, an entire wall of bookshelves, and a coffee table. To the right of the living room, through another archway, was a spacious kitchen. Carolyn loved to cook. She kept labeled jars of spice mixtures in her cabinets, including some used for spell casting.

Adjacent to Render's bedroom was a walk-in closet, which at first had been his to use but which Carolyn had recently negotiated taking back. Though tiny, it had become a sort of mini guest room, which she used as an office and sometimes slept in when she would Airbnb her bedroom to pay the rent. She kept some of her clothes on a rolling rack in her bedroom and would roll it into the walk-in closet on those occasions as well. Pamela had slept in the small room when she Airbnb'ed her own apartment, and Jenny slept there when she was in town too.

Carolyn's bedroom was smaller than Render's, but she had easier use of the common areas. Her door was to the left of the living room and opened onto it. Render rarely used the living room. Like the hallway closet, Carolyn's bedroom shared a wall with Render's room. When Airbnb guests stayed in it, he was surrounded: they were on one side of his room, and Carolyn was on the other.

Like Carolyn, Render was an alum of Bard College. He was a year ahead of her; he is older than Carolyn by exactly nine months, February 19, on the cusp of Aquarius and Pisces, to her November 19 Scorpio. They linked through another Bard alum after Carolyn's first roommate in 2A moved to California. Carolyn described Render to Pamela as the ideal roommate because he paid his rent reliably and rarely left his room when he was there, which wasn't often.

Despite spending a good deal of time at Carolyn's, Pamela seldom saw Render. She'd interacted with him directly only once when she couldn't get the front door open, and Carolyn texted him to let her in. He ran down, opened the door, then ran back into his room without even saying hello. She remembers thinking it was kind of weird. They may have said hi in passing otherwise, but he never stopped to chat or ask how she was. "He was the kind of person who would wait until you were animatedly having a conversation in the living room so that he could sneak into the bathroom and not have to say hello," she says.

Jenny spent most of her week in New York with Carolyn, but there was one night near the end of her stay when she texted Pamela to say she was craving spaghetti. Carolyn was out doing something and Jenny had the night to herself. Pamela invited her over. "She just came in and commandeered the kitchen," says Pamela, and she started asking for spices she didn't have. Pamela isn't a slouch cook, but both Carolyn and Jenny had learned to cook from their dad, and Jim Bush was a star in the kitchen. He'd cooked for the family throughout their childhoods, and that night, Jenny wanted comfort food.

"So, what's the deal with the roommate?" Jenny asked Pamela over the spaghetti. "I haven't laid eyes on him." She'd met him briefly in the hallway when she'd first arrived but hadn't seen him since; he just stayed in his room. She'd asked Carolyn at one point, "Doesn't he hate the fact that we're being loud and staying up all night and talking in the kitchen and smoking cigarettes and blah, blah, blah, in the house?" Carolyn had brushed it off. "No, it's fine. He's fine."

"I remember Jenny saying that she was worried about Carrie, the direction of her life," says Pamela. "What's going on with Carrie? Is she going to be okay?" Jenny had asked her. Carolyn was not always totally forthcoming; she could keep certain things private or compartmentalized. She wasn't secretive, just selective about what she shared. "I didn't even know that Carrie got kicked out of Bard," Pamela says. Jenny told her that night while they were eating spaghetti. "It's not something she talked about." She wonders if Carolyn was embarrassed about it; she had high expectations for herself. "Remember being twenty-five?" says Pamela. "Outwardly, you presented as excited and adventurous, up for any challenge, but inwardly, you were terrified of failing."

"She just wanted to be in the city," she says. At times it was a struggle; New York can be ruthless. Pamela's own parents didn't want her to go there. "They would have been very happy if I moved back to Florida and worked at Walmart," she says. As long as she was nearby. All that did was make her want to prove them wrong.

There's a sense, at least to those living in New York, in which the resilience of the city's inhabitants is born of the necessity to rationalize away their collective suffering with delusions of superiority, via that same suffering, as though their ability to survive—and "thrive at times," as Carolyn had put it—in extreme circumstances makes them better, stronger, more determined than others. While Jenny has always disliked New York, "she really, really leans into the Pacific Northwest," says Pamela. When she visits Jenny in Portland, everything is quaint and picturesque: "We're going to the farmers market, and everything is so beautiful." As a New Yorker, Pamela thinks, "Loser, don't you want to be in this disgusting place with these mutant pigeons?" She imagines this was Carolyn's thinking too.

"I was so excited about who she was going to be," says Pamela. "She was figuring everything out." Jenny had a hard time finishing college as well, repeatedly dropping out in the middle of the semester and graduating from Portland State University at twenty-eight.

Pamela thinks about that when she remembers her conversation with Jenny. Maybe Jenny hadn't wanted Carolyn to struggle like she had. "Carrie mentally has her shit together," Pamela recalls telling Jenny. "She knows who she is. The rest will work itself out."

After dinner they walked to Aunt Ginny's, a new neighborhood bar with a kitchen and a pool table. Carolyn met them there wearing a black dress that showed off her legs; wherever she was coming from, she had wanted to look vampy. They sat outside under an umbrella while Jenny smoked. Pamela was stressed about work.

Once Jenny finished her cigarette, they found a booth inside. They had the place to themselves. Carolyn went to the bar and came back with a beer and a shot of well whiskey. Her sister and Pamela teased her. "Is she always going to be that cool, or will she outgrow it like we did?" They all did the photo booth—Pamela still has the pictures.

Finally, Pamela was tired and had to go. "I didn't really want to. I just couldn't stay awake anymore." Jenny and Carolyn walked her out, and they stood smoking under the streetlamps. Over the years, when Pamela had hung out with the sisters together, there'd been a palpable big-sister-little-sister dynamic between them, but she remembers feeling they were all friends that night, "like Carrie was a peer, and just happened to be a little younger." It was a warm and happy feeling. "I felt like we were all on the same level, vibing, enjoying ourselves."

Pamela wouldn't be seeing Jenny again this trip; for their last night together the following day, Jenny and Carolyn were going out just the two of them. "I wanted to have a special meal to remind us of being in this moment, and so we decided that we would do the very New York thing and go to Russ & Daughters," Jenny says. Carolyn was excited about getting to eat organ meat after reading *Nourishing Traditions*, a tome from the 1990s about eating it "combined with lacto-fermented pickles," Jenny says, and "how that was the healthy thing." Of course, now those things are all the rage. The sisters also wanted caviar and Bellinis.

Pamela said goodbye. She remembers Jenny saying, "Come to Portland," because that's what she always says.

"She certainly doesn't want to come back to New York," says Pamela.

Then Carolyn said something like, "I'll see you at your thing next week."

Then Pamela walked home.

"That was the last time I saw her," she says.

• • •

On the night of September 28, 2016, around 8:00 p.m., Render arrived at his brother Finnegan's apartment. He had brought his set of power tools with him to make a desk in Finn's bedroom smaller. He's good with tools and Finn is not. Render had worked in construction in Rhinebeck since he was a teenager and was currently employed as a crater for the art-handling company Atelier 4, in the city. The job required physical fitness, and Carolyn had told her aunt that Render went to the gym often. Finn, on the other hand, is a classical composer and freelance musician and studied violin at Bard, two years behind Render.

According to Finn, as each other's only siblings, he and Render were quite close in childhood and remained friends into adulthood. They closely resemble each other, nearly identical in the face, though Finn is shorter and slenderer, and Render wears a beard and mustache. Their coloration is similar: white men with wood-brown hair. They're both handsome.

The desk only took Render half an hour. Afterward, Finn went across the street to the deli for a case of beer. Within the hour, the brothers ordered pizza. Finn invited a friend to come over and hang out with them. They watched TV, drank beer, and ate the pizza. "At this point in time he was perfectly amiable, [in] perfectly good spirits, friendly to everyone that was in the apartment," Finn would later testify. That included Finn's girlfriend and a friend of hers, who were mostly hanging out in another room, not interacting with the guys. Finn said Render was "visibly under the influence" but acting normal.

Render told Finn he'd started seeing his ex-girlfriend, Sofia Bonami, again, within the last two weeks. He felt good about it and hoped they were going to stay together this time. He'd slept over at her East Village apartment the night before and they'd had sex. Sofia would say later that the morning afterward was awkward and emotional. "Between two people that don't know what's going on, it was uncertain," she'd say. "It was uncomfortable for me."

In recent months, Render and Sofia had discussed his disaffection with New York and with Ridgewood specifically. They'd also talked about moving in together, though that conversation had stalled since they'd broken up in May. They had grown apart, and it felt to her that "he was suffering from a depression that seemed to be consuming him." It was painful to let go of a relationship that had defined their early adulthoods—they had first met as juniors at Bard—but both felt it was the right choice.

Render, Finn, and his friend were smoking weed too. Finn had bought it through a friend, who had gotten it from an underground delivery service. The three smoked it from a pipe. Finn had been smoking weed since he was fourteen and still smoked weekly.

Soon after smoking, Render texted Sofia to say he'd hit a milestone in his life: "Sof, my brother got me high."

She was surprised; Render rarely smoked weed.

"I've never smoked with my brother before," he said, calling the product "serious weed from Colorado."

She texted him back, "Ha ha ha."

"I have only been this high like two other times in my life," he responded. "And he and his friend are even higher and they're just talking about weed. My brother is one of those guys who talks about weed when he smokes weed. Sof, I'm so high right now."

"Oh my God, stop calling me Sof ha ha," she said.

A little while later, he texted her again. "I'm at my brother's. Are you there?"

"Yeah," she responded. "Are you okay? Do you want to come here?" She lived alone.

"Yeah, I'm about to go home," he responded. "No, I'm good. I have stuff with me I have to drop off at home."

"Okay. Will you let me know when you get there?" she said.

"I will," he said.

"Be careful sweetie, all right?"

"I will, Bubba."

Finn could tell Render was tired and knew that he had to work early the next day. "He said his farewells and made a point of saying goodnight to everybody that was there, and gave everybody hugs," he would testify. Render left in an Uber between 10:45 and 11:00 p.m.

Sofia texted him again while he was in the Uber. "How you feeling?"

"Great," he responded. "I love you."

Four minutes went by, and she didn't respond. Then Render called her. This was the first of two three-minute calls between them, made at 11:08 and 11:14. "Render called me and he sounded very jittery," Sofia later testified, "and his voice, he was speaking very fast. I couldn't really . . . his voice was at a kind of different register than normal and he wasn't really making much sense. And he was trying to find a way to come to Manhattan. He sounded very disoriented, like he was on the street. It sounded like he wasn't wearing shoes."

She was scared. She heard him yelling at someone. "The whole phone call was highly alarming," she said. She had never witnessed Render like this. "He didn't seem to know where he was and I was trying to make sure he could be okay. I was just trying to help him figure out where he was." She asked him, but he couldn't give her an answer. "I may have suggested he go home, but I don't recall." She asked him if he could get an Uber to her apartment and texted him her address. He said okay and hung up.

She texted Finn, who at this point was watching a movie with his friend. She and Finn didn't have a close personal relationship, but they knew each other well enough, since she had been dating his brother on and off for six years. "Finn, what the fuck is wrong with Ren?" she said. "I'm so pissed right now. He's on the street alone freaking out and I don't know where he is." She had texted Render again saying, "Can you send me your location?" He didn't respond.

"Really?" Finn replied.

"Yes."

"Let me call him."

"This is not good."

"He's fine."

"No, he said he wasn't dressed. Did you talk to him?"

"He smoked weed at my place and I think he's just super not used to it. He was acting normally here, but I'm sure he's not used to it and that's why he was being weird."

Finn called him. He asked Render why Sofia was so freaked out and what was going on. "He was outside of his apartment," Finn later testified. "In the first phone call that I had with him he described why Sofia had been . . . why he had thought Sofia had been disturbed, and in explaining, he said that he was trying to be almost like Superman and run to her, go to her apartment." Render was talking quickly, like he was on fast-forward, and didn't seem able to finish his thoughts. "It was a very short phone call," said Finn. "Though confused, I believed that the situation seemed okay enough to hang up." He returned to the movie.

At 11:14, Sofia called Render back. It sounded as though he had gone inside from the street and calmed down a bit. He apologized for scaring her. He said that he had to check on Carolyn. He thought he had scared her too. "And then he said he was just super high and he needed to sleep, and I tried to keep talking but then he hung up."

"Oh my God," Sofia texted Finn. "He said he's home now. I think he just fell asleep."

"He just talked to me and he's being really silly," Finn replied. "I'm just trying to make sure he is home and safe."

"You don't know his roommate's name, do you?" Sofia responded.

"No, I forget," said Finn. "He told me he was just getting home. I'm going to his apartment now in an Uber just to make sure he's okay."

• • •

At 11:15 p.m., Render and Carolyn's downstairs neighbor, Joshua Cruz, left the basement apartment of 1861 Stanhope to put a load of laundry in at the Laundromat two blocks away. He had lived in the building on and off for the last nine years with his mother and was employed as a security guard at the time. The basement apartment had a separate entrance in the building's backyard, down an alley that Joshua and his mother accessed through a metal door to the left of the main entrance. He was in the alley, returning to the apartment to get another couple of loads, at 11:20, when he heard Carolyn scream twice, on the second floor, only he didn't realize it was Carolyn. Another neighbor had a rodent problem and she'd sometimes ask him to handle it.

He looked up but heard nothing more, and no one came outside. He exited the alleyway to the front, through the metal door, to see Render exiting the main entrance of 1861 Stanhope. Render was talking on the phone, approaching a car parked in the street. Joshua had met Carolyn before and knew her by name because the mailman had once accidentally put a letter for her in his mail. He'd delivered it to her in person. He had never seen or heard Render before. Render was dressed only in boxers, with blood on his stomach. The night was chilly; other passersby on the street wore coats. One of them, seeing Render, crossed the street quickly and ran away. Joshua couldn't tell whether or not the blood on Render's stomach was from an injury.

"I think I am not going to have a lease anymore," Render said into his phone. Joshua was unable to hear the other side of the conversation. The person on the other end was Finn.

Render held in his hand a Spartan-George V-14 Dagger, 6¾ inches long and ¼ inch wide, with "an ergonomic and textured handle specifically designed for maximum comfort and a confident grip," according to the company's website, where it sells for $495. "Simply put," the site reads, "this is a true combat dagger!"

Render had posted it on Reddit exactly one month earlier, next to a Lucas Forge ProSkinner knife with an aged oak handle, with the caption, "Started a new collection this year."

As Joshua watched, Render shattered the window of a car with the hilt of the dagger. Joshua tried to take cover back in the alleyway. Before he could get away, Render noticed and approached him. Joshua remembers him saying, "I've never seen you before," in an even tone of voice. Joshua was close enough to notice his eyes were blue and that he didn't smell of alcohol or marijuana. Render was aggressive, but he didn't seem like he was under the influence of anything. He asked Joshua what his name was. He thrust the dagger at him, missing him, and Joshua backed up and shut the metal door between them.

Joshua called 911 and watched through the gate as Render continued down Stanhope, south toward Onderdonk Avenue. He told the 911 dispatcher there was an "armed white man popping people's windows."

Render was still on the phone, Joshua said. When he reached the corner of Onderdonk, he hurled the phone overhand across the street, "like a pitcher would throw a ball."

Then he turned around and approached 1861 Stanhope again, smashing another car window with the dagger. He came within eight feet of Joshua, who had exited the alleyway and was standing behind the low metal fence encircling the building's courtyard, to watch Render. Hearing Joshua on the phone with NYPD, Render said,

"Yeah, tell them I'm upstairs," and reentered the building. Joshua ran out into the middle of the street to flag down the police.

Render's second phone call with Finn had prompted him to call the police as well. He dialed as he was leaving his apartment. "In the second phone call that I made to him I heard footsteps," Finn said, "and heavy breathing, and what sounded like a confrontation with somebody, as well as glass breaking."

"Did he say something was wrong?" Sofia texted him.

Finn responded, "He seemed to be in a fight, I called 911 to be safe."

Sofia asked who the fight was with and what Finn had said to the 911 operator. By this point she was on her way over as well.

"It sounded like he was in a fight and I heard yelling, and he said he had a cut on his leg," Finn replied.

Hearing that Render was injured, Sofia also decided to call 911. Then she tried to call Render four times. He didn't answer.

"Oh my god, I hope he's okay," she texted Finn. She said the 911 operator had told her an ambulance was on the way. Finn replied that he was the one who had called it.

. . .

Officer Onur Cumur arrived on the scene of 1861 Stanhope along with two other officers within minutes of receiving a radio run for an assault in progress with a knife. Upon arriving, he noticed blood on the sidewalk. Joshua directed them to the second floor.

Cumur yelled "Police!" as he went upstairs. There was blood on the steps and on the landing. He remembers a man responding, "I don't have any weapons."

Cumur entered apartment 2A. He reached the landing, also bloody, and in the first bedroom, at the top of the stairs, Cumur found Render lying on his back on his bed, in his underwear. There was blood on the bed and on the floor.

"What happened?" said Cumur. Render said he stabbed himself. Cumur observed a two-inch stab wound to his right thigh. He asked Render what had happened and called for an ambulance.

"I was upset," he recalls Render saying in a normal tone of voice, not seeming to be in any pain.

Cumur asked if anyone else was in the house.

Render said his roommate was. Then Cumur recalls that he said, "I stabbed her. She's in the other room."

Cumur asked if there was a reason he'd stabbed her.

He remembers Render telling him, "I won't give any confessions but I stabbed her. I just went up to her, she was on the phone. She didn't have a chance to react. I went up to her and said, 'Guess what?' And I stabbed her."

Cumur surveyed the room. Render directed him to the dagger standing upright in the floor, its blade sunk into the wood. He told Cumur there was another one in a drawer. Cumur searched the drawer and found the ProSkinner wrapped in a piece of clothing.

. . .

At 11:28 p.m., Sergeant Charles Choi was dispatched to an assault in progress, a woman stabbed. He arrived at 1861 Stanhope approximately three minutes later. Other units were already on the scene, and he followed other officers upstairs. On the landing, he looked through the entryway to the living room and saw Carolyn, unconscious, lying in a large pool of blood in the doorway of her bedroom, with stab wounds to her throat, shoulder, back, and arm. EMTs arrived within two and a half minutes, but there was too much blood in her bedroom to start care on her there, so they pulled her into the living room. When they rolled her over onto her back, she took her last breath. They started chest compressions and ventilations. When paramedics arrived, they administered IV fluids and surgically bypassed her severed trachea, to give her oxygen.

In the ambulance, they cleared the blood from her chest and were able to apply cardiac monitor pads to get an EKG. Carolyn's heart showed no electrical activity. She was pronounced dead at Wyckoff Medical Center.

At about 11:45, Render said to Sergeant Choi, "I stabbed her. I am not making any more confessions after that."

Officer Gregory Teti heard him say: "I stabbed her, then myself."

• • •

Sofia was still on her way. "I am confused," she texted Finn. "I thought he went to bed." Finn thought so too. He reached the scene about fifteen minutes before she did. Render was being led out of the apartment in handcuffs.

"He is safe, he is alive, he is in trouble, though," Finn texted Sofia. Render looked completely dazed. Finn had seen him less than an hour earlier, and now he looked like he was in shock. Being led by officers, Render was able to see and look at Finn, but he "didn't quite look like he understood fully who I was." Finn called his name and Render turned toward him. "He seemed almost unaware of his surroundings." Render's leg was bandaged. He was cuffed to a stretcher and loaded into an ambulance.

By the time Sofia arrived, Render was gone. Stunned, she didn't even notice the blood on the street. She found Finn. This was the first time the two of them had ever been at Render's apartment together. Both were taken to the 104th precinct for interviews.

• • •

Render was transported to Elmhurst Hospital. According to Officer Vahan Bayizian, in the ambulance, Render said, "I drank a lot of beer, I smoked some weed at my brother's house. I then took an Uber back to my house. I called my girlfriend. I stabbed myself."

He arrived at Elmhurst just before 12:15 a.m., with "blood on all four extremities." Dr. David Cherkas treated him in the ER. "He didn't have any apparent paralysis or severely altered mental state," said Cherkas, but he seemed to have a "constricted affect." In other words, he wasn't very interactive. Usually, people who come in after being involved in violent crimes, whether victims or perpetrators, are agitated or emotional, so this struck Cherkas as strange. He ordered a psychiatric evaluation.

"His recollection of the events in question is sketchy and, as such, his story is disjointed," Render's hospital report reads. "The cannabis was not his and the patient is unsure of whether it was all cannabis or some other drug. He reports taking an Uber home to his apartment in Queens, 1861 Stanhope Street. Patient remembers getting into bed then getting out of bed and calling his girlfriend. After this, patient states he remembers running down the street trying to flag down cars to catch a ride to his girlfriend's home in Manhattan. Patient states that he was smashing car windows with a knife, but he cannot recall how he came into possession of the knife. Patient suspects that his stab wound was self-inflicted, but he is unsure of this. He also states, 'I think I may have hurt someone.' He recalls his brother, police and firetrucks, as well, stating that he is currently in a dream-like state. Patient reports feeling depressed lately due to financial and occupational stress, but denies any history of treatment. He currently denies suicidal or homicidal ideation. When asked if had been hallucinating, patient stated, 'It's hard to say.'"

2.

Ally

"It matters which beings recognize beings."
-Donna J. Haraway, *Staying with the Trouble*

arolyn's maternal aunts, Ann Caywood and Carol Heidausen,
are eating pizza across the street from the Queens Criminal
Courthouse in Kew Gardens, New York. Outside, sleeting rain has
turned the city block into a frigid gray sarcophagus. Carol is drinking
a beer. It's December 2019, and they've just heard testimony from the
father of the man who murdered Carolyn. Ann is older than Susan
Balfe, Carolyn's mother, and Carol is younger, and the two are nearly
identical to their sister with their high cheekbones and sharp, all-seeing
eyes. "Susan and I were like best friends growing up," Carol had told
me earlier. "In a lot of ways, Carrie matured because Jenny was older
than her. Maybe that's why I related to Carrie, as well, because I hung
out with Susan. I was always looking up to Susan."

Pamela sits across from them, next to me in the booth. She's also
drinking beer, even though the only options are cheap domestics. Her
blonde bangs fall in her eyes. Everyone is tired, wet, cold, and hungry.
They're exchanging stories of the morning of September 29, 2016,
when they learned Carolyn was dead.

"Susan had been hanging up on the detective the morning it happened for several hours," says Carol, "saying—"

"Because she couldn't accept it."

"Saying that this has got to be a bad joke."

"She'd hang up," says Ann. "And he'd call back again."

"She couldn't face it that day."

"And she called me about five o'clock, hysterical," says Ann. "And said, 'We've got to get somebody up there to identify her.'" Ann imagined Carolyn had been hit by a car, but not dead—only difficult to identify for some reason. "Susan never told me she was dead. I figured she was in the hospital, unconscious, and they wanted to make damn sure the wallet they found with her went to her."

"And then you knew that she was dead," says Carol.

"Then she called back," says Ann. "Susan called back." By that time, Ann's husband was already making airline reservations. Ann arrived in Florida the same day, Carol a day later. Susan struggles with her health and couldn't travel to New York to identify Carolyn; she would be cared for by Ann and Carol back in Florida.

"I asked Carrie a thousand times" about Render, Susan would later tell me over text. I had gotten in touch with Carolyn's family in 2017, when I first started researching her murder. But every time Susan would ask Carolyn about Render, she would shrug and say, "He's the perfect roommate. He's never there. He went to Bard. What more do you need to know?"

"That's all I had," Susan told me. "She was private about damn near everything. She was open and honest, happy and lovey and cheerful and cooperative and all that, yes. When it came to deep shit that she was unsure of, I don't know. The kid was over twenty-one."

Susan kept telling herself, *She wants to be a grown-up. I should let her be a grown-up.* But it was hard. She would text Carolyn but only hear back on one of every three texts. This went on for two or three years. Finally, Susan would ask her, "Are you alive?" and hear back, "Yes." The last time they saw each other, Carolyn had let Susan brush her hair and tuck her into bed. "She was somehow different," Susan told me. "Maybe she was just growing up."

Jim Bush and Cindy Marden Bush, Carolyn's father and step-mother, had celebrated their ninth wedding anniversary on September 28, the night Carolyn died. On the morning of the twenty-ninth, at five thirty, the phone rang. It was the detective, calling him after Susan.

"Jim had been the one to tell me," says Pamela, drinking her beer. "He was on his way to the airport to catch a flight to JFK." He was flying to New York City with Cindy to identify Carolyn. "He told me over the phone that he'd need my help," she says, "and then he started to cry. I told him of course."

• • •

After receiving the news from Jim, Pamela was lying on the floor of her friend's apartment, down the street from the NYU Kimmel Galleries. She had been on her way to work when he called, then redirected her route. She was afraid to call Jenny. They had known each other since Carolyn was in kindergarten. She picked up the phone and watched her fingers move over the screen, disembodied, dialing Jenny's number, and pressing the call button before she could stop herself. *Carrie is dead* repeated over and over in her mind.

Jenny answered. Their conversation was recorded in the subterranean zone of memories never meant to be exhumed. "Endorphins are so strange," Pamela remembers Jenny saying. "I feel like I'm on ecstasy." Pamela hung up to make the round of calls to friends from childhood, sharing the news, because "that's what you're supposed to do," though it felt like someone else was doing it. Even her own thoughts felt like someone else's. "They'd been scooped out and I was just a human body making human body movements," she would later write.

"I didn't think she was murdered," Pamela says. She too thought Carolyn had been in a car accident or something. Somehow, she learned that whatever happened had made headlines. She told her friend to look up the story.

He read the first article. "Look, he probably had a sexual fixation for her," he said. She'll never forget how true that statement seemed. He read other articles, relaying the facts. He said that it had happened at Carolyn's home. That she had been stabbed. "It would have been quick," he said, though there was no way for him to know that.

He told her not to read the articles, but she would, a week later, drinking half a bottle of Buffalo Trace in the process. She would email each reporter, one by one, to tell them what horseshit it was to write stories with titles like "Artist Fatally Stabs Female Roommate" because Carolyn was the real artist, and her murderer was "just some psycho-pathic piece of shit who probably wanted to fuck her and didn't know how to deal with it."

• • •

Jim met Pamela at her apartment that first evening after the murder. He had just identified Carolyn's body from a picture on a computer screen at the medical examiner's office. Pamela made tea and put out cookies. Jim sat at her kitchen table, and she asked about Carolyn's cat. He didn't know she had one.

Jim called the detective, who called the cops still stationed outside the apartment, which would remain a crime scene for months. It had only been fourteen hours, and police would be at the building around the clock for another six days. No one had seen a cat, but Pamela insisted, repeating over and over: "She has a cat. The cat's name is Ally. She's black. We have to find the cat. It shouldn't be in there." Finally, something she could fixate on, so she latched on hard. The police said they'd look again for Ally. "I hate cats, but I couldn't stop thinking about that damn cat and how she was in there all by herself with the whole mess and everything."

When Jim left to go check into his hotel, Pamela poured a glass of red wine and called Jenny's other best friend in Seattle. "I started to cry for the first time since I found out what happened," she says.

• • •

As news of what had happened spread, Carolyn's friends started two online fundraisers, separately, to raise funeral expenses for the family. "We didn't need money to bury Carrie," Jenny says. The campaigns hadn't been authorized by her family, which tried to tamp them down before realizing they could just donate the money to Wendy's Subway. "We raised a lot of money for them, and I'm glad we did," says Jenny. "It meant a lot to Carrie."

In one of the campaigns, a friend recalls Carolyn sharing what a great roommate she'd had in Render, and how well they got along. "It was a seemingly ideal housing situation," she writes. She herself had lived with Carolyn in a rambling old house in Red Hook, New York, five minutes from Bard, while they both were students there. Their relationship had deeply affected her. "Coco, you are missed by a sea of anguished people."

One friend among many taking to Facebook describes smoking on a fire escape with Carolyn; talking about *Cléo de 5 à 7* and drinking wine from paper cups with her; sitting in a circle on the floor and listening to Éliane Radigue; sitting on a radiator one August night, talking about astrology; Coco asking him what he was translating, and how he was genuinely moved by her warmth and interest. He remembered seeing her recently in NYU's Bobst Library, in the West Village, where she often would spend days writing.

"Jenny does have sensitivity about things," says Pamela. "All of the people posting nice things about Carrie on her Facebook," it confused her. "Who are all these people?" Jenny had asked her. She had never heard of any of them. "Jenny is and should always be the queen in that regard. That was her baby sister," says Pamela.

Jenny's husband, Mike, did most of the talking for her for about six months, while she was incapacitated from grief and unable to speak about what had happened. "I don't want to upset Jenny ever," Pamela says now. "So I don't bring it up."

"Me too," says Carol. "When you lose someone, it's hard. People generally want to hear about that person and talk about them. But I don't think that's true for Jenny."

"Jenny and I, we've said some things, we had some stories, and then it'll be like, 'Okay, new subject.' Very quickly," says Pamela.

"Now I am fundamentally alone in a way I can't describe," Jenny would write in her victim-impact statement. "Carrie held all the keys to my past," and their futures were meant to be shared. "We were going to live next door to each other, grow tomatoes in the space between our houses." She often thinks of the days when their parents will have passed, and there will be no one left who truly knows her, aside from her husband. "A day will come soon when I will carry my memories of my childhood entirely alone. It will make me unknowable, and in a way Carrie and I will both be gone for good."

I remember finding that in the margins of Carolyn's copy of Simone Weil's *Gravity & Grace*, she had written, "Time heals all wounds, unless the desired body ceases to exist. Then it is a wound, disembodied."

"Susan has said, 'Jenny may look like a big, strong girl. Inside she's a little, tiny, fragile . . .' You never get that from looking at her," says Ann.

"She's very sensitive," says Pamela. "Jenny feels things very deeply."

"Carrie was way stronger than her sister," says Carol.

"I don't know what Carrie would have been like in five years," says Pamela. "But Carrie always had a lot of 'I'm not going to give up' bravado."

"Absolutely," says Carol. "That's what I saw."

"What you think is bravado of youth I feel would have carried forth forever," says Pamela. "She wasn't going to be knocked down."

. . .

Police found Ally that night. They called Jim, who told Pamela to meet him outside of Carolyn's apartment. She walked over, the few blocks. Pamela had moved nearby because it's important to have friends as neighbors in case something bad happens. "But something bad did happen and there wasn't anything to be done," she says. "I was ten minutes away and I had no idea what was happening while she was dying."

As she walked she looked down at her shoes, placing one in front of the other, lit by the orange-yellow lampposts on Onderdonk Avenue. She looked up and saw she was approaching Stanhope, barricaded with police cars and yellow tape. Jim was already there. He offered Pamela a cigarette. "I took it because if there were ever a reason to start smoking again, this was it." There was blood all over the sidewalk and glass everywhere.

"Suddenly my head felt light, like when I was a little kid." She used to pass out whenever she skinned her knee. "Jim told me I looked pale, and I dropped the cigarette." She puked up the wine and it splattered over the shards of broken glass, mixing with the dried blood. A cop caught her as she started to faint. He took her to the back of a police van, where he laid her down and gave her water and a cold compress. She felt her blood pressure plummet. *If Render hadn't run outside*, she thought, *and no one had called the police, he might not have been arrested. If he hadn't been arrested, he might have covered up the murder. Carolyn could be a missing person.*

In the pizza parlor, she reconstructs this scene for Ann and Carol. Our conversation over lunch has centered on a collective sense of overwhelm. A trial is a series of minute details held up and examined through a prism, scattering bright sober light in every direction: on a time stamp on the closed-circuit footage, the weather that evening, the pleading opinion of a father. The trial started the week of Thanksgiving 2019. At this point we've sat through over a dozen hours of argument and testimony. We've seen the surveillance footage from across the

street, showing Render's confrontation with Joshua Cruz. We've
heard Cruz. We've heard the testimony of the responding officers and
EMTs. We've just now heard Render's best friend, Arun Saxena, and
his father, Danny Shanahan. We obsessively analyze the minutia.

"It was Render's phone found outside?" Ann asks. "What made
him drop it? Does that come up?"

"He was punching, beating up on a car," says Pamela.

"And he dropped it at that time?"

No. Render smashed the Subaru's window with the hilt of the dagger, accosted Cruz, and then continued shouting into his phone at
Finnegan, "I think I am not going to have a lease anymore," as he
proceeded toward Onderdonk. Then he hung up and tossed his phone
overhand across the street. "Like a pitcher would throw a ball," Cruz
testified.

"There was glass everywhere," says Pamela, her eyes focused on
her memory.

"If he punched, his hands would be bloody," says Ann, "if he broke
windows."

"That's true."

A reasonable guess, but no one had mentioned that his hand was
injured. Plus, he was later able to stab the dagger into the wood floor.

"Car glass pretty much stays together," says Carol.

"It would break the knife," says Ann.

It didn't.

The police had seen Ally, but she kept hiding. Finally, someone
caught her. An officer brought her out to Pamela, who had somewhat
recovered and was sitting up in the police van, color drained from her
face. She pressed the all-black cat against her chest and walked back to
her apartment. Upstairs, she turned off the lights and fell asleep on top
of her covers.

3.

It Was Like I Was

Someone Else

"Dissect him how I may, then, I but go skin deep;
I know him not, and never will."
—Herman Melville, *Moby-Dick*

On the morning of Friday, September 30, 2016, Render was arraigned on charges of second-degree murder, second-degree menacing, and fourth-degree criminal possession of a weapon. If convicted, he faced up to twenty-five years to life in prison. He wore a white shirt and gray sweatpants to the arraignment, clothes that one reporter would write were stained with blood. At the family's request, Render's lawyer for the arraignment, Philip Middler, asked the judge for a psychiatric evaluation to be performed on his client. On the court's request for a mental health evaluation, the judge wrote, as the reason for the evaluation, "used deceased as contact info."

Later that day, Melkorka Licea visited Render at Rikers Island's Anna M. Kross Center (AMKC), which houses a mental health ward. Back then, as a daily breaking-news reporter for the *New York Post*, Melkorka was expected to publish between two and six stories a week. Coming up with original ideas and writing them to completion in four days was a lot of work, she says, sitting in a pastry shop in Williamsburg.

Breaking news daily required nonstop research and reporting, "really a six-day-a-week job," she says.

Melkorka had read about Carolyn's murder in the first news reports. "I live really close to where they lived," she says. "Blocks away." Herself, Carolyn, and Render were in the same age group and seemed to have similar interests. "I might as well try and talk to him and see what happened from his perspective," she decided.

Melkorka arrived at AMKC in the morning. "I ended up getting in, which is kind of hard," she says. "I just went. We do that a lot at tabloids, jailhouse interviews. The only way is you can't alert them in advance. You just show up and get through all the security." There are multiple buses you have to take and screenings you have to go through. She wasn't allowed to bring a recording device inside, or even a pen. For that reason, quotes in jailhouse interviews are not expected to be 100 percent accurate; instead, the reporter is expected to make her best effort to be faithful. Melkorka says that she left her pen in an available locker and wrote down as much as she could remember as soon as their meeting was over.

At AMKC, there are many waiting rooms that you have to pass through in successive order. The last one has visitors seated at a long table. The incarcerated person is notified they have a visitor but not told who is visiting: it could be their mother, a total stranger, or a reporter. "It's nerve-racking," she says.

There was a small glass partition down the center of the table, but people were hugging and kissing over it. The inmates were called out one by one and sat about as far apart as we are now, across from each other at the pastry shop. In her recollection, there were no handcuffs or shackles on anyone: "They were just totally free from restraints in any way. It seemed very casual." She had visited other people accused of murder and they had met in small rooms, separate from the others. This relatively laid-back setting surprised her.

Render came out limping, leaning on a cane. "He looked very frail and kind of sickly," she says, "pale in the face." He was thin and seemed weak. *I can't imagine that you overpowered somebody*, she remembers thinking.

Historically, Render has been athletic. A classmate from Bard recalls him going to the gym in college and describes him as "buff." Carolyn's aunt Robin remembers her niece saying Render was often gone, working out. Render's father would write in his letter of support, "He ran cross-country in high school, played a season of rugby at Bard College, and successfully completed a very rigorous, years-long study (along with his best friend, Arun Saxena), in the Korean martial art of Tang Soo Do." Perhaps he had gotten ill or stopped taking care of himself. Perhaps the previous twenty-four hours had deflated him.

Melkorka waved Render over, and he sat down. They were at the far end of the table, and she was nervous that a security guard standing along the wall would hear their conversation. She was technically allowed to be there and ask him questions, but sometimes prison personnel will change their minds and kick reporters out for no reason. She told Render who she was.

"Actually, I'm relieved you're here," she recalls him saying. In her article, Melkorka describes him as a "tortured artist" who turns his "bright blue eyes" down at the table when answering questions. "I just don't want to have to keep talking to my family," he told her.

"He seemed relieved not to have to discuss legal matters and face people who love him the most," she says, assuming it was due to the guilt he felt. "To talk to somebody who was removed from him" was a breath of fresh air.

"There was something weird, I think, relationship-wise, with his family members," she adds. "Oh, they're great. They're great," Render kept telling her, but her gut impression was that something in his head wasn't sitting right where his family was concerned.

It appeared at the time of Melkorka's visit that Render was still trying to comprehend what had happened, she says. "He was articulate. Seemed like somebody that I could easily meet here sitting at a coffee shop. He didn't have anything emanating from him that seemed creepy to me in any way." He didn't describe any of the hallmark symptoms of psychosis, like believing in conspiracies or detachment from reality, where perception is "completely misconstrued in every way," according to Melkorka.

"I mean, he was definitely able to carry on an intelligent conversation," she says. "He seemed very aware of the fact that he was mentally ill." He didn't offer a self-diagnosis, "but he felt very strongly that he had been battling with mental illness and had never gotten help for it, and that he should have." Looking back now, she ventures that he could suffer from something like narcissistic personality disorder, "where his whole world is just about himself, and his self-worth is completely wrapped up in his reputation." Studies show that narcissists are more likely to react to anger or disappointment with violence. She also wonders whether he felt any jealousy toward his family. "They were all successful in their respective fields," she says. It's possible, compared to his father, a *New Yorker* cartoonist who is a household name, and his brother, a rising star composer, that Render, by trade a construction worker and an art handler, "never felt like he was given the recognition he deserved."

To be sure, Render is a talented illustrator. He'd designed poetry books for friends and teachers, painted signs and murals for stores and restaurants in downtown Rhinebeck, and was trying his hand at designing movie posters. He'd also collaborated with Finn, who released his first full-length album in February 2016. Render drew eighteen intricate "dream map" illustrations as album art.

The Wayback Machine is a website that takes pictures of other websites receiving notable traffic to preserve their appearance over time. On July 5, 2016, it captured Render's website. Maybe Finn's album was driving the traffic. His bio read, "Render Stetson is an artist, illustrator, and signmaker with experience in carpentry and fine art handling. He graduated from Bard College in 2012 with a B.A. in History. He currently resides in Queens."

On October 3, 2016, with the murder driving traffic, his bio was captured again. This time it said, "Render Stetson is an artist, illustrator, and signmaker," leaving out carpentry, art handling, and Bard College. "He currently resides in Queens, New York."

Melkorka imagines that after Render was arrested, he could have been thinking, *Now that I'm in jail I can become who I really was meant to become. As long as I can create art, I'm still pursuing my dream.*

Render talked to her for an hour. Their conversation would result in the publication of a story that would later be used at Render's trial. He told her he had a regular job as an art transporter. Later, in a letter of support to the judge overseeing Render's trial, his boss at Atelier 4 would write that Render was being trained as a master handler and considered for a promotion into a management role in the packing and crating department. He'd praise his "talent" and "willingness to accept new challenges," and he'd write, "he gave the impression of being far more serious and mature than many of his peers." Render had daily open access to "sharp cutting implements and power tools" but was always found "to be working closely with his team in a calm and collegial fashion."

There is other evidence that attests to his wellness of mind prior to the murder. One year earlier, the previous fall, Render had run into his former Spanish professor from Bard in downtown Rhinebeck, while he was home helping his father recover from an emergency open-heart surgery. In her letter of support to the judge, she would write that he told her he'd found a job he loved and that he most enjoyed "the design phase of the process," for which his talents were well-suited. He also enjoyed the "physical labor of preparing art works for mailing." He said he'd "found an apartment with a friend and was generally enjoying his social life in the city." It was a long conversation that she remembers clearly because he "seemed to have found a clear path in life: satisfying work and friends." He seemed "happy and at peace."

A year later, in August, one month before the murder, Render's attitude toward his life may have shifted. Render and his father, Danny, went on a camping trip with their friend, Gregg Haefelin. Gregg is a golfing buddy of Danny's and owns the bespoke construction company in Rhinebeck that Render had worked for since high school, Handcrafted Builders. It is next-door and upstairs from the candy shop where he'd also worked through high school and occasionally after college, and it's around the corner from his childhood home. Gregg had grown to be close with his friend's son, with whom he shared a love of history and motorcycles. Just that month, the same week Render posted a picture of the dagger he used to kill Carolyn, he had also placed for sale his prized restored red 1973 Triumph T100R Daytona.

The three men planned a fly-in camping trip at an otherwise inaccessible lake in the Adirondacks. Danny was still in a weakened state from his heart surgery the year before, so Render took care of packing gear, setting up and breaking down the campsite, collecting wood, and beaching and launching canoes. On that trip, he confided to Gregg that he was starting to feel frustrated with the direction of his life in the city and was considering moving, possibly to California. Gregg told him to see the world.

That year, Render was often in Rhinebeck, helping his parents pack his childhood home, which they were preparing to sell. It was blue, two stories, large and pretty, with a spacious kitchen, restored wood details, sloping roofs on the upstairs bedrooms, lots of sunlight, and Danny's cartoons all over; he worked from home and his studio was off the kitchen. Neighbors recall Finn practicing his violin on the back deck, overlooking the yard. The property sits on the site of a demolished turn-of-the-century hospital. In their yard was a stone cold-storage house, where bodies were once kept. Nearby was a former stable for ambulances and dormitory for nurses, which is now an apartment complex.

A neighbor says that Danny and Render's mother, Janet, had decided to separate the year prior but were still friends and living together. They say that Janet stayed with Danny through the open-heart surgery, for which they postponed selling the house. Render had been traveling back and forth from Queens to Rhinebeck every weekend, for months, to help with the preparations, since he didn't want his father to exert himself. He painted, shingled roofs, did yard-work, split wood, packed and moved dozens of boxes, and helped prepare the family's yard sale. The sale of his childhood home, a signifier of his parents' separation, would close just a few days after the murder.

While home, a month before the murder, Render told his mother that he was about to be offered a promotion at Atelier 4 and that, if it came with a substantial raise, he'd accept it. If not, he would move back upstate to start his own art-handling business. Two investors had expressed interest, he said. He also told her that he'd recently started seeing Sofia again. Janet told Danny afterward that Render seemed happy about his prospects.

At the yard sale he had been helping them prepare for, a neighbor and close friend of his mother's, Rachel Cavell, purchased a beach umbrella, and Render walked it two doors over, to deliver it to her door. Rachel teaches at Bard and in the Bard Prison Initiative and is married to the school's then-dean of graduate studies, Norton Batkin. She and Render chatted in the backyard, and he told her what he'd told his mother about his promotion. Rachel shared with Janet that she thought Render seemed optimistic about the future.

However, Render told Melkorka at AMKC, "Even if I had the option to get out of here, I wouldn't want to go." And he said, "There's something very wrong. I need to be in a psychiatric hospital."

Melkorka wrote, "The tortured artist said he has long been depressed but was not being treated for it and never sought help."

"I'd become really good at hiding it," he told her. "I chose to ignore it and just dealt with it on my own."

He also told her, "I've always buried my anger at small annoyances."

"He said he had a lot of anger," says Melkorka now. "He didn't necessarily recognize it as anger, but in retrospect, he didn't know how to handle it. I think there's something that he's harboring emotionally that was affecting every single relationship in his life."

"Render Stetson-Shanahan may not remember the merciless moment cops say he plunged a kitchen knife into his roommate three times," Melkorka wrote in her article. Render stabbed Carolyn seven times, not three, and the seventh stab attempt resulted in a surface wound. The use of a kitchen knife may imply a spontaneous outburst. It was a dagger he'd recently purchased.

Melkorka wrote, "He does know he shouldn't walk free," and also that he "claimed he could not remember the grisly act, but pieced together in detail the moments before and after it."

However, in that same article, she also writes that she asked Render to "recall the brutal crime." He turned those blue eyes down at the table. "I'd rather not talk about that," he told her.

"Who really knows if he remembers that moment," she says now, admitting, "it's not in his best interest to explain those details to me as a journalist."

"Maybe out of safety his brain blocked it out," she wonders. "Maybe he just had to come to terms with it." With that said, "He definitely seemed to recall the events leading up to it. He was doing normal things before, and then he freaked."

"When he was describing the events, according to him, he completely blacked out during that time period," she says. She adds, "He just felt like somebody else completely took over his body and mind, and that it was just so separate from who he felt that he was."

"The illustrator may have been self-medicating," she wrote in her article. Narrating the events for her, Render "didn't deny drinking" but said he "wouldn't exactly say he was drunk" after leaving his brother's apartment. He did not tell Melkorka about his conversation with Sofia in the Uber. He said he remembered taking his clothes off and telling himself that he needed to go to sleep.

Then, he told her, "I felt my mind shifting states. It was distinct and very sudden. I started being really loud, stomping around, calling people and talking loudly on the phone. I was also talking really fast. It was like I was someone else." These sound like classic symptoms of mania, which include elation, rapid speech, delusions of grandeur, heightened energy, irritation or agitation, insomnia, doing things that are out of character or that others see as dangerous or that have disastrous consequences, and, also, psychosis.

He turned his attention to Carolyn. "At one point I . . . asked Carolyn how to use my phone," he told Melkorka. "She laughed, gave me a weird look and asked if everything was okay. She knew something was off." Melkorka wrote that this is when police say he killed her. "He then maniacally sank the knife into his own leg."

Render told Melkorka, "The next thing I remember is running down the street barefoot in my underwear. I was almost euphoric. The pavement under my feet was wet and I was a bit cold, but I didn't feel any pain. I started smashing people's car windows with my fist and a knife, I think. I was also going around asking people how to get to Manhattan. I don't know why."

She writes, "His single moment of lucidity came . . ."

". . . when I registered that I wasn't wearing any clothes and felt a bit embarrassed," according to Render.

Melkorka had seen Render's statements to EMS in the police report, which had him saying: "I drank a lot of beer. I smoked some weed at my brother's house. I then took an Uber back to my house. I called my girlfriend. I stabbed myself." She asked about his girlfriend. This part of their conversation didn't make it into the article. She didn't know that Sofia lived in Manhattan.

"He was very much just like, 'Yeah, my girlfriend is nice. She's cool,'" says Melkorka. "There was no detail. All that he really said about her was, 'She's there for me.' I think they broke up for a while and they got back together." Render told her they'd met at Bard, which made sense because "it seemed like, as far as being in New

York, he had no friends," she says. He painted a very bleak picture for Melkorka, one with no passion.

Render had at least one friend in the city, one of his coworkers, who would write a letter of support to the court. The two share a love of David Foster Wallace. He and his wife sometimes invited Render to barbecues and movie nights, where he got along with their friends. To Melkorka, though, "He did not seem very social," she says in the coffee shop. "He just worked and they hung out together, him and his girlfriend, and that was the bane of his existence. And he was just in his room a lot."

Melkorka asked him over and over: Why did you do it? "Did your roommate do something to you? Did she piss you off? Did your dad piss you off? What happened?"

"He just wouldn't get there with me," she says. "Because I don't think he knew." Render insisted Carolyn was a great person, that there was no friction between them at all. "According to him, they lived pretty harmoniously. There weren't any issues." Her impression was that Carolyn was in the wrong place at the wrong time.

He repeated what Carolyn had told others: they didn't interact all that often. "We just did our own thing," he said. They were roommates, not friends. "I sort of thought it was weird," says Melkorka. "Here you are living with somebody who's so intertwined with this community. How are you not better friends?"

"Though depression and rage had been building inside of him, he harbored no ill will toward Bush," she wrote.

"It was all about me, not her," Render told her ("wincing," she added). "She was a very nice person. Of course, it's terrible she's gone."

"I could see in the way he was moving his face when he was speaking, he was definitely in a lot of pain," says Melkorka. "I could visibly tell that. While he was trying to recollect and talk about this, it was difficult for him. He didn't smile. He was tearing up. He was having a really hard time. It was tough for him to say all that."

"I'm actually glad the police arrested me when they did," Render told her. "I think if I had kept running I may have done more harm to myself." He was on suicide watch at Rikers. Melkorka asked him if he might have killed himself that night. "It's possible," he said.

"Stetson-Shanahan said he does not want freedom, but does want help," she wrote.

"I'd like to be put somewhere upstate," he told her. Presumably he meant a state-run mental health facility, of which there are several in New York, not all of them comfortable. "Somewhere I can draw, paint and read. That's really all I need. It will of course put a strain on all my relationships with family and friends."

"That was really big for him," says Melkorka.

"I just want to get out of here," he told her. "I want to be somewhere peaceful where I can read and write and draw and do art."

"That's all he wanted to do," she says. "That's all he wanted to think about. That was really big for him. He needed peacefulness. He was not at peace in that jail, as you could probably imagine." Arraigned that morning, he had been there for only a few hours.

At the end of the interview, Render said to her, "I truly deserve to be in jail. I should be in jail. I should not be out of jail."

She had gone into the interview thinking, *He probably just snapped. Something set him off.* Afterward, it sounded like the trigger was "deep-rooted."

. . .

"I think he's definitely insane," says Pamela. "I just need to process how I feel about what happens to him. People who plead insanity are basically locked up for life anyway." They can be. If they are found fit to stand trial. Then win their case. Which is difficult. And very expensive. And very rare. In December 2016, several weeks after the murder, forensic psychiatrist and frequent expert witness Dr. Alexander Sasha Bardey published an essay on CBSNews.com in which he writes about a case for which he had served as an expert witness earlier that year. He says that the insanity defense "is used in less than one percent of felonies and succeeds at trial in less than a quarter of cases." The law in New York "states that an individual is not responsible by reason of mental disease or defect if, as a result of the illness, the individual lacked the capacity to know or appreciate the nature and consequences of his actions, or their wrongfulness." The problem with this, in his opinion, is that people with mental illness sometimes cannot resist doing things they know are wrong.

In 2013 Bardey had coproduced a star-studded psychological thriller, *Side Effects*, with Steven Soderbergh. The premise is that a woman is prescribed an experimental drug by a psychiatrist, the side effects of which lead her to kill her husband. It's a scenario similar to what Render would later plead had happened to him, if you consider his brother a sort of psychiatrist and marijuana an experimental psychotropic drug. Bardey would serve as the expert witness for Render's defense team.

One year after Carolyn's murder, Gabriel Mac would publish an in-depth feature in the *New York Times Magazine* called "When 'Not Guilty' Is a Life Sentence." It details the nightmarishly stalled lives of those who have been deemed mentally unfit to stand trial and those who have successfully won insanity pleas in New York State. If you're deemed unfit to stand trial, you may languish in a carceral mental health facility for the rest of your life, unless you can somehow manage to prove you're once again fit. If you're deemed fit, winning your plea is nearly impossible. It requires proving that, although you are well enough to understand the proceedings of your trial and repent your actions, nonetheless, at the time you committed the crime, you grasped neither the illegal nature of your actions nor their consequences. It's a legal Möbius strip: you cannot be held responsible for what occurred, but, going forward, you can be trusted to be responsible. Further, although at the time of the crime you had dangerously lost touch with reality, you now no longer pose a threat and should not be incarcerated. If you fail to prove this, you're placed in an indefinite mental health hold.

If someone were found not responsible by reason of mental illness, it would mean, since there is no conviction, there is also no sentencing. However, because of this, there's no limit to incarceration. If he is deemed dangerous due to a mental illness, the condition underlying his threat is assumed to be a lifelong one. "The laws that govern the practice of committing people who are acquitted because of mental illness dictate that they be hospitalized until they're deemed safe to release to the public, no matter how long that takes," McClelland writes.

. . .

Like many of Carolyn's loved ones, Cameron Seglias read whatever articles came out in the first days, looking for any information, an explanation. "I was very disturbed," he says of Melkorka's interview with Render. As fellow Bard students, he'd grown close with Carolyn, who called him "Cammie." He also knew of Render by reputation, because Render's mother, who has worked in the admissions office at Bard since 1999, often talked openly about her "well-raised boys." "I was trying to understand why somebody would kill my friend," says Cameron. "I, of course, also just assumed that he was insane, whatever that means. How could you not be?"

Reading Melkorka's article, though, Cameron was appalled. "That person is really a serious danger to society, and he's thinking about his artwork? He said that he was looking forward to his prison time so that he could focus on his art. That just was so repugnant to me." That's when he stopped reading articles altogether. "I think a lot of our friends did." An earlier one describing Render as a "struggling artist" had been difficult enough to swallow. Now it seemed as though Render believed "this was going to be part of what made him an artist."

Alexis Graman is Carolyn's former roommate from Bard and was her close friend. "It's a funny thing to say," he says in reference to Render's line about drawing, painting, and reading. "When I'm stressed out or something, I say that: 'I just need to go be alone and get my things done.' I know I'm being selfish. But I didn't just murder somebody."

A former classmate and tutor of Render's at Bard remembers that in Render's compulsory tutoring sessions with him, he seemed like he was "waiting to be delivered from this mortal plane, which he had to share with a bunch of imbeciles who weren't as smart or talented as he was."

"I try and think about Render's inner life, and honestly it's a black hole," says another Bard classmate, Moira Donegan. "You can try and look in there, but you're not going to get an answer. Carolyn was reading. She was directing this organization that was doing a lot for people. She was writing and producing a lot of criticism. I could see him being very proximate to art in his job and being very proximate to this person who was living a creative life at home, and in those post-college years, where everybody's insecure about what they're doing with their lives. I could see it," she says, meaning blowing a gasket.

"It just makes me sick because I knew him," says Maximus "Max" Agrio, who requested his name be changed. Max was Carolyn's close friend and had published a book featuring Render's artwork on the cover. "They were friends. They got along. They lived together. They were friends, and they got along."

"It's an awful tragedy," says Melkorka. One person could have gotten help for mental illness. Instead, "two people's lives are ruined." Two families, really.

4.

The News

Carolyn was Max Agrio's first friend at Bard College. The two met in a freshman poetry workshop. Prompted to talk about themselves on the first day of class—"Tell us something you do"— Max said he performed exorcisms. "I kind of did at the time, this weird little poetic ritual I called 'exorcisms.'"

After class, Carolyn came up to him. "Max, right?" she asked.

He said yes.

"I need you to perform an exorcism in my room. My room is haunted."

That day, they drank wine in her room in Tewksbury, a dorm for freshmen. They burned candles, read poems, and then performed a ritual that involved reading from random pages of a book to try to dispel the locked spirit.

"I was a real weirdo back then," says Max. "She immediately is drawn to that outsider energy. We both had an interest in alternate theology, and she's always been drawn to the poetry boys, that kind of milieu, because it included a lot of weird people. Each time we'd hang out, it'd get progressively weirder."

Like Carolyn, Max didn't connect with many of the other kids at Bard. The campus is rural, the winters are long, harsh, and isolating, and the student body appears to boast a larger-than-average contingency of corporate heirs and heiresses and celebrities' wayward children. Carolyn echoed Max's impression: "Who are all these pretentious New York types?" she'd rant. "I'm from Saint Petersburg. I'm the daughter of Jim Bush."

"That's what I really liked about her," says Max. "She didn't care about class." The most important question to her was: Do you have something interesting to say?

Max was working as a software engineer in the newsroom at the *New York Times* on the morning of September 29, 2016. "I was in this really odious, awful meeting, just so boring," he says. Something had gone wrong in the code and people were yammering about procedural stuff. "They were talking about stories, and then they brought up this story."

"For instance, the *New York Post* just reported this story about a woman . . . ," someone said. The *Times* wanted to know how the *Post* broke the story. They sent a link to everyone in the meeting's chat. Max clicked and began to read. *Wait a minute*, he thought, as he realized he was reading about Carolyn.

"I was just sitting there, ruined," he says. His fellow reporters dryly discussed strategies for landing more stories like that one. In this style of meeting, called a "postmortem," they analyzed how the *Post* is embedded with the police department and listens in on 911 calls. Max was in such shock he couldn't speak. *I need to leave*, he thought, but he didn't. He stayed. Then he finally went home after "fucking something up." He doesn't even know if he told anyone why. "I couldn't open up," he says.

At home, he drank whiskey, cried, and tried to write down everything he could remember about her. All the odd interactions they'd had. He was looking at photos: there's a funny one that he cherishes. Carolyn was strangely obsessed with how only one of his arms was covered in freckles and the other wasn't. "She was into them for this weird astrological reason," he says. He remembers a cute picture of her at the Bard cafeteria: she had put a bunch of pepper on her arm and tagged him in it. "I'm Max Agrio," the caption said.

He thought a lot about the fact that he knew Render too. "How awful and lurid it was, and how it was this weird Bard tragedy in a way" because the school is so "close-knit." He had always written Render off as "just this weird type that hangs out around Bard and is a disaffected white artist." Render had always seemed antisocial, but Max couldn't understand why Render would do something like this. He was totally taken aback. The only person Max knows who was close to him, other than Carolyn, was a poet named Tamas Panitz. Tommi. Tommi was, Max thinks, one of Render's only friends.

Tommi's 2014 Bard senior thesis, *Blue Sun*, was the second chapbook Max had ever published on his small press. The book featured Render's artwork on the cover. "I couldn't believe that I had published that," Max says. "That I had used that image." He knows it's irrational and silly. "I couldn't handle the fact that I had literally put a murderer's work on the front cover of a book that I believe in." He destroyed a lot of the copies because he was so upset. "I had a bunch. I ruined them. I tore them up and tossed them out."

Tommi and Carolyn had been friends since meeting at Bard. He was the one who'd suggested Render move into her apartment, when her previous roommate moved out. He would write in his letter of support for Render, "As I've known him, he has been an ideal friend, and a model person in his own right." For most of 2016, Tommi and Render had worked together publishing poetry books, which Render designed and formatted, for Tommi's own small press. "This required daily contact between us, and I saw him several times a month," Tommi wrote. "He performed this work out of his own generosity, and we hoped eventually to publish a volume of his drawings." He says that Render's responsibilities required contact with "difficult authors" and "difficult templates and websites, for which he showed unflagging patience."

Tommi is a recluse, Max tells me, so it could be hard to contact him. He might know a little more about what happened that night, though. Maybe he had talked to Render beforehand.

"Someone told me what happened," Tommi writes to me, after first declining an interview, then acquiescing to answer some questions in writing. "I didn't believe it, thought it was a bizarre tasteless joke. A fake article with fake reporting. But as I saw it was getting picked up and developed through different media outlets I had to accept it." His initial response to hearing the news was "utter disbelief."

"It seemed impossible that this was true," he wrote in his letter of support. "I thought a practical joke was being played on me, and not until reading several horrendous and disgraceful 'reports' did I take in the situation."

I ask him: Did he talk to anyone about it? Did he grieve?

"Many people," he says. "Yes, I did, and still am grieving. I don't wish to elaborate."

• • •

The first article had come out hours after the murder, at two minutes to eight, in *DNAinfo*. It said that Carolyn and Render had been fighting before he repeatedly stabbed her inside her bedroom. "I heard a high-pitched scream," it quoted neighbor Joshua Cruz as saying. It said that Cruz had been outside the apartment when he saw Render on the phone telling someone, "I don't think I'm gonna have a lease anymore." Cruz told *DNAinfo* that Render seemed intoxicated.

Their building manager, Pat Castellar, appears in the article as well. He had been asleep and woke to the cops pounding on his door at midnight. "I was brought upstairs by the police, to identify her," he tells me on the phone. Render was still in his bedroom when Castellar entered the apartment. There was blood all over his room and in the hallway. Cops led him into Carolyn's room. "There was too much blood," he told reporters. They couldn't save her. "Her head was to the side. Her eyes were closed. They tried doing chest compressions, but she wasn't responding."

He hasn't been able to make sense of it, he says now. It doesn't help that he still lives in the building. "It was crazy. I was crazy. I mean, imagine. I live here. Such a beautiful girl, such a beautiful daughter." He's a father of daughters himself.

He also knew them both. His unit is on the building's first floor, and he would see Carolyn and Render coming in and out every day. He and Render are both smokers, and Castellar's window faces the street. He used to leave his front door open all the time because his children spent time outside, in the gated courtyard out front. Render would walk away from the front door or even cross to the other sidewalk when Castellar wasn't outside smoking with him, so his second-hand smoke wouldn't drift back into the apartment. When smoking together, Castellar and Render would talk. Short conversations, what's new, that sort of thing. "His drawings, the weather, beer. He used to want to make homemade beer," says Castellar.

Carolyn was a very nice girl, too, according to him. "We would talk about so much," he says. One of their shared passions was books. "I remember telling her about how rich is our Spanish literature in comparison to the famous 'English literature,'" he says. "We are so diverse, in twenty-one different countries."

"You got Shakespeare and who else?" he ribbed her.

"Believe me, they were two great kids," he says. "That was the shame. I never thought of them never being on the same page, ever." He suspects there might have been a disagreement between them. At least, that was the rumor circulating the next morning. "According to what they say, Carolyn might have told him to move. He did tell some people here that he was told to move. That's how I think it started. I think a couple of days before." Castellar says Cruz was the main peddler of the story, though he never saw Cruz talking to Render or Carolyn. "He was victimized too," says Castellar of Cruz—Render had lunged at him with a knife. "He had a story to tell everybody."

"You know, he's a kid," he says of Render. "It wouldn't be the first time I saw myself kicked out, I'm gonna do some drugs, and alcohol, and he's not the same person no more. Now we got an animal." Castellar had called Render an animal to his face when he saw the scene. "She was beautiful. A beautiful life. A young life."

• • •

The second article on Thursday morning came out an hour after the first one, in the *New York Post*. It bore the clickbait title "Artist Stabs Female Roommate to Death, Gripes about Finding New Apartment." In typical *Post* style, the rest of the language was exaggerated and grotesque. It described Render as a "struggling artist" and "psyche-delic illustrator" who "butchered" Carolyn and "plunged" the knife into her then "fumed" about not having a lease anymore. "He was wearing just underwear," it quotes Cruz saying, and "he was covered in blood."

The *Post* reports that Carolyn was a waitress struggling to pay the rent, who was "letting Stetson stay and pitch in." It does not explain how reporters learned she was struggling to pay rent, but her landlord would later tell me she always paid on time. It's possible the use of "struggling" is more typical *Post* melodrama, a way to pump up a nor-mal New York–roommate scenario in which one person pays another person for a room. The *Post* does not elaborate on their description of Carolyn as "waitress struggling" alongside Render as a "struggling artist." Nor does the *Post* examine the discrepancy of this arrangement of her "letting Stetson stay and pitch in" with Render's overheard complaint that he wouldn't have a lease anymore.

The *Post* incorrectly describes Carolyn as a Bard College gradu-ate. Soon afterward, Bard would tell *DNAinfo* that she had never graduated.

The *Post* describes Render stabbing himself in the leg as inexplica-ble. But he stabbed himself just after the murder. We can speculate that he felt overwhelmed. Self-injury is not an uncommon way of coping with emotional overwhelm, though it's not the only possible explanation.

The *Post* wrote that Render "has his own website with trippy sketchings and lithographs, including a movie poster he drew up for the Hunter Thompson flick, *Fear and Loathing in Las Vegas*." They embedded his Twitter post showing the illustration. They also embedded a headshot of him with a beard and a backward baseball cap, licking his lips.

They describe him as "scantily-clad" when he ran outside, a phrase conjuring lingerie photo shoots. They report that cops said he "posted up" on a street corner and waited for them to arrive, when in fact he ran back to his bedroom and waited, and that's where they arrested him. The *Post* broke the story. Is this true if the facts were wrong? What story were they breaking?

• • •

Matt Ossias was dating Carolyn when she died. He found out on Facebook. "I remember seeing a bunch of posts on her page. I thought it was for her birthday, and I didn't know it was her birthday," which seemed strange. Then it sunk in. He read the articles.

They had met on a dating app one month earlier and then met in person for the first time outside The New School's campus in Union Square. Carolyn was designing her own major there, and Matt was studying philosophy and writing his thesis on film. "No one looks like her," he says. "She had these stunning, sharp facial features. Her expressions were always so poignant. The way that she would emote was distinct and genuine and open." She would constantly gesticulate; "everything was emphatic." They shared a cigarette, and she pecked him on the lips.

Matt also lived in Ridgewood. He and Carolyn would often meet at a dive bar midway between their apartments. When they stayed the night together, it was at her place. "I remember her apartment very vividly," he says. "It was really fitting for her," he says. "I think she really loved that apartment. She loved it. It was a beautiful place." The ceiling's molded tin tiles had been painted with some kind of ugly material, and "the clash of the two was just beautiful." They would smoke cigarettes inside. "She had these two big windows behind her couch. We would hang out on the couch."

Matt never met Render nor had any interactions with him, though Carolyn mentioned him. "He was never there, I don't think, or maybe he was," but he wasn't interacting. "It felt more like her space, in a way. It didn't feel like it was a shared space." Still, "she only talked well of him. She said he was just calm, quiet, Bard graduate. It didn't seem like they had much of a connection from what I could tell. I don't know. I don't know. I don't know. I don't know. I don't know the history there at all. Just from my impression of her, she did not seem in the least concerned about him.

"She was very intuitive," he says. Matt remembers her asking him for his astrological sign when they first started talking, and she told him about her interest in the occult. She was also very smart and opinionated. Sometimes they would get into political or philosophical debates. "Never fights," he says. "Her and I never fought." Matt is a far-left socialist; he and Carolyn agreed on most things. "She would rage against things; I would rage against them." She would stoke him. "Usually when I rage against things, people just say, 'Shut up,'" but Carolyn encouraged him. They both had sharp edges. She was the sharpest person he'd ever met. "Not just sharp in the sense of witty," he says. "She was very tender, but she also had fangs. If she needed to rip in, she would. She let me have it a few times." They were both appalled by Donald Trump. "We were convinced that he was going to lose."

Matt and Carolyn didn't see each other during the week Jenny was in town. He was busy, and they were transitioning into being friends. He last saw her on Saturday, the day after Jenny left. She was very sweet. "I wanted you to meet my sister," she said. She had a surprise for him. "It's a statue of an animal but you have to guess what animal it is." They had never talked about animals. Matt guessed his favorite: a whale. "What does she unleash from her hands?" he says. "A little tiny whale statue." She grinned. "I knew it, I knew it, I knew it!" she said.

Four days later, Wednesday night, he was headed to plans with a friend when she messaged him. It was around 10:30 p.m., about forty minutes before the murder, and she asked for a movie recommendation. "I think she just wanted to hang out," he says. He didn't want to respond while walking, so he put it off until he could sit down. Back home later he recommended a film by Pier Paolo Pasolini. She didn't reply. "I remember hearing a lot of sirens in the neighborhood and not thinking anything about it, because it's New York. You hear sirens."

• • •

The news continued to spread on Facebook. People shared the articles and posted on Carolyn's page. Christine Pfister, who met Carolyn during her freshman orientation at Bard, remembers, "She always radiated a confidence that I envied immensely, which paired beautifully with her sharp wit and sharp tongue." She describes Carolyn as having a "deep, raging fire in her soul" and how she had told Christine that it was fire that connected them. Carolyn had carried the astrological *Secret Language of Birthdays* everywhere with her, and she read about Christine's "dormant but omnipresent fire" in it. "Carrie's astrological chart was all fire," Pamela says. She was a Scorpio, a fire sign. "She had so much fire."

Danielle Sinay, who met Carolyn when she lived down the hall from her their freshman year at Bard, wrote on her Facebook, "It was the Black Moon on Friday, the day after you passed, which, as I'm sure you know, is most connected with goddess Lilith . . . hypnotic and magnificent, [who represents] sexual energy, creativity, rebellion, and feminine power." Carolyn had told another of her Bard classmates and close friends, Elizabeth "Lizzy" Crawford, that she was very connected to the moon. "I felt that moon-ness around her," says Lizzy.

"I would like to actually tell you a dream that I had a couple of nights after Carolyn died," says Cameron Seglias. It has happened to him more than once with people who have died, he says. Not too long afterward, he'll dream about them. "I'm not suggesting that it's some sort of esoteric insight," he says, "but that maybe it's my own mind telling me to sort of accept their death. But Carolyn, it was a very strong feeling." They were at a house with a large lake and Carolyn came. Cameron said, "Oh, Carolyn, I heard about what happened to you. Are you okay?"

She said, "Well, I'm dead, basically." They had a long conversation.

"I can't tell you—it just felt really, that we were having a conversation," not like it was his words in her mouth. "It really was as if she was there again. Then we held hands and flew around this huge lake together." It was a moment of seeing each other one last time, he says.

It occurs to him now that the last time he saw Carolyn in real life, they went to a lake together. It was on a trip to see Tommi in Catskill. Maybe that's why he dreamed of a lake.

Then he says, "I don't see a lot of connection between how she died and how she lived."

5.

The Vigil

"Survivors look on and must make sense of something
both violent and tender."
 -Brenda Iijima, "A Lesson in Dead Language"

Kevin Cassem is a small, sandy-haired fellow with round glasses and a serious, old-timey demeanor easily interrupted by quick laughter. "Carrie had such a crush on Kevin," says Jenny. On Thursday, September 29, it was Kevin, Carolyn's cofounder at Wendy's Subway and a fellow Bard alum, whom Jenny called first, when she knew that she had to let the Wendy's people know about Carolyn's death. He was at NYU, about to give the first presentation of his PhD studies in comparative literature. "I never answer, it's always debt collectors," he says.

Then he got a Facebook message: "Call me now."

Shit, he thought. He called her. "There's nothing you can ask of a person in a moment like that," he says. "You just stare at the line as the sob begins."

He asked if he should tell other people. Jenny said yes, "We have to start the chain of information somewhere," but asked him not to post it online.

"It's not my first rodeo," he says. He lists the rest of the Wendy's Subway inner circle, whom he called one by one to give the news. "Adjua, then Chris, Gabe, Rachel," then Matt Longabucco, then

Macgregor Card, two poets and founding members. "There was a time when we were very close," he says.

. . .

Carolyn and her fellow Wendy's board member Christopher "Chris" Prioleau had been casually dating for a few months. She'd even been trying to get Chris to meet Jenny while she was in town. "You're both very verbal," she'd said. It felt considerate. *I am very verbal*, Chris thought. *You're paying attention.* The night Jenny left, Carolyn had invited him to her place. "I came over and was pretty drunk," he says. "We were both upset about people that we were dating, and kind of falling apart, and we slept together."

The next morning, Carolyn rose very early to clean in preparation for some Airbnb guests who were arriving that day. Chris says she was "perpetually annoyed" by managing the needs of her Airbnb. "She was cleaning her house really manically," he says. He was still waking up when she came into the room and said, "You don't have to leave, but you need to wake the fuck up and get out of my bed." Then, "I'll cook you breakfast."

They talked and hung out until the afternoon. At one point, she was in the bathroom when her doorbell rang. "I didn't answer the door," Chris says. Instead he yelled, "Carolyn! Your doorbell!" She didn't respond and he thought, *Fuck it.*

When she came out, he said, "Dude, your doorbell rang."

She let loose a string of profanities.

Chris was surprised. "Were you waiting on a kidney?"

She ran downstairs and came back inside with the yellow USPS slip.

"Why didn't you tell me?" she said.

"Dude, when the doorbell rings at my own apartment, I don't answer it."

She was mildly "Carolyn" irritated about it.

"I don't live here. I don't know what you want from me," he joked.

Finally, it was time for him to leave. "It's such a cliché that I wasn't sure about our relationship," he says. "I just knew that I had a really good time when I was with her." A friend of his whom he had talked to about Carolyn told him he was stupid: "That girl's going to fall in love with you. You can only do this so many times before someone develops feelings."

Chris was slowly coming to the realization that he didn't mind that. "But when I left that morning, we just kind of hugged awkwardly and said, 'That was fun.'" He didn't know how to describe what was going on between the two of them. "She had a lot of funny ideas," he says. "She was really sharp, cocky. But was also extremely vulnerable, extremely sensitive."

"I have this image burned into my memory of her sitting on the couch," he says. "She had this way of looking at me. She was so cute. And beautiful. She was really smart. She was prematurely like a seventy-five-year-old spinster. She had all of these headbands and was always smoking. But she was also really young. She was twenty-five years old." For a moment, looking at each other, her bravado fell away. Not as though it were a veil, or false—she was the same person all the time; she would always talk shit to him. But in her expression, he saw that, overnight, he'd peeled back a layer. He remembers looking her in the eyes, feeling overwhelmed. Then leaving, down the stairs.

"I shut the door. That was the last time I saw her," he says.

· · ·

Two days later, on Monday, he got a text message. "Hiii," said Carolyn. "Just paid nine dollars for an Uber to get to a very far away post office before close and have been waiting in line for fifteen minutes to pick up the package I would have received had you effectively notified me the doorbell rang." The package contained a new iPad.

"Carolyn, I'm not your doorman," Chris responded.

"Thank you for letting me send you this shitty message," she said. "I feel better now. I know it's not actually your fault. I'm not mad, I'm just disappointed."

She sent him a picture of a dog patting the head of a cat.

"Am I the dog? Am I the cat?" he says, laughing. "She was so much all the time. I loved her for that."

· · ·

At the time, Chris was the development and communications manager for NY Writers Coalition. He would usually wake at ten thirty or eleven on his days off. Thursday morning, he was lying on the couch watching an episode of *South Park* on his computer when Kevin called. In his memory, Kevin said, "Are you sitting down?" He warned Chris that it was bad. He said Carolyn had been murdered by her roommate.

"I remember screaming," says Chris. "Just a long scream." He collapsed on the ground in a fetal position with his forehead on the floor and his butt in the air. His mind was all over the place. *I was just over there. Her roommate, she was maybe talking about him. What about those Airbnb people? Does somebody need to talk to me?*

Kevin told him they were meeting at Wendy's.

"No," Chris said. "I don't think I'm going to do that." He doesn't know what he thought he was going to do. He just needed to get off the phone.

He sobbed for fifteen minutes. Finally, his roommate, Liz, came home. "What the fuck is going on with you?" she said. She had been to Wendy's for events and readings. She'd met Carolyn there, and Carolyn had been to their apartment a handful of times. She was shocked. "If people are going to Wendy's, you should go over there," she said.

In other words, "You should get up from the floor," says Chris. "Then I just walked over there." He was supposed to wait for Liz while she brushed her teeth. "I just left."

• • •

The day before, on Wednesday, 1861 Stanhope Street had been over-filled with healing herbs. That afternoon, Carolyn's friend and fellow Wendy's member, Adjua Greaves, received a Facebook message from her, surprising since Carolyn had never messaged her there before. The subject line said, "Hi! Do you have any interest in this?" with a link inside to a Craigslist post advertising "Bulk Organic Medicinal Herbs, Spices, Beeswax, and More."

"A bunch of free medicinal herbs I'm trying to get rid of," said Carolyn's Facebook message. "Giving up on my dreams of becoming a witch this year. Anyway, I could bring them to Wendy's even. If you think you'd use them or can think of any other folks who'd be down with some healing?"

Adjua responded, "Yeah? Oh great. This is incredible. What time is good for you?" She bedazzled her response with the "blowing weed" emoji.

"It makes me so happy to give them to someone who will really value it," said Carolyn. "I've been hoarding this shit for so long now and I had a kind of crisis deciding to finally part. I'm fairly flexible. Will be at home or in my neighborhood all day and tomorrow."

"Raaad," Adjua said, and then, "Tomorrow is likely best. May I confirm with you in the morning?"

And Carolyn said, "Yes, give me a call."

Then they traded hearts. Carolyn saw Adjua's heart.

• • •

Adjua awoke on Thursday morning with a plan to attend the final meeting, that afternoon, of an administrative arts fellowship she was due to complete at the Rap Research Lab. She is a poet and perfor-mance artist, an "ethnobotanic literary critic," and that year she was also curator for the Segue Reading Series. In the morning, she ran through her mental checklist. Before the meeting at Rap Research Lab, she had to text Carolyn and make a plan to meet up for the herb handoff. She did so at noon, saying she could meet at any time before four o'clock that coming Sunday. Then she brought her phone into the bathroom.

"I'm in the shower and the phone rings, so it interrupted the music," she says. She got out because she saw that it was Kevin. He would usually text, not call. She answered expecting the crisis to be about his personal life, "so I'm getting into Mom Mode for him," she says. He sounded awful. Like he was bracing her for something. She was terrified.

"I wish I knew how to say this," he said. "I have to tell you something."

"I don't have words for what that shift was," says Adjua. "But it was a leaving. It was a departure from something. Something like, 'All my friends are alive.'"

He said they were gathering at Wendy's. She told him she needed to finish getting ready and then stop by the fellowship meeting. Then she would head there.

"I think he couldn't believe that I wasn't going right there," she says. But she didn't feel the immediacy or devastation of it, yet. "I was thinking about it, but I was not feeling it." She wasn't deeply involved in the organization at that point either—she had distanced herself in the last year, due to life circumstances. Also, nobody in Adjua's life had ever been murdered before. "My body just didn't know how to do that."

She got back in the shower. Then she got dressed in a totally different way than she usually would. "I adorned myself in extremely feminine funereal garb," she says. She wore lacy black tights and a black dress that she'd gotten for a wedding. She wrapped her natural hair in a cloth headband like the kind Carolyn would wear, "perched up." She put on makeup and made herself smell like roses. "I have chills all over saying this," she tells me.

Some might say she was in a trance, but Adjua doesn't like that word for it. Other people have died in her life and she's felt "really, nothing." It has surprised coworkers. When her aunt died and she needed to leave work early for the day, her coworker was stunned by her offhand explanation that she was going to a funeral. "I didn't feel connected to it at all," she says. But Carolyn "was in my blood, then my humors."

Half an hour later, she wrote an email, her first negotiation with how to let the people in her life know that something extremely terrible had happened without upsetting them. "That's something I deal with a lot, the day-to-day of this," she says. "Deciding whether to tell people that my murdered friend is, like, right here," by which she means spiritually present in the room with her. She said she was heading to Wendy's and would be in touch again when she knew more. Everyone responded with condolences and concern. "Love you guys. Fuck this society," she replied.

"Then, I was in another dimension," she says. She went to *Gothamist* for information on what had happened and felt some grounding in the familiarity of being able to find it. "I knew it would be there, and it was," she says. "This was a *Gothamist*-level thing." That Carolyn's murderer was someone Carolyn knew added a layer of understanding as to what had happened; it was probably personal. She tried to read between the lines of the *Gothamist* article to see what she could glean from those first details. "Why he did it, or who this asshole was. Anything." She was terrified by her suspicion that Carolyn had been sexually assaulted and was relieved to confirm that she hadn't been. "I haven't been able to say that," she admits. "It's so intense."

· · ·

"Wendy's was a body with no blood," says Kevin of that Thursday afternoon, as they gathered in the library storefront, no larger than a small studio apartment. The metal window covers were drawn down, flanked by canary yellow trim. The lights were off, and the only door, shaded by a large tree just starting to turn autumn gold, was unlocked to the triangular intersection of Bushwick Avenue and Moore Street. A housing project stood across the street from Wendy's, green with its own abundant trees, and a few doors down was a DIY art space for skateboarders and graffiti artists, some of whom the group had befriended. Inside Wendy's, people were silent. For hours and hours and hours. Chris arrived before noon. A new person would show up and they'd hug. Then more terrible silence.

Rachel Valinsky, director of the organization, was there with Matt Longabucco, her partner, a founding board member. Rachel is an editor and art writer. Matt is slightly older than her and the others, a soft-natured poet and professor, who had taught at Bard College.

Gabe Kruis and Emily Reilly were there. Emily was the director of public programming at the Bard Graduate Center. Her presence in the room elevated Adjua's understanding of how serious their relationship was—she was here in this "family moment." Macgregor Card, a poet and professor and founding board member, was also there. People were slumped on the floor in front of the "little brown stupid" couch, says Adjua.

The way some people displayed grief made things complicated, Chris says. Kevin had lost other friends recently and had lived through horrific tragedies in his life. His family is from Iraq and he has a keen awareness of what life is like in countries with less privilege. He has an attitude of "things like this happen," says Chris.

In general, Kevin tended to have a doom-and-gloom outlook. "Everything was the end of the world, and everything was so fucking Edgar Allan Poe," Chris says. "Everything was just really dark and depressing. There was a time that he was more directly mourning Carolyn. It just wasn't immediate."

"Some people were destroyed," says Kevin. "Just completely. Some people stepped up." Some, like Adjua and him, fit both descriptions.

"Both of us kind of kept our shit together," for the sake of the group, he says, "then lost our minds a little later."

. . .

For Chris, one of the weirder, uglier parts was the guilt that started that morning and stayed for a long time. "It's this feeling of being a Black person in America," he says. Like when he's in a clothing store and the alarm goes off. He'll feel a tinge of *Oh, no. Someone knows that I did something*, even though he hasn't done anything. Assumed suspicion, "watching my behavior from the point of view of someone who wants to tell me that I'm bad."

He felt it intensely the morning after the murder. "Did I do something? Are people going to think that I did something?" He knew it was Carolyn's roommate who had killed her; there was no mystery. He still felt guilty.

"I was also a person that had penetrated her in her room, and I was just there, and should have seen something, should have done something." He wondered if he'd just been there for his own selfish purposes. Or to exploit someone he should have protected. "Which is bullshit," he says. "Because she didn't need my fucking protection."

"I was just destroyed," he continues. In the months after Carolyn's death, he was suicidal and taking a lot of Xanax. "Suicidal thoughts, I'm no stranger to them," he says. "I knew what was happening." But it was rough for months and months and months. It was hard to be in social situations at all, though it was especially hard to be around people who didn't know about Carolyn. "It was hard to work; it was hard to live," he says. "There was a morning, I remember waking up and seeing all of these takeout cups of urine in my room." He'd been relieving himself in them and had forgotten to dispose of them.

"I thought I saw her everywhere," he says. "I think that happens to a lot of people. That still happens."

The morning after staying over at her apartment for the last time, he'd walked from her place in Ridgewood to his in Greenpoint, a little over an hour. *I have the best time when I'm with her*, he'd thought to himself. *We have such a good bond, and relationship, and understanding. We'll see what happens.*

In the months afterward, he would think about that walk. "I'd feel like . . . I felt that . . . or I did, fall in love with her after she died," he says. "I thought about her all the time. I talked to her all the time. It was just such a deep hurt that I was lost in it."

As someone who tries to be a good person but doesn't always get it right, he admits that he's had shitty experiences with women that have been completely his fault. "What has ever stopped me from losing it and hurting someone?" he says. "What has ever stopped me from doing something that I can't take back? There's a whole spectrum of behavior that men put women through." He felt implicated by an entire pattern.

And then, "Why do I have the right to learn something from her? I would give all of it back for her just to be here."

. . .

"Some coping mechanism had turned me into a caretaker," says Adjua about how she responded to seeing her friends in "various states of wordless grief and holding each other," crying, at Wendy's Subway, the day after the murder. She wasn't crying, or couldn't cry yet. She kept thinking, *I don't need help. They're the ones who need help.* She hadn't spent much time at Wendy's in the last year, but these people had been part of Carolyn's life every day. She felt so bad for them, she says, repeating this. "So sad. So, so sad."

"I flung myself back into the organization, in order to help them be okay during this time," she says. "Then I started to realize how much I needed this too."

Wendy's Subway came about in early 2013, within the first few months of Carolyn moving to the city. Kevin had been pitching the idea to his friends, and it was gaining steam when he approached Carolyn. They knew each other from Bard and were working together at the SoHo independent bookstore McNally Jackson Books—where Adjua and I both worked as well. "The second I told Carolyn what the general outline of it was, she was on board," says Kevin. "Immediately. Completely. Even before the space existed. She was part of those conversations in the six months it took us to put it together."

"Wendy's Subway invites you to become a member starting January 15, 2014!" Kevin had written in a mass email. "'A reading room.' Said aloud, this small statement sounds beautiful. It is the image of some space in a far-gone time. With an ever-growing library, Wendy's Subway is a community offering you the possibility to work, read, and come together in an open environment with and around like-minded peers." The email advertised Wi-Fi, 24-7 hours, a "growing, and at present, unassuming but ambitious non-circulating library," kitchenette and bar, wall space, projector, and bicycle storage. There were quiet hours during the day and "bookings for exhibitions, readings, performances, reading groups, screenings, rehearsals and more." Membership was seventy-five dollars a month, with a seventy-five-dollar security deposit to help maintain the space. "Let's sustain our practice and come together to create a space where we work, create, discuss, read, or write. One that is ours for collaboration, action, or exegesis."

Emily Toder was one of the first members. Her roommate was a bookseller at another bookstore and had invited her to the first meeting. Kevin held it at "this little Moroccan place" called Café Orlin that he liked because it was always open late. When Emily arrived, he was there with Matt, Rachel, and Macgregor. She sat and listened to his pitch. *This is unrealistic*, she remembers thinking. "It just seemed too good to be true. The idea in the beginning was just a space to read and write." Which, honestly, she admits, really appealed to her.

• • •

On the Saturday after Carolyn's murder, of which Emily had not yet caught wind, she was at Wendy's Subway teaching an informal letterpress class. She was with two other poets, talking about typography design and listening to music with the door open to the street. It was the afternoon. "Carolyn's parents came in," she says, referring to Jim and Cindy. She had never met them, had no idea who they were. Now they suddenly materialized in the room, asking her if they were in the right place. They had never seen Wendy's before, only heard about it.

"I never understood what Wendy's Subway was," says Jim. "First of all, it has this really quirky name."

"I think the people who started it would say it cost time and stuff like that, but this was them," says Cindy. "This was all a part of them."

Now Carolyn's dad and stepmom saw the library's large wall of simple industrial bookshelves, which their daughter had helped assemble. The curtains in the window, which she had hung. The stacks of plastic chairs she would set out for gatherings. The communal table, and the individual desks, where she preferred to work alone.

"I don't think I ever understood the mission," says Jim. It wasn't until now, standing in the room looking around, that it began to make sense to him. This was a place where people who loved writing gathered to talk about literature, art, publishing, and social justice. Where they held film series, poetry readings, book clubs, and classes, and where they wrote their own books.

"Did you know Carrie?" they asked Emily.

At first, she didn't know who they were talking about. "I didn't remember anyone ever calling her Carrie." Then it registered. And she realized they were speaking about her in the past tense. She had to sit down. She couldn't think of what to say. The scene was so casual: there was loud music; people were eating. "It was not ceremonious," she says.

Once they left, no one could return to work. Someone had looked up the news and given the others the details of what had happened. "Nowhere on the mind is there such a horrific possibility," says Emily. She had always thought of Carolyn as so tough, in a way she admired. Her murder still frightens her.

• • •

I ask Adjua what those first days were like for her. "I entered a version of a Bardo state," she says. "I felt her come into my body." She bought a book on astral projection and told her friend, "I'm going to hang out with Carolyn." Her friend warned her, "It's really important to have clear communication with spirits that are ripped from the world like this."

"I think that's wise, caring advice," says Adjua. "I think it was responsible adult friending. But it really upset me because I lost her." The new sense of caution caused her to loosen her grip on the connection with Carolyn she had been fomenting. She hopes the portal is still open, "that there's still cosmic access to her. I would really like that."

In those first days, a very specific image of Carolyn persisted in her mind. Carolyn was leaning back in a chair, legs crossed, smoking. She would say, "Can you fucking believe this?" She was so present and so bodily herself. So angry.

Adjua thought a lot about Carolyn's admission to her over Facebook the day before the murder, that she had given up on being a witch. Adjua thought of her own growing identity as a witch. Carolyn had decided not to pursue a particular path in that moment, and because of that, she had directed her resources to Adjua. It was a potent message, allegorical.

"I didn't intend to be alive and for my friend not to be," Adjua says. "I'm the person who's alive. I'm the person who will have the healing plants. I was going to take on a mortal responsibility, not because of my own choosing. But I wasn't going to reject it."

. . .

Wendy's Subway was set up for the vigil on Sunday, four days after the murder. Plastic chairs were arranged in rows facing a microphone, which faced the door to the street like a sentinel. On a table inside the door sat a guest book, a vegetable platter, wine, and whiskey. Rachel remembers Lizzy Crawford putting on Josephine Foster's song "Child of God," a favorite of Carolyn's. People embraced, smiling through tears in the space's soft white light. When the chairs filled, people stood around them and spilled out onto the sidewalk.

"In that moment, I was documenting," says Adjua. "I was like the archivist of this horrible thing that was happening, this beautiful response to it." She had told Carolyn's parents she would take pictures of the gathering and would record the audio.

Walking in, Matt pulled Adjua into a long hug. He asked how she was doing. She was finally catching up to the fact that she shared this grief with everyone. "I feel so tender right now and I really don't want to ever feel another way," she told him. He said he felt the same. "I refuse to harden myself," she said. She was so angry at the world that "I'm going to be softer and softer and softer in response."

This was when I arrived. I hadn't seen Adjua in ten months; we'd had a fight just after the New Year. I had thought about her a lot. We'd first met in 2010, when I'd applied to work at McNally Jackson. At the time, the store had a hiring policy that involved passing your CV across the front counter and a bookseller asking you questions on the spot, while taking notes on you. That day, Adjua was behind the till. She probably asked me what kinds of books I liked to read, and I probably told her what I was reading in grad school that semester. She wrote the words *quick and lively* on the top of my CV, and the store's owner called me a month later. We worked together for three years and quickly became close.

"I didn't know how to get back in touch," I told her now.

"Me either," she said.

We hugged. I can still feel that hug.

• • •

"Hi. Thank you all for coming," Adjua said into the microphone. Everyone quieted. People took their seats together and held hands, or they leaned against walls or into corners. "This room means so many different things to me," she said. She informed those present that she would be taking photos for Carolyn's family, who couldn't be there.

Kevin replaced her at the front. He wore a rumpled collared shirt and held a plastic cup of whiskey. His eyes were glassy with tears. He welcomed everyone to the new space.

Wendy's had moved in January 2016, when the owners of the building on Metropolitan Avenue had sold it, ejecting the many ad hoc galleries and studios inside. In my memory the old building lovingly calls to mind 1980s punk squats. One could look through the cracks in the floorboards to the story below. I had helped power-sand the floors because they didn't have any chairs, and people kept getting splinters from sitting on the unfinished planks. "Carolyn was thrilled by the new space, it's so fancy," says Kevin. "It was nice wood floors, I mean . . ." At least the wood was sealed.

"Oh my god, glass?" he remembers Carolyn saying about the street-facing windows. "White walls? Some flourish on the ceiling? The checkered bathroom?"

"It was very cute," says Kevin. "It was also nice to be on the ground, on the storefront. I think both of us were very excited to be more public facing, to be able to look through the windows and see eyes."

Rachel and Macgregor were out of town when they had to move in the dead of winter, so Matt, Carolyn, and Gabe had loaded everything into a van and moved it over in a snowstorm. "She was always making very practical things happen," says Gabe, "like making curtains and making it more of a home, a space that was nice to study in."

Along with the change in location came internal shifts. In the beginning, the aim was so broad—a place to read and write, and make art together—that no one imagined disagreeing about execution. After the move, "It was becoming, very quickly then, a literary and art institution," says Macgregor. Rachel was a sophisticated and visionary administrator and Kevin an enthusiastic fundraiser. Macgregor feared that if they weren't careful, Wendy's Subway would no longer be an intimate place for friends and fellow artists.

"I mean, we're not an institution really," Kevin said to those gathered at the vigil. "We're, like, friends that kind of hang out and love books. These bookshelves on the left are the new bookshelves we built. Carolyn helped build them. The tables on the right are tables that Carolyn helped carry here. Every single book here is a book that Carolyn helped bring here. That couch is one that Carolyn and I carried upstairs, at the old space. Everything in this room is something she touched. She slept on this couch, many, many, many, many nights. This was her house," he said.

She had her own apartment, sure, and probably many of those gathered had spent time in it, and shared thoughts, feelings, love, he said. "She also did that here a lot: feelings, love, books, writing, being annoyed with us for interrupting her writing." Even as she was also excited to talk about what they were doing, and about what she was doing.

"We are very happy and confused and lost and distraught and—supply the adjective, please; I don't know it—but this is her house, and you're in it. She was our family. She was our sister and our comrade and our colleague and our friend.

"And, man, people didn't know Carolyn really like Bard people," he says. "I see you."

Kevin invited others to come up to the microphone. "We're going to feel this together," he said. The microphone was the "conduit."

"Oh, and her notebooks," he added. "We put notebooks around. She loved writing. I'm sure a lot of you love writing." He invited everyone to sign them. "Jim, her dad, he would really love to see that."

Gradually, former classmates, roommates, friends, coworkers, and lovers approached the microphone. A close friend from Bard described living with Carolyn when she first moved to the city. She hadn't thought, coming to the vigil, that she'd say anything, but she'd say it: it was a little crazy living with Carolyn. "We didn't know about Home Depot and bought all our hardware at the dollar store." They were lost and jobless. They fed off each other's chaos and argued about typical roommate issues but reunited after Carolyn moved out. This week, she'd begun to realize how much of Carolyn was still around the apartment: bulk toothpaste, like sixteen tubes; beauty products; a shower hat; an ashtray; her favorite T-shirt. She slept in Carolyn's pajamas.

Gabe approached the microphone. He remembered Carolyn working on the original Wendy's space in Williamsburg. "We'd be doing construction and drinking Four Roses and it was not really work," he said. "She had this kind of beautiful incredulity to things that were bullshit, and this"—her being dead—"is the most bullshit."

Early in their friendship, they'd sometimes be at a Wendy's event that neither of them was digging, and they'd be talking in the back, instead of listening to the performance. "Do you have any whiskey?" she'd ask him, unable to stand whatever it was any longer.

"Yeah, Coco," he'd say, endearingly. "Here, just take it."

I got up to speak. I told everyone that Kevin had connected Carolyn with her job at McNally Jackson in early 2013, and that's how I'd met her. Kevin had been working at the store for a few months already, managing the philosophy section while I managed the adjacent poetry section. Soon after he started, we collaborated on a display that paired poets with philosophers whose work they seemed to be in conversation with, in our pretentious, twenty-something opinions. Another bookseller contributed book stands that were jury-rigged to hold tiny cigarettes and cups of coffee.

Carolyn had been hired into the bookstore café instead of onto the sales floor and hated it. She wanted to be a bookseller, not serve coffee. "After the holidays, they'd put her back in the café and she was really pissed off, because she loved books," I said to the room. Carolyn loved Simone Weil, a French feminist mystic and philosopher, and Mina Loy, a British novelist, poet, and playwright. I'll never forget her coming to the Essays Book Club I co-ran. The first time she came, in March 2013, we had selected Anne Carson's hybrid work *Decreation*, a book that combines poetry, essay, screenplay, libretto, oratorio, and opera. I had struggled with the text, but Carolyn came prepared to dominate the conversation. We all sat in awe of her as she talked circles around us.

Afterward, she and I stood shivering outside the store, smoking rolled cigarettes from her bag of loose tobacco. I asked Carolyn where she'd learned so much about Weil, on whom Carson centers *Decreation*. She told me about her studies at Bard, where Carson had briefly taught. I wasn't aware that Carolyn had gone there before moving to the city, or that she was friends with some of my other friends who'd gone there, who were now working around and alongside us at McNally Jackson.

What I can't remember is whether we knew by this point that we were from the same hometown and knew a lot of the same people from Florida. We discovered this one day while I was refilling my endless cup of free coffee, available to all booksellers, all day—a nonstop annoyance to the café workers who were forever navigating around us in the tiny space. During one of these maneuvers, I happened to ask Carolyn, who was still relatively new, where she was from. Or maybe she asked me.

"Wait, you're from Saint Petersburg?" one of us said.

We stared at each other in recognition. Suddenly, her scuffed kitten heels, slip skirts, and skinned knees made perfect sense. She was aloof but funny, at times brash, and sophisticated, yet rough around the edges in a way I recognized as a hallmark of Saint Pete natives. She wore long necklaces that hung between her breasts and her hair pulled back in a tight, messy bun with a headband, revealing defined cheekbones and a sensitive mouth, features that could have belonged to a classic film star.

She asked me if I knew Pamela. I said yes. I had met her in 2009, when she took my parents and me on a tour of the Raymond James art collection in Saint Petersburg, which she managed at the time. I'd also seen her since she'd moved to New York, as I'd moved there soon after she did, and had once had her over for dinner. Carolyn said they were best friends.

She asked if I knew a guy named Michael Assiff, whom she'd been dating. Stunned, I said yes. He and I had gone to high school together, at an arts magnet school where I studied singing and he studied visual art. He was a grade above me, and I rode the school bus with his best friend. One of my favorite memories involves getting stoned with them in a cemetery when I was fifteen. Carolyn looked sad, so I asked why. They'd broken up recently, she said. She'd really liked him.

I thanked everyone and returned to my seat. Kevin came back to the microphone. "I wanted to read this weird exchange, which she would probably be pissed about," he said. "So, we had this event Sunday," four days before the murder, "and I've told every one of the Wendy's people, she sent me these really funny texts."

The arrangement among Wendy's members was that they'd rotate running events. "We all took our turn," he said. "There's three fucking events" on the Sunday before. "There's only ten of us that do any of the events shit. So guess what, Carolyn?" He laughs. It was her turn this time, and she was mad.

"Hey, Carolyn, are you good for this event?" Kevin had texted her Sunday night.

"Yeah, probably!" she'd responded.

Thirty minutes later, she texted again. "Wait, unless you're close by?"

"I'm home, alas," said Kevin.

"Like a bajillion people are here, all of a sudden, totally fine though," she said.

"Okay. Oh really?" he said. "Well, that's good, right? There's beer. Hope that works out. I'm sure it'll be fine, let me know if you really need anything. I just started cooking."

Twenty minutes later: "This is very garbage," she said, about the readings. "I'm dying. I can't not talk shit."

"That bad, huh?" said Kevin.

"Intermission. They're playing emo pop rock. No irony. No. No." She described a few of the pieces being read, in cringeworthy detail. A little later, still during intermission, she said, "Actual Dashboard Confessional actually was playing." This is funny to me because I know that she used to like Dashboard Confessional.

Kevin, seeing all these texts, decided he definitely wasn't going to the event now. He responded, "Fuck, sorry dude. Yeah. Today was bad too. Sorry."

"There was a story about buying a bridesmaid dress. Another about 'adulting' as a writer." Several sad screaming emoji faces. "K I'm done," she said.

Then later, she reported, "Yay, yay, that's done! Sorry, that was shit."

. . .

Chris thanked everyone for coming. "It feels really wonderful to see the amount of people that are here in this space that meant a lot to her," he said. He admitted that, over the last few days, he'd felt a lot of emotions. He kept thinking of the last time he saw her, how she adoringly teased him. "I just keep thinking of her, rolling her eyes. I keep thinking of her smoking her cigarettes. Like Adjua said, if you asked her how she was, she would tell you everything. And if she asked me how I was, and I wasn't going through the best time, she was open and she listened and she was a really good person, and I will miss her for a very long time, as I'm sure everyone else will." He became emotional and paused, stepping away from the microphone.

"Sorry," he continued. "Recently, we were joking around and I was telling her about my complicated love life."

She made a joke. "I don't want you to fall in love with me," she said.

"Carolyn, don't worry. I won't," he'd responded. Now, he said, "I feel like I didn't live up to my part of the bargain."

• • •

Rachel stood to say a few words, reading from something she'd written. She told the story of meeting Carolyn three years earlier, when Wendy's was beginning. "We were huddled in a great big loft drinking whiskey and wine to ward off the winter cold and dreaming of a space with others, which became this home for us." Three years later, it still felt like the beginning. "The beginning of really knowing her, of being let into the complex world of such an infinitely creative and intelligent and witty person. To know what she dreamed about and thought about and wanted to do. She was applying to graduate schools. She was writing ferocious texts. I had never seen her so passionate."

A few months prior, they had begun working on a compilation of essays they would write with the rest of the group at Wendy's Subway, "around the question of how to live together." They were basing it on the book by Roland Barthes called *How to Live Together*. The format was an abecedarium. Participants selected terms to define in their own language later. Carolyn had selected the term *parataxis* and defined it as "simultaneity, alone together," signing with her initials to signal to the others that she would expand on the definition later. She never had the opportunity. "All of her thoughts were incredible departures into new territories, which I could only hope to read more about as we wrote this month," Rachel said.

Last year, Carolyn had shared an essay she was writing with Rachel and Matt. "She was tentative about it, as it was just the beginning, but she wanted to share it with us and hear our thoughts," Rachel said. It was rare for Carolyn to show her writing to others, so they knew this was a treasured opportunity to know her more deeply. "She wrote about angels, about Maria Callas singing Verdi arias, and about how pathetically mediocre Maria Callas was but how beautiful it was."

Rachel read aloud from Carolyn's essay. "It was like parataxis," wrote Carolyn, "and the chance operation of parataxis, the accumulative algebra of parataxis, its absolute certainty, which is felt precisely as a continuity of emptiness."

Her essay is written like an extended prose poem blending memoir and criticism. In it, Carolyn is walking around the city in the gentle rain intermittently crying, listening to the opera singer. She admits that she knows very little about opera, but nonetheless, she is swept away by the emotion. She looks at her phone and sees that the shattered glass on the screen makes heart shapes. She appreciates it the way that she would a beautiful landscape.

Rachel keeps that image with her, of Carolyn walking through the streets of New York City and sobbing to Maria Callas in her headphones, "thinking about debt and angels and embodiment and infinite deferral and catharsis."

"And also, all the images of her dancing here and writing and reading and chain-smoking and bursting in," she said. "Always perched on a heel the right height."

6.

The Plea Deal

In March 2019, I'm living in Saint Petersburg and teaching an hour south in Sarasota, at New College of Florida, a small public liberal arts school that Carolyn had considered attending instead of Bard. It's a Saturday night around ten o'clock and my new boyfriend, Patrick, and I are both peaking on psychedelic mushrooms, melting into our living room furniture, giggling uncontrollably, when I get a call from Pamela. Given the hour, I'm afraid it's serious, so I answer, deciding I'll keep my condition a secret.

"They offered Render a plea deal," she says.

"What?" I've missed any clues in the preceding months that this was coming. By now, two and a half years have passed since the murder. I had been attending pretrial hearings while living in New York City, but since moving to Florida, I have not been able to attend any. Each of Pamela's words floats separately inside my skull, like the negative ends of magnets repelling each other. "Say that again?" I step outside.

"He's saying he had marijuana-induced psychosis," she says. "It comes with a sentence of ten to fifteen years." I would later learn the charge being offered to him in the deal was "criminally negligent homicide."

I grow suspicious of the conversation. "Marijuana-induced psychosis," I say. "Is that real?" I'm suddenly laughing and unable to stop. "Wait, are you fucking with me?"

"I'm serious."

Still laughing, I now also begin to cry. The absurdity is hysterical, tragicomic. I hear Patrick inside talking to our cats and I stare into our empty street, without streetlights.

"This conversation is real?" I say again.

"Sarah, it's real."

"Oh my god." I can't tell her what I'm experiencing, embarrassed not to be prepared for this moment. "Pamela, I can't believe this is happening right now."

"I know."

"No, like, right in this moment. This makes no sense."

"I know."

. . .

On Monday, I call ADA Jack Warsawsky, who has retired and handed the case to another prosecutor, whose identity Pamela and I don't yet know. "You never know what a jury might do," he says, explaining why the DA's office might want to avoid an expensive trial. "He's saying this was caused by ingesting marijuana." He goes on to tell me that Render's lawyers are claiming that in high school Render had suffered an episode where he smoked weed and had to go to the emergency room. "There's plusses and minuses with that theory of the defense.

"Our medical reports indicate that there was no marijuana in his system," he says. "Blood was taken at the hospital. We sent them to a private lab to see if there was synthetic marijuana, and that came back negative. That obviously would be a plus for us and would possibly negate that defense."

I mull this, whether it's possible for Render to have smoked weed in an amount small enough not to show up in a blood test yet potent enough to induce a psychotic reaction. In addition, a psychotic reaction wouldn't explain the actions he took in that state, since most people who experience psychosis, even untreated, do not commit violent crimes. And those who do can still be held responsible for them, if a prosecutor can prove they knew what they were doing was wrong, despite their psychosis.

"You also have to understand," says Warsawsky, "look, for all intents and purposes he was leading a law-abiding life. It wasn't like he was beating up somebody every other day of the week or had run-ins with the law. This is something out of left field. For jurors, it's: How do they come to understand what happened in this situation when he's really had no previous record of violence, and then all of a sudden he commits a violent act? It's going to be hard for twelve people to look at this kid and say, 'You're guilty,' knowing it's going to take a large part of his life being spent in jail."

At this point, I think to myself, *Really?* I imagine being a juror. I was once called but not selected for jury duty, for a trial involving someone being injured—a car accident or medical malpractice, I can't exactly remember. I imagine that most trials came with points of moral contention. But this one? Render? He stabbed Carolyn seven times.

"Even though they're not supposed to think about that, we don't live in a make-believe world," says Warsawsky. "We as DAs and lawyers know that jurors think about that. The jury, they do what they want to do. They don't have to explain why. If they feel that they can't bring themselves to do what the law says they should do, they can say, 'Not guilty.' You have to pick the right people to be on a jury, and we don't always succeed."

I ask him if a sentence of ten to fifteen years seems a little light to him, given the crime.

"I've been doing this for a long time and it's not unusual," he says. "We look at a case differently than a family does. It's a traumatic experience. Their life will never be the same. We have a bunch of cases. Nobody has just one case, except maybe the bureau chief and some executives have that luxury. But the line assistants have a multiple caseload. Normally, when both sides agree, it's a way for the judge to resolve the case and the judge nine times out of ten will accept that."

. . .

In the summer, the DA's office pulls the deal. Jim says, "I really, really got upset when there was a plea bargain. I got on the phone with Brian and his boss," meaning ADA Brian Hughes, the new prosecutor. "I was very demeaning to Brian and the justice system he worked with. Then it was silent for a couple of months, and then we found out, 'Oh no, they've taken a plea off the table and they're going to trial.'"

"The DA hadn't been in touch with the family," says Ann to Carol, Pamela, and me in the pizza parlor across from the courthouse, after one of Render's preliminary hearings soon after. By now, I've moved back to New York City. Together, we are learning the terminology: Sandoval hearings, Molineux hearings, motions in limine. Ann has created a vocabulary bank and shared it with all of us over email, in one of many ongoing threads.

"They hadn't been in touch with the family, or they didn't know that the family would object," says Carol. "Then they found out that the family did object. Susan said, 'That can't happen! That can't happen!' That's when I got back into it because, I mean, nothing happened for three years." Everyone was wondering if Render would ever go to trial. "It was like, 'Oh, well it's going to be at least a year,' and then a year stretched into two."

"I think the defense took that long to do the research, wind up the psychiatric exams, get the results," says Ann. "Line up another one. Get more results. But apparently the plea deal had been offered. It had been accepted. And the judge had not ruled on it. So the defense was very taken aback that it was pulled off the table."

"But I mean, marijuana-induced psychosis," says Pamela. "Does that always mean you attack somebody? Is it a violent thing?"

"It's something that we didn't know existed," Jenny would tell me eighteen months later, on the phone, "that I thought was so laughable. I mean, I've smoked pot. You've smoked pot. I have never even considered killing somebody. How do we walk in as grown-ups who understand what pot is and think this could have happened?"

. . .

In the fall of 2019, Render officially waives his right to a jury trial. He'll have a bench trial, heard by a judge whose identity is changing weekly or daily, along with all the trial's details, including the date of the hearing to set the dates for it. "Hughes felt that the judge would want to schedule the trial as soon as possible since it has been postponed for so long," Ann writes to us in one of our threads. She'd spoken to Hughes directly and he'd explained that the cannabis-psychosis plea had been defended successfully in other parts of the country but not yet in New York. Because of that, "There are no precedents that he can use as a prosecutor."

. . .

On October 3, 2019, there's another continuation. The trial dates will be set on October 11, then the 18th, then the 22nd. It's looking as though the start will be in November, during the week of Thanksgiving. A few days later, Ann emails us, "I believe Jim will not make it up for the trial."

"Susan very much wants to be there, but who knows," Pamela responds. "Carol is likely to attend if either parent doesn't, or to support Susan if she comes. Jenny won't as she will be into her 8th month and already doesn't feel like traveling." She was pregnant with her first child.

When I later meet with Jim and Cindy, I ask them about their decision not to attend. "I struggled personally about whether I should go to the trial and the trial wasn't about Carolyn," says Jim. "It was about Render. I don't think I could have lived through that test."

"Those are the final things you're going to see of Carrie," says Cindy. "When I think of Carrie, first thing I think of is that picture on the computer when we had to ID her."

"Me sitting in that trial would imply a respect for Render in a court that I don't have," says Jim.

. . .

Carolyn had started visiting Pamela in dreams. "The very first dream that I ever had with Carrie is that I was waiting for a call on a land-line," says Pamela. "I was in a Florida sunroom or on a porch. Finally the call came. It was a bad connection, then finally it was crackling and came in, and it was Carrie."

"Hi!" Pamela said.

"Oh my God, I'm so sorry, I should have called sooner," said Carolyn. "I've just been so busy over here."

"What are you doing over there?" Pamela knew that she was call-ing from the other world.

Carolyn was like, "Oh, I had to get my new house in order, and I had to go through all of this training for my new job."

"Whoa," said Pamela. "Well, what it is like over there?"

"Well, it's just like how it is there, except there's less men." Then she started laughing. "It makes sense when you think about it, because we're all made up of mostly female energy."

"Aren't we all female first?" asks Pamela. "Then the extra chromo-some is added."

Pamela had started writing a novel with Carolyn as a character. "It's forty thousand words so far," she says. "I had this other dream where Carolyn told me her only regret was not publishing her book, that it was all done. I told her to give it to me, that everyone would believe I had found it. She said she would. In the dream, it felt literal, like she'd give me a physical copy. Now I realize that wasn't it at all, because some of what I'm writing is just her."

"I told you about the dream that I had about Carrie where she was being interviewed by Terry Gross, right?" she says. "I only remember hearing the interview. It's Terry Gross's voice. It's super iconic."

"Okay, so we're here with Carolyn Bush who was . . . ," said Terry.

"There's this introduction," says Pamela.

"Tell us what happened," said Terry to Carolyn.

"Well, it was really surprising," said Carolyn, laughing. "You really don't expect for your friend to stab you. I thought he was joking at first when he held up the knife, but now I understand a lot more about what's happening there."

"Well, what was happening then?" said Terry.

"It really had nothing to do with me at all," said Carolyn. "I had no choice in the matter, because I had signed a contract before I was even born."

"Then Terry was asking questions about that," says Pamela.

"Oh yeah, no, no, really," said Carolyn. "You make all of these arrangements because actually death has very little to do with the person who dies. It has to do with everyone else around them."

7.

Grieving Giver

Riven River

One year earlier, in 2018, I'm interviewing Adjua in a coffee shop in the West Village. It's cold and overcast, and it's the first time we've talked at length about Carolyn since she died. "I wrote about her," she says. She tells me she agreed to participate in a reading at The Poetry Project called "It's After the End of the World, Don't You Know That Yet?: Writing in the Shadow of Human Extinction." The reading was just a few weeks after the murder, and the piece she read "was an early draft of trying to pull together my understanding of Blackness and femininity, and the parallels with plant life, and how that resource is not valued," she says. She was working as a flower courier then, "bringing the dying carcasses of floral material from human to human in acts of celebration." Humans raise these beings only to kill them. She felt compelled to write about that, and about "that trans-moment of turning myself into an extremely delicate version of myself in order to rage, fully grieve, how this beautiful young woman was taken from the world."

Then she caught wind that Matt had written something about Carolyn too, and that his work was connected to the tarot. At the Met, Matt had bought a poster of a tarot deck by photographer Bea Nettles, made in the 1970s, featuring people she knew. *I really want to write something about this*, he'd thought. Then Carolyn was murdered, and he used the poster as a prompt to write about her. Soon after, he was asked to read at a series on the Lower East Side called GUTS, described as "bare-bones" and encouraging experimentation. Writers were invited to read new work and discuss it in an intimate setting.

In October, less than a month after Carolyn died, Matt shared the tarot-deck-inspired essay into which he'd poured a lot of his immediate thoughts and feelings. After, he "felt super weird about it, actually," he would later tell me. Following the reading, another poet came up to him and said, "I don't think I could have written something so soon after I lost somebody." *Oh no*, Matt thought. *Did I just do a terrible thing?* "I had worked on it really hard, and it was a little bit polished," he says. "I had turned it into a very structured piece of writing very quickly." He feared the other poet's comment meant his grief wasn't real.

It's been a file on his computer ever since. He's never thought to do anything with or about it. He's written about Carolyn since then, but only once, and "she's mentioned so tangentially that if you weren't paying attention, you'd barely notice." He sees it as a reaction to the way that first piece was written, so raw and immediate. Now that he's written about her twice, he thinks maybe he should stop. He really loved Carolyn and she meant a lot to him, but they'd never had "super deep" conversations. Others were closer with her, and he feels "nervous about claiming more than is my right to claim."

Is memory a limited resource? Is grief? Should they be carried alone or shared? Matt worries that, in writing about Carolyn, he was "tearing through the memories that feel really vivid to me." He explains, "I don't want to process them out of existence." He found himself asking, "Does all of this have to get turned into writing?"

"You overwrite it and then shape it a little bit," he says. Writing about anything, you reduce it, in giving it form, language, and meaning, when truly, what you experience is beyond words. He shared his feelings with Rachel, who admitted to having them too. When she talked to people about Carolyn, she noticed that "the things she was saying turned into a little script," says Matt. She would hear herself telling more than one person the same story in the same way, using the same words. "It would start to take on a shape. I think she got very spooked by that."

After the GUTS reading, Gabe reached out to Adjua to let her know about Matt's piece. They exchanged what they'd both written. "I called him crying such cathartic tears of gratitude and grief," she says.

That fall, for Adjua, "everything was so hard that my brain went into categorizing," she says. The story of Carolyn and Render took on fairy-tale and allegorical tropes in her mind; everything became metaphor. "It was a stress response," she says, but it was also an interesting thing to observe about her own brain, as an artist. It has helped her understand the importance of fairy tales and mythology. Sometimes there are too many details, too many feelings; the meaning of them gets lost. You need "a structure so that you can talk about it."

As an example, Render's name "short circuits" something in her mind, about the various meanings of that word, *render*. She didn't at first consider *draw* as a synonym; she'd only thought of it in terms of melting, such as at a *rendering plant*, where one sends the cadavers of dead animals to be reduced into other materials, for human use. It also means "to bring about," or "give," such as in *rendering services*. *Render* is also a synonym for *deliver* or *impart* or *administer*, such as when *rendering judgment* in a courtroom.

Leading up to the presidential election in November, which was to take place just five weeks after the murder, at one point Adjua became very ill and was home with a fever. She saw Donald Trump on television. "I just started crying," she says. In her fevered, fairy-tale understanding, refracted through immense grief, anger, and confusion, she thought, *He's the villain that wants to end the world and he's on TV. We're praising this monster. My society is fucked.* "I saw it really clearly," she says. "I felt such frustration." *The only person I want to talk to about how crazy this is is the person who was killed.* Her highly intelligent friend Carolyn with whom, she knew, she would be able to talk about anything.

"I have to say something that I feel embarrassed by," she says. "As a young child, I wanted to know what this felt like. I wanted to know what losing somebody felt like. I envied the emotional extremes of grief and tragedy."

Author T Kira Madden writes about a similar feeling in her memoir, *Long Live the Tribe of Fatherless Girls*, but from another angle, imagining herself as the one people are grieving for. I happen to have a copy with me in my backpack, so I read a passage aloud for Adjua in the coffee shop. "What I wanted was my freckled cheeks printed on cheap paper, stapled around the ears, the flyers torn from telephone poles and the scales of palm trees, a sliver of my face left flapping in the wind." Madden describes someone jogging past a trash compactor and seeing her "beaten blue knees with their warm fuzz of kiddie hair." But did she want to die? "Not really, no. I wanted the beauty of the doomed." Adjua pauses over this last line, "beauty of the doomed." "Missing girls are never forgotten, I thought, so long as they don't show up dead," writes Madden. "So long as they stay missing."

If they stay missing, then they become the stuff of legend; they can be for us whatever we make them. But Carolyn didn't stay missing, we say. What does that mean for her? Does it mean she will be forgotten? Or is there another meaning of *missing*? Like the way we miss her now because we can't talk to her anymore. We worry about what kind of legend she may become. "I cannot tell you how much *Law & Order* I have watched in my life," says Adjua. She hasn't been able to watch it since Carolyn was murdered; it feels wrong to her now. "I would think about what happened to her, and I was having flashes of this really manipulative crime show." *What the fuck have I been watching?* she thought. *Why have I been entertaining myself with this thing that's so painful?*

I relate to this. Growing up, one of my favorite movies was the 1968 adaptation by Carol Reed of the stage musical *Oliver!*, based on the Charles Dickens novel *Oliver Twist*. I rewound our VHS tape a hundred times between the ages of three and thirteen. I knew every line of dialogue and every trill to every song. Still, some of the finer details of the story eluded me. I did not understand that Nancy, Oliver's surrogate mother on the streets, was a sex worker. I didn't fully grasp the enormity of the scene in which the burglar Bill Sykes, her boyfriend, in an alley at night, stabs her until she stops screaming. Yes, I understood that it was murder. I understood that Nancy was dead, and that Bill then eventually flees with Oliver as a captive, and that he then gets shot and accidentally hangs himself from a rooftop and dies too. I did not understand the seriousness of what Bill did to Nancy, though—maybe because it's so quickly overshadowed by what happens to him; maybe because I was too young, too naive, to grasp the finality and agony of death; maybe because death delivered as entertainment by its very nature robs mortality of this finality and agony.

In 1989, my parents taped *A Cry for Help: The Tracey Thurman Story* off the TV. It's a made-for-TV movie based on the true story of Tracey Thurman, a woman who was attempting to escape her abusive husband, Charles "Buck" Thurman, in 1983, when he stabbed her thirteen times in the chest, neck, and throat, and then, in full view of a police officer, their toddler son, and several neighbors, stomped on her head, breaking her neck. She survived but was partially paralyzed. Her lawsuit against the Torrington, Connecticut, police, for failing to protect her, brought the epidemic of domestic violence to national attention and led to the passing of the Thurman Law in Connecticut, which requires police to treat domestic violence like any other violent crime. At that time, and arguably still, domestic battery was considered a family matter. Despite having a restraining order against Buck, Tracey's fears were treated differently because she was a woman and because she was still married to her abuser.

I was four when the movie came out. My mother was the director of a domestic violence shelter in Clearwater and spent her extracurricular hours lobbying the Florida legislature for laws protecting victims. The movie was likely an inspiration to her. I was an only child with parents who let my curiosity roam unfettered, and I discovered the VHS in our cabinet. *A Cry for Help* doesn't shy away from dramatizing Buck's violent attacks, including the final one, the way he continued beating, kicking, and stomping on Tracey while she lay bleeding on the ground. In the movie, he forced their young son, C. J., to look at his dying mother, telling him, "I killed your fucking mother." The actor playing Buck orders bystanders to let her die. He tries to climb inside the ambulance to interfere with paramedics fighting to save her.

Over the course of several weeks, I remember rewinding the tape ten or so times. I remember thinking the actress who played Tracey was pretty. How the quiet suburban neighborhood reminded me of my own. How her son looked to be near the same age as I was, with brown hair like mine. How her screams reminded me of Nancy's in *Oliver!* and gave me the same sense of fear, tension, and release.

Finally, my dad sat me down. My mother didn't want me to watch *A Cry for Help* anymore, he said. It made her sad. I felt guilty and ashamed for making my mother sad. I knew that, before meeting my father, she had been married to a violent man. I did not know how much like Bill Sykes and Buck Thurman that man was. I did not know what that meant for my mother; that, in another life, she might have ended up like Tracey or Nancy. I did not know until writing this that the real Buck Thurman was released on probation after serving only eight years of his twenty-year prison sentence. That he later moved to Massachusetts, remarried, and had another child. That, in 2008, when asked about Tracey, he told *Republican-American*, "I am tired of hearing about it."

When I tell people that I'm writing about Carolyn, what happened to her and what happened to her murderer, often they ask me if I've read Maggie Nelson's poetry book *Jane: A Murder*, about her mother's sister, who died before Nelson was born and whose killer escaped capture. Or whether I've read her memoir *The Red Parts*, about attending the trial of Jane's murderer, when he was finally caught. I have; I read many books about murder when I started writing this one. I hadn't previously read any in the genre known as "true crime," and I still don't read many books about murderers, though I've enjoyed some books about their victims, such as James Ellroy's memoir *My Dark Places*, about his mother's murder when he was a child.

Sometimes, when I tell people I'm writing about Carolyn, they tell me not to. They are afraid that a book about her will flatten her for easy consumption, turn her into entertainment, glamorize her murder. Michael Assiff, my high school classmate and friend who dated her, told me, when we met to talk about this project, that he wished there could be a rebuttal to whatever I wrote, published simultaneously, to capture her complexity. I agreed. He said, "She's smarter than both of us."

Around the time I started my research, I asked for recommendations for true-crime books on Facebook. Matt told me that the post had inspired a conversation between him and Rachel. "I remember our feelings then being complex," says Rachel. "What does it mean to write about someone's death? What is that writer taking on? And why?" I was glad for the questions. I knew nothing back then about the inner workings of the justice system or how to write about it. I knew nothing about how to write about murder, or how not to write about it. I needed to know how to do it wrong, so I could know how to do it right. I needed to know what motivated other people so I could figure out what was motivating me. Was it a thirst for justice? Fear for my own safety in a sexist culture? Grief—though, like Matt's, mine wasn't as profound as those who were closer to Carolyn? Entertainment, fame, or money? Fascination and curiosity with death? A desperate desire to know why?

I wanted to know why it happened; I can't deny that was a motivation. I wrote Render a letter in prison immediately, simply asking him why, though I knew he wouldn't answer. I was shocked and disgusted and hurting for the people around me. More important, I wanted to know Carolyn. We had only just begun to form a friendship. I liked her and was intimidated by her, and there was potential for so much more and then she was suddenly gone, and I regretted the time we didn't have. We had planned to hang out again but didn't have the opportunity. Life got in the way and then death did. There were so many ways to keep knowing her. One was through the people we both knew. Once I began talking to them, I feared the stories they told me would be lost, so I started recording them. I cared very much what happened to them.

In her book *Dead Girls*, Alice Bolin writes about the cultural phenomenon of the dead white woman, including a consideration of *The Red Parts*. She interrogates a strange twist the story takes when Nelson's family participates in an episode of the true crime show *48 Hours Mystery*. "Nelson becomes a character in *48 Hours*'s version, the writer niece whose work is fascinated with her aunt's death," writes Bolin. "A producer tells Nelson that their episode will help other people mourn." Given the show's previous episodes, with titles like "Where's Baby Sabrina?" and "JonBenét: DNA Rules Out Parents," Nelson asks the producer "if there's a reason why stories about the bizarre, violent deaths of young, good-looking, middle- to upper-class white girls help people to mourn better than other stories."

Bolin says these stories "help us to work out our complicated feelings about the privileged status of white women in our culture." It's true that white women hold a privileged status in comparison to other groups, even after they die. But I'm not sure our complicated feelings about their privilege are driving the frenzy around stories of their death. That perspective frames those stories as a sort of revenge for that privilege, which would suggest that the people writing them don't have the same privilege, or perhaps have it but feel guilty for having it.

A white woman is "the perfect victim," says Bolin, and I agree with this, insofar as there is such a thing ("perfect" by what measure). She's white and therefore more people will watch her on TV and listen to podcasts with her easily pronounceable name for the English tongue.

Because racism is woven into the fabric of our culture, white women drive views and clicks, alive or dead. The dead white woman is a woman, and our culture, for some reason that I still can't explain, seems to hate anyone who isn't a man, so a white woman is easy and convenient and marketable to kill. Since Christian theology is also woven into the fabric of our culture, and since the dead white woman is a woman, in stories told about her, she is depicted as virginal, maternal, or promiscuous; her death is surprising and tragic, or it is to be expected; we can easily understand and consume it without too much reflection.

Bolin writes of dead white women "effacing the deaths of leagues of nonwhite or poor or ugly or disabled or immigrant or drug-addicted or gay or trans victims," and she's not wrong. In 2016, just a few days after Trump's election, American journalist Gwen Ifill died. She had coined the phrase "Missing White Woman Syndrome" to describe the disparity in the media attention given to missing white women versus missing people of color. One study found that missing white women were ten times more likely to receive media coverage than their counterparts of color. Consequently, missing people of color are less likely to be found.

Maggie Nelson's aunt's story became satisfying under *48 Hours'* gaze. The "years of compulsion, confusion, and damage," writes Nelson, were sublimated into a narrative to be consumed by the masses, "a story of struggle and hope," or so the show would like you to think. "But to achieve that seductive conclusion, the story must be over before it begins," writes Bolin. What is Carolyn's story? Is it over now that she's dead?

· · ·

Danielle Sinay and Carolyn both lived on the third floor of Tewksbury Hall their first semester at Bard. Tewksbury was the party dorm, and much of it is a blur, she says. "I remember I mispronounced her name, and she corrected me," says Danielle—she'd said "Caroline." She remembers Carolyn seeming older than others around her, more worldly, a woman among girls. They spent days and nights together and accrued a group of friends that included Casey Romaine, Ally Davis, and Carolyn's roommate, Taylor "Iggy" Isaacson, all of whom received a group text from Danielle with the news of her murder.

As Ally remembers, the text included one of the first-published articles and Danielle's question: "Why is this journalist Facebook chatting me about Carolyn and Render's murder?" Ally looked at her own Messenger. A journalist had messaged her too. She ran outside and called Iggy, who went outside at her own job and smoked a cigarette, then took the rest of the day off. Iggy was living with another Bard alum at the time. A few days later, the two of them met up with other alumni in Los Angeles, everyone bewildered and devastated.

A month later, Danielle spread Carolyn's "ashes" at Blithewood Manor, a historic three-story Georgian mansion at Bard, where everyone would hang out when it was sunny on campus and tan and day drink. "Carolyn sat in a can of ground sage," Danielle wrote about the one-person ceremony she held. "She loved sage, and I didn't have her ashes. But I had to make do: I promised I'd spread her spirit where we'd seen her the happiest."

Blithewood is famously haunted. The Hudson River flows past. There are English gardens of statuary and flowering trees, and there's a wide field leading down to woods. Trails connect to a protected preserve called Tivoli Bays, where in 1997 a Bard student and her seven-year-old daughter were raped. The attack came just two years after a similar attack on another Bard student. The dean of students at the time said they could not rule out that the attacker was a Bard student. He was never caught, and it didn't help that Bard did little to aid the investigation.

Danielle remembers another classmate passed away since they had graduated, of an overdose. He knew Carolyn too, at Bard. Danielle enjoys imagining them reuniting in the afterlife. She and Ally, by the time Carolyn died, had already conceived of an entire afterlife in which all of their many dead friends from Bard College were hanging out again. One way, I have noticed, that people make sense of Carolyn's death is by placing it within a larger pattern. "They all live together," says Danielle, "but Carolyn does not live with them. She lives next door and uses their Wi-Fi. They're too loud for her. I have a whole narrative to make me feel better about all of this."

"There's so much crazy shit that has happened at Bard," says Alexis Graman, who lived with Carolyn in Tivoli during one of the semesters that she was taking a leave of absence from her studies—according to her family, at the administration's behest. "I knew a bunch of people who killed themselves," he says. "Usually in the yards. Two boys." And a roommate of Alexis and Carolyn in Tivoli. He struggled with severe mental illness while he was a student and killed himself about a year before Carolyn died.

Alexis knew Render. "There's people like that" at Bard, he says. The violence of the school adds up to something less than accidental in his mind. He tells me of two previous incidents by Bard students. The first was in 2011. Alexis was in class with a kid whose girlfriend had been hit by a car about six months prior. While she was comatose in a nearby hospital, he infiltrated it and stabbed her in the ribs. She miraculously survived for another two months.

Also, many years before Alexis came to the school, in 1998, an art student was murdered by her boyfriend, a recent Bard graduate. She had transferred from Reed College to Bard to be with him. They were arguing when he used his friend's camping knife to slit her throat in a parking lot in Barrytown, a mile from Bard. About Bard, and its history of associated violence, Alexis says, "I think it's something about the culture."

8.

Day One

———

"He assaulted another inmate," says Ann, at the end of the first trial day, November 25, 2019. She's referring, of course, to Render. "He punched him in the face and did not stop when ordered to." We are talking on the phone via Pamela's car Bluetooth as she drives Ann and Carol back to their Airbnb from the courthouse. ADA Brian Hughes had described the incident to Justice Richard Buchter in the courtroom that day before giving his opening arguments.

Days later, I will obtain the transcript of the opening arguments and read about the incident. On October 16, 2019, Render had punched another inmate after a verbal exchange in the dorm area, and the two had to be separated. "Defendant did write a statement in connection to this incident," Hughes said in court. "He acknowledged having punched the other individual in the face, though he refused to plead guilty to the infraction because he stated that the cellblock that was written on the paperwork was incorrect; he couldn't in good faith plead guilty. He ultimately was convicted of a violent infraction."

The defense would hold their opening statements until it was their turn to present their case, after the prosecution had presented theirs. But they cross-examined the prosecution's witnesses. "His attorney Margulis is very slick," says Pamela on our call, of Zachary Margulis-Ohnuma, Render's cocounsel alongside Philip Smallman. "They're definitely trying to gear up for this insanity plea. He asked a few leading questions like, 'Doesn't he look like a crazy person in this picture?' which was a surveillance still. Asking about the weather, try-ing to lead toward, like, 'Obviously, only a crazy person would be walking around in their underwear.'"

Margulis-Ohnuma had also asked Officer Cumur, of Joshua Cruz, "Pretty much based on what you remember he said a crazy guy attacked him out of the blue, right?"

Hughes objected. Buchter allowed it.

"No, he didn't say 'crazy guy,'" Cumur had answered.

"All the people on the other side were retiree age," says Carol, referring to those in the audience who had come out in support of Render.

"They were all wealthy," says Ann. "They look like aunts and uncles, grandparents, a few younger people. His brother was there. His brother left and sat in the hall for a large portion of it. It might've been too much for him."

"He was sitting there quietly with his head down and his eyes closed," says Carol.

Adjua had also been there. She was the only other person sitting on Carolyn's side of the courtroom, with Pamela, Ann, and Carol. Hughes had warned that it would be emotional for the families to see each other, and potentially difficult to avoid confrontations, so the courtroom had naturally divided itself. Ann, Carol, and Pamela had arrived at the courthouse with printed-out photos of Carolyn. "Brian can't allow the audience to hold the photographs, but we still had them on the seats with us," says Ann. Four days earlier, Jenny had given birth to a girl. She came two days after Carolyn's twenty-ninth birthday.

9.

The Woman's Club

There were daisies blooming everywhere at Carolyn's memorial at the St. Petersburg Woman's Club, on Snell Isle, on the west central coast of Florida. In lieu of flowers, the family had asked for contributions to Wendy's Subway. "I can't tell you how much Mike and I appreciate all the kindness, flowers, meals, Carrie anecdotes, well-wishes, GoFundMe donations, and compassion you've shown us over the past few weeks," Jenny wrote on Facebook, inviting people to the service. "My family and I would be especially touched if you'd like to stand and share a memory or two, as we're not sure we'll be up to it." It would take place on November 20, 2016, the day after Carolyn's twenty-sixth birthday.

Snell Isle is a lush green neighborhood of historic brick streets and waterfront mansions. Its location on a peninsula gives it a feeling of privacy. It's named after its developer, C. Perry Snell, who in the 1910s bought 275 acres that were mostly underwater; registered his own business to do dredging, lay streets, and install utilities; and literally moved earth to build homes there for the ultra-wealthy. He then donated the land for the Woman's Club, one of the first clubs of its kind, giving a home to what he considered to be the most important local organization. The building features Mediterranean revival architecture, arched windows and doorways, a shady courtyard, terra cotta tile, and a picturesque view of the bay. Today it is salmon pink.

Snell Isle held personal history for Carolyn as well—the peninsula was the site of many a group ride during the days of The Skirts, an all-girl bicycle gang she cofounded with Pamela. Through it they raised money for organizations serving victims of domestic violence and they promoted getting girls on bikes. This was in 2008. Jenny had moved to Portland and told Pamela, "Take care of my baby sister," a charge she took seriously. Pamela already owned a house in Saint Petersburg and Carolyn had her own set of keys. She and Pamela spent most of their time together, going to punk shows and riding their bikes, and each finishing school—Carolyn at St. Petersburg Collegiate High School and Pamela at USF St. Petersburg.

The two years in between Jenny moving to Portland and Carolyn's own move to Bard at the age of eighteen were deeply formative for her. She started driving. She worked her first part-time jobs, tutoring, assisting at a preschool, and working at a dermatology clinic. She worked toward her associate's degree. She started asking people to call her Carolyn instead of Carrie. "Carolyn is just a better name," says Pamela, who started going by Pamela instead of Pam for the same reason.

Then there was The Skirts. Pamela and Carolyn started brainstorming with their friends, other women who rode bikes, and came up with a mission statement: "We believe a bicycle represents independence, self-sufficiency and mobility. Through cycling, we strive to empower women and girls." Pamela was president and Carolyn was vice president. "We decided that it would be stupid not to try to do some good with it, so we would have fundraisers and sell cupcakes at the races," says Pamela. They hosted night rides on the beach, bike polo matches, safety classes, mechanical workshops, vegan brunches, and races that began and ended at locally owned businesses. They carpooled to races in Sarasota, Tampa, Orlando, and Atlanta and competed and placed in them.

• • •

I was not able to attend Carolyn's memorial in Florida. I was working out of state at the time, living paycheck to paycheck, and headed toward a divorce, and I could not afford the ticket. Nor could Adjua, Kevin, or Emily afford to attend. Carolyn's friend from Bard, Masha Mitkov, had originally planned to stay at my parents' house about thirty minutes north of Snell Isle. Then, a week before the memorial, she and her partner got lost in the desert in the Imperial Sand Dunes, about a hundred miles south of Joshua Tree National Park, and were missing for six days. They had resorted to drinking their own urine. They were found on Friday the eighteenth, the day before Carolyn's birthday. Masha did not make it to the memorial in Florida two days later.

Chris and Rachel did attend the memorial, however. "That entire time period felt so unreal," says Chris of Masha and her partner getting lost, then found. "It just felt like they were the mascots of everything that was happening." Chris and Rachel took separate flights down to Florida. Chris had originally missed his own flight. "I almost missed my second," he says.

When he finally got to Tampa and met Rachel in the airport, "Her eye was inexplicably swollen shut," he says.

"I just woke up this way," she told him. "I don't know."

"First it was me and Chris figuring out what the fuck we were doing there," says Rachel. "And then the strange feeling that I had this whole time . . ." Masha lost in the desert; Chris missing his flight. It was like they "couldn't be there," says Rachel. "Just could not. Just on a purely logistical level, it was really hard to be there. To get there. To leave. It was just a hard situation to come in and out of."

"This is all correct," she said to Chris at the airport. "My eyes should be swollen shut. She's lost in the desert. We shouldn't have to be doing this. This isn't something that should be happening. It makes sense that all of this is going on."

Chris had reserved a car, but when he called to ask if he could pick it up later after missing his first flight, he found out his reservation wasn't for another two weeks. Life felt like some sort of bait and switch. They finally reserved another and drove to my parents' house.

. . .

Amanda Roper met Jenny and Pamela just after high school and was absorbed into their group of girlfriends—the kind who burn hot and fast together in their early twenties, when friendships play out like love affairs. "All of those girls had a lot of problems going on at the time," she says. "There was a lot of fighting in that little group." Some people had grown apart while others grew closer; there were unspoken resentments. "Before the funeral we all got two hotel rooms together, and everybody just squashed all their problems."

Pamela had brought photos of Carolyn and frames, so that people could take them home from the memorial. The night before, they cut the photos to size, drank champagne, laughed, and cried. There was still tension, but they were determined to be there for one another, and Carolyn.

. . .

"We got ourselves there despite all sorts of apprehensions," says Rachel. They stopped at Hooters on the way to the memorial, to try to eat something. "It was absurd," she says. "I mean, it was the most absurd. We were dressed all in black. We'd printed out all the poems that we had of hers. We were reading her poems out of a binder in Hooters, trying to figure out what to read at the service. It was insane."

"We went to Waffle House that morning," says Pamela. "I think we went to The Emerald beforehand too," she says, referring to the locally famous Saint Petersburg dive bar where they'd all hung out in their teens and early twenties, and where Carolyn used to do her homework. "I'm not walking into this thing sober," one of them had said. Then they went to the memorial.

"I wished that I could have been recording it," says Pamela. Crossing the lawn at the Woman's Club, she saw people in leather jackets, friends of Carolyn's from the downtown punk scene. "Somebody should have gotten a picture of that," she says. "There was this dirtbag-looking dude, and everyone was chain-smoking and wearing black. Then there was Carolyn's family, which was a contrast."

"It felt like all these people were coming together," says Carol. "They were shit circumstances, but everybody did their best."

Jenny and Chris had picked out music. "I'd had too much to drink," says Jenny. She told Chris beforehand, "Gosh, I realized I probably screwed up the music. It was probably the music she liked when she was nineteen and I did it wrong."

"Yeah," said Chris, oblivious, and he walked away.

Right, thought Jenny, left to herself. *Of course. I picked the songs that reminded me of our relationship, which was at its strongest when I was home. He knew a different version of Carolyn.*

Light fell through high windows inside the ballroom of the Woman's Club. A two-tiered stage with mauve curtains faced somber rows of white folding chairs. The framed photos sat on a table in the doorway. Pamela had also made a slideshow filled with childhood photos in which Carolyn appeared unrecognizable to her New York friends. "That was horrible to look at," says Rachel, "because none of those photos look like her."

"They are her," says Pamela. "So many people knew a different Carrie. New York Carolyn, Bard Carolyn, high school Carrie, baby Carrie."

Jim's minister from the Unitarian Universalist church led the service. "The service itself was just heart-wrenching," says Rachel. "It felt impossible to be sitting in that chair. It was just a lot. It was too much." After the minister spoke, anyone who wanted to tell a story about Carolyn was invited to go up to the stage.

"They made me go first," says Pamela. It was hard to think of a story that was appropriate for the setting. "The things that I remember about Carrie are her raunchy sense of humor and her unabashed comfort with her body, with herself. How refreshing that is. How she could hold you accountable and make you feel incredibly loved at the same time." With some friends, Pamela may appreciate their honesty but it can be "caustic." Carolyn never judged. "She was fluid in her way of interacting with me," she says.

She can remember more than once Carolyn saying to her, "Don't sleep with him."

"But . . . ," Pamela would say.

"Or do," she'd shrug.

Pamela knew she couldn't share this. She wanted to share how kind and generous Carolyn was. She finally decided to tell a story from when Carolyn used to work at the Union Square Holiday Market. It was November or December 2012, when she'd first moved to the city. "She was always doing weird jobs; she hustled all the time." A lot of Bard women were working for a particular jeweler. They would drink to stay warm and listen to music and dance around, trying to convince people to buy "really basic" jewelry pieces, a task they found hilarious.

"It was these little gemstones on earrings or a necklace," says Pamela. One day, she was taking a break from NYU and walked up to Union Square to browse the market. She liked to visit Carolyn's booth for a few minutes to chat sometimes. That day, she really liked one of the rings on display, but she wasn't sure if she wanted to spend money on it, so she said she was going to come back.

"Then the next time I saw her, she gave me the ring," Pamela told the room at the Woman's Club. "It was just like Carrie to be thoughtful in that way."

• • •

Carol remembers Jenny speaking at the memorial, her posture, the beautiful things she said, the eloquence she managed in her grief. She remembers wondering, *How can people do this*. Pamela remembers Mike speaking, and how she appreciated his presence for Jenny. Chris "gave an extremely moving speech," says Rachel. "People came up to him all night afterward. We brought Carolyn's poetry there in a binder that we read from but then just had open at the service for people to read at their leisure."

"I learned at her memorial that she had given so many poems to people and she didn't even keep them," says her aunt Robin.

Outside the ceremony were the photos and frames that Pamela had prepared. "I have one of the pictures of her and Jenny, in one of the frames," says Alexis Novak, Carolyn's English teacher at St. Pete Collegiate. Recently, she came across it while moving. *I can't think of her as my student who was murdered*, she thought. *I can't define her that way in my mind, because she was so much more than that.*

"I remember her sister recalling their last phone conversation," outside after the memorial, she says.

Jenny recounted that she'd been feeling depressed, and Carolyn had told her, "Get into the ocean. You need the water. Florida girls need a way to float."

Alexis thought, *God, she was so wise*. She intrinsically understood people so deeply.

• • •

"I met her mom," says Rachel. "It's kind of amazing to meet her. She is like nothing that I could have expected but exactly what I should have anticipated. She's the parts of Carolyn that are irreverent and brash but so sophisticated." Susan is a "very small woman," she says. She was sitting in the Woman's Club's courtyard, "chain-smoking all night." Sitting outside, not drunk, but a little tipsy. "Super glamorous looking. The way she speaks, it's honest and genuine, but also, kind of the way that Carolyn talked—it didn't matter if you liked what she was saying. She said the truth. That is from her mother." Susan curses.

She has a Southern drawl. Rachel can't even remember what she said exactly, only that she was impressed.

• • •

After the service, Rachel received a text from Kevin. An acquaintance of theirs had died back in New York, and Kevin seemed to have forgotten that they were physically at Carolyn's memorial service in Florida. *Sorry, dude, can't go with you there*, Chris recalls thinking, *because we're here, very actively mourning your actual friend that was just murdered.* His own feelings for Carolyn at the time were confusing, and Kevin was entangled in them. *When I was spending the night with this woman, she was talking about you*, he thought. *It feels like I'm mourning and you're not. You don't even want to talk about it.* Kevin knew how Carolyn felt about him, Chris believed. *It sounded like you did, and you were kind of a dick around it.*

"Time would have sorted all this stuff out," he says now. In the months following Carolyn's death, he felt protective, but he swallowed his anger at Kevin. "I didn't know if it was my own intense feeling," he says. "Who am I to tell people the way they should feel and mourn?" He wondered, even then, whether Kevin's grief was operating at a delay, and he would later learn from Kevin that it was.

• • •

Chris's strongest memory from the day of the memorial is from after. "We went to this bar," he says. "When we told Jim that we were going there, he grabs me." Jim was sitting down. He took Chris by the wrist. "I used to have to pull her out of there when she was sixteen years old," he told him.

The bar, called The Emerald, is an anachronism. Straight out of the 1970s, it's a vaguely Irish-themed pub thick with smoke, every surface sticky: the tile floors, the wooden barstools, even the wood paneling, on which hangs local artists' works for sale. Even the drop ceiling and the Christmas lights suspended from it are probably sticky. It's on Central Avenue, downtown, between Fifth and Sixth Streets, virtually the only business in that area that hasn't been forced out by gentrifiers. They serve domestics on tap and in bottles and cans, well liquors, and sugary carbonated hard beverages. Mixed drinks are poured into clear plastic cups like the kind you find at water coolers. There's a cigarette machine because smoking in bars is still legal in Florida. There's also a dart board and live music several times a month.

After the memorial, a dozen or so of Carolyn's loved ones took up three of the round particleboard tables while others cycled in and out from their houses near downtown. "No one was ready to be alone just yet," says Pamela.

"It was really special," says Chris, about The Emerald. When Carolyn was still alive, he would sometimes look at her and think, *Who is this person? Who is the headscarf, cigarette?* Here was his answer. "There were just all of these beautiful women, sitting around this table, smoking." *This is where she's from,* he thought, looking at them all. *She was born in this bar. This gives me so much understanding and weird solace.*

"We went to The Emerald until two in the morning and got absolutely trashed," says Rachel. "It really made sense to me, that Florida part of her, from going there."

"Rachel and I talked about it months later," says Chris. "It was actually sort of too surreal. That fucked with her. She thought that Carolyn was in the room. For months, she couldn't shake the feeling that she was in the room."

"It felt like she could have walked in the door any minute, she was so present," says Rachel. "It felt like she was there with us. I feel that a lot."

Jenny and Mike were sitting at a table in the corner, sharing an ashtray, smoking from a pack of Camel Lights.

"What are you thinking about?" Jenny asked Pamela, at one point.

"Being here with Carrie," she said, remembering a night when they'd gone to a show there. "The fact that we'll never be here with her again."

"Yeah," said Jenny. "It's such shit."

10.

Day Two

D ay two of the trial, I am in the courtroom. Patrick and I married on November 24, 2019, in Florida, and flew back to New York the following day, missing the first day. Several middle-aged white women in stylish boots and shawls hold hands on the other side of the courtroom, around Janet. Finn sits beside her. Danny is at the far end of the row, separate from his wife and son. ADA Hughes wears socks with a football pattern on them, which is visible when he leans over the table to examine his notes.

Hughes calls Sergeant Charles Choi to the stand. He was one of the first to the scene, and discovered Carolyn. Hughes warns those assembled that he will be showing her postmortem photograph. He does so and asks Choi to identify her.

Choi had observed her bleeding from the neck and lying unconscious in a large pool of blood when he'd arrived on the scene. EMS began care while he proceeded to Render's room. He found that Officers Onur Cumur and Gregory Teti were already in there. "What happened?" he asked Render, who freely told him he'd stabbed Carolyn, then himself. Choi ordered the other two to cuff him, and they did so.

On cross-exam, Margulis-Ohnuma asks Choi what else Render had said.

Choi says, "He said: 'I'm not making any more confessions after that.'"

"But he had just made a confession, hadn't he?" says Margulis-Ohnuma.

Hughes asks on redirect, "Sergeant, during the period of time that you were in the room with the defendant, did it appear that he had any difficulty responding to your questions?" Choi says no. "Did he seem confused by the things you were asking?" No. "Did he seem able to understand what it was that was going on?" Yes. Hughes asks if Render seemed intoxicated. "No, to me at that moment he didn't look intoxicated to me," says Choi.

On recross, Margulis-Ohnuma says, "So you're saying you came upon this man lying in bed in his own blood on him, you asked him two questions and he answered that he had just stabbed his roommate, and other than that he appeared totally normal; is that what you're saying?"

Hughes objects. Buchter sustains it.

"I'm trying to understand," says Margulis-Ohnuma. "Sergeant, your characterization, didn't he seem totally out of his mind?"

Hughes objects. Buchter sustains again.

"I am not asking if he seemed rational," says Margulis-Ohnuma.

"He is not qualified to make a diagnosis of illness," says Buchter.

"You just said," Margulis-Ohnuma says to Choi, "I am not remembering the exact words you used—but he seemed normal, right?" Yes. "He didn't seem intoxicated?" No. "Did you smell alcohol on him?" No. "Was his speech slurred in any way?" No. "So again, given the scene you came upon, there was nothing at all unusual about Mr. Stetson himself; is that what you're saying?" No.

"Nothing further," says Margulis-Ohnuma.

"Just very briefly," says Hughes. "Other than the fact that he was lying in a pool of blood, in his underwear, so on and so forth?" Choi agrees that this was the part that was unusual. "All right. Nothing further," says Hughes.

Hughes calls Officer Gregory Teti. He was a neighborhood coordination officer near the end of his shift when he received a radio run and proceeded to 1861 Stanhope Street. On his way up the stairs, Choi exited Carolyn's room and told Teti there was a possible homicide. Teti proceeded to Render's room, where he found Cumur. None of the officers that night drew their weapons, a point Margulis-Ohnuma ensures each conveys during his cross-exams. Render was lying on his back, on his bed. Teti and Cumur rolled him over when Choi ordered them to cuff him. When EMS arrived, he was cuffed to a stretcher in the ambulance. Teti rode to the hospital with him. "And were you present when he told the EMS technician that he smoked weed and drank beer, then stabbed [himself] with a dagger?" says Margulis-Ohnuma.

"I was with him," says Teti. "So possibly. But I don't recall that being said."

"And do you recall him being very uncooperative and spitting at the crew in the police department?"

"You're referring to the vehicle?" says Buchter to Margulis-Ohnuma, clarifying the setting, since they had previously been talking about the ambulance ride.

"Yes," says Margulis-Ohnuma.

Teti says no.

Margulis-Ohnuma then furnishes Teti with the FDNY pre-hospital-care-report summary from the ambulance ride and directs his attention to the last page. "Just look up once you have read that, I'll ask you a question," he says. Teti does. "So does that refresh your recollection that Mr. Stetson was very uncooperative and spitting at the crew and the police?"

"I just, I don't recall what happened in the ambulance, so . . ."

Teti agrees that the ambulance ultimately arrived at the hospital. There, he heard Render tell a doctor, "I stabbed myself with a dagger," and that it was about six inches long.

"And at that point did you notice anything unusual about the way he was talking?"

"No," says Teti. "Not that I could recall. Nothing seemed off."

"Let's be absolutely clear," says Margulis-Ohnuma. Then, he once again seems to forget the setting of the story, which is now in the hospital. "Are you denying that he stated that in the ambulance or you don't recall?"

"I don't recall what happened in the ambulance," says Teti.

"I have nothing further, Your Honor," says Margulis-Ohnuma.

• • •

I go back to Pamela's apartment with her that afternoon to have tea and decompress. She will be welcoming Airbnb guests any minute. After she lets them in, Ann and Carol will meet us nearby and we'll walk together to Wendy's Subway, so Ann can see it for the first time. We sit at the kitchen table. Ally the cat gazes out a window, obscured by numerous vining plants adopted from Carolyn's apartment.

Pamela rents out the back bedroom of her railroad-style unit on Airbnb. She never feels uncomfortable with strangers there. "But it's my apartment," she says. "It may be more stressful with a roommate."

That's why she had encouraged Carolyn to oust Render. "I just remember her seeming a little nervous about having conversations with him," she says. "She wanted to keep him as her roommate because he was paying the bulk of the rent." She isn't sure whether Render was aware of this fact. Pamela recalls Carolyn's total rent for the unit being very low for the neighborhood, possibly below $1,500. "I think he was paying $1,100. Carrie just got an insane deal on the place. It's the kind of place they could have been renting out for $1,800 or $2,000. It seemed suspiciously low."

"In that scenario, she was making money off of Airbnb," she says. "I remember she was afraid that it was going to piss him off."

Then Carolyn would say, "Well, it's my apartment."

"But she seemed kind of worried that he might be mad." To Pamela, in retrospect, Carolyn's concern was uncharacteristic. "She wasn't somebody who was concerned about other people's feelings when she had the power in a situation. Maybe he was moody." But Carolyn didn't want to have to find another roommate.

• • •

"So, I heard that for Airbnb he was paying less that year, fifty dollars," says Carol. It had come up in the trial that Carolyn had decreased Render's rent by $50 because he was unhappy with her booking Airbnb guests.

We're on our way to Wendy's Subway, pooling our collective knowledge. It's a little before seven o'clock and we've just had dinner. The sun is setting behind the buildings of Bushwick and shows rosy between them.

"He brought that up with Carrie and was really pissed about it," says Carol about the Airbnb situation. "'I'm not paying this much money if you're going to be doing Airbnb.' She agreed that he didn't have to pay as much."

Pamela concurs. Then she tells us that as she was leaving the courtroom this afternoon, she had slyly slipped Hughes her business card. "I kind of played him a little bit," she admits.

"Good," Carol says. "How'd you do it?"

"I wasn't aggressive," she says. "I was like, 'Just in case it's helpful, I know a few things about this,' and I gave him my card."

"Really freaking brilliant," says Carol.

"Instead of just being like, 'You should be doing this and this,' because with men, it always has to be their idea." She says that she and Hughes had agreed to meet on Friday.

"I don't know how Brian has put together the situation, because he mentioned the side tension about Airbnb," she says about Hughes. "This is something else he said specifically, and I don't know why— I'll ask him on Friday—but somebody who can 'speak to her state of mind around the time period of the incident.' Adjua was there, and she said that she had a Facebook message from that day, from her, and that she seemed cheerful. Last time I saw Carrie she was in a really good place. She was excited about the future."

"You, I think it was you, yesterday morning we were talking, remember we were talking about this?" says Carol. "That Hughes said something about, Carrie had a 'sharp tongue.' Where did that come from?"

"I don't know who he's spoken to; it's not been me," says Pamela.

"Is that what he said, that she had a sharp tongue?" says Carol.

"Yes, he's the one who said that," says Pamela.

"Because she didn't," says Carol. "She didn't have a sharp tongue. She had a quick wit."

"A quick wit," says Ann. "A biting sense of satire."

"But she was never unkind," says Pamela. "She would say something that was a little sarcastic maybe, but it was always playful."

11.

Saint Petersburg, Florida

"Studies of racial profiling have shown that police
do, in fact, exercise their discretion regarding
whom to stop and search in the drug war in a highly
discriminatory manner. Not only do police discriminate in their determinations regarding where to
wage the war, but they also discriminate in their
judgments regarding whom to target outside of the
ghetto's invisible walls."
–Michelle Alexander, *The New Jim Crow*

One week before Carolyn's family moved to Florida, on the evening of October 24, 1996, on the south side of Saint
Petersburg—a term referring to the predominantly Black area south
of Central Avenue—two white police officers, James Knight and his
partner, Sandra Minor, pulled over a Black teenager named TyRon
Lewis. In the passenger seat was TyRon's friend, Eugene Young. The
pair were en route to buy hot crabs when TyRon stopped his Pontiac
LeMans behind another car at an intersection. Officer Knight would
later claim the LeMans had been speeding. Eugene would claim that,
in contrast to police testimony, the cruiser did not turn on its lights
when it pulled up behind them.

In 1996, a majority of Saint Petersburg's forty-six thousand Black citizens lived on the south side. The south side is generally thought to end at about Thirty-Fourth Street and Thirtieth Avenue South, not far from my high school, which established a magnet program in 1984 as a means of addressing de facto segregation. Magnet programs throughout the county were designed to coax white students into Black schools through bussing but did not always integrate those schools within the classrooms. At my high school, just a few years after TyRon refused to roll his window down for Officer Knight a few blocks away, classes offered to students in the magnet program—such as classical instrumental and vocal music, theater and musical theater, ballet and modern dance, and visual art—took place in separate classrooms and were largely not offered to students who lived in the neighborhood.

When TyRon did not roll his window down for Knight, five minutes away from that high school, Knight stepped in front of the LeMans. Stepping in front of the car was against Knight's training. A month earlier, he had been shown a video about why this was dangerous, but he would later claim he didn't remember this instruction. According to some versions of the story, this is when he drew his Glock 17 pistol. Minor exited the cruiser and approached Eugene's passenger window, which she directed him to roll down. Eugene also did not. Minor then returned to the cruiser to move it to block the car but abandoned that idea and proceeded to TyRon's driver's side window. She peered around the windshield post in front of the car, until she could see Eugene's gold teeth. Eugene had both his hands up, which Knight later testified to seeing. TyRon had one hand up, but Knight claims he couldn't see the other one, which may have been on the steering wheel. According to Eugene, TyRon said: "Please don't shoot, please don't shoot, I ain't even got nothing!"

What's important to know is that the LeMans did not have a driver's side rearview mirror. TyRon could not see Minor over his left shoulder nor see what had produced the sound just behind his head that made a six-inch hole in the window—it could have been Minor's nightstick, or, for all TyRon knew, a bullet. This was probably the sound that he, at that point, turned around to see. "The location of the first two wounds and the stippling indicate that when Knight opened fire, Lewis was probably not facing him, said Dr. Joan Wood, Pinellas-Pasco's chief medical examiner," the *Tampa Bay Times* would later report. "Instead Lewis had to be turned fairly far sideways in his seat, with his right arm across his body about chest high."

The car rolled forward slightly. Knight would later claim the car veered left and accelerated, which threw Knight onto the hood, causing him to fear for his life and shoot. Plenty of witnesses—and a handprint on the car—seem to say differently: that the car was not speeding up, and that Knight was never on the hood at all.

Knight fired his pistol three times, a choice he would claim was in response to the car rolling. Two shots hit TyRon in the right arm, extended across his body. The shot that killed him pierced his heart. His last words were, "Dawg, I'm shot."

Eugene threw himself out of the car. Knight handcuffed him, though he had broken no laws and was unarmed, then put him in the cruiser. Soon, more than a dozen officers were at the scene, along with a few dozen witnesses, devastated and appalled. TyRon was taken away in an ambulance, dead, and bystanders began chanting about another Black man murdered by police on the south side.

Night fell. Emotions mounted and a crowd of several hundred gathered in the intersection where Lewis had died, growing to cover several blocks. They threw rocks and bottles at windows and at officers. They set fire to parked cars and buildings. The riot raged overnight and into the next morning. More than 130 officers in riot gear barricaded the streets, and police declared a state of emergency. The White House announced it was watching. Two hundred Florida National Guardsmen were dispatched and kept on standby. Lewis's brother spoke to TV stations. "My little brother is gone. And I don't know, I don't know," he said. "I don't think burning down no buildings is going to bring him back."

. . .

One week later, Carolyn's family moved to Seminole, twenty minutes north of Saint Petersburg. Carolyn was a month from turning six. The family had previously been living in Texas, but when Jim's banking job was made redundant, he was offered relocation to either Virginia or Saint Petersburg. The choice was obvious for a family of water lovers. They packed up the minivan and headed east. In the back seat, Carolyn devoured her massive bag of Halloween candy. Jenny remembers being told to keep an eye on her sister's pupils.

Bill Clinton was campaigning for reelection, making his final stops in Florida, "preaching to the choir" (his words) at an all-Black AME church in Tampa, across the bay from Saint Petersburg. He told the congregation, "You know after the events of last week, when we are divided we defeat ourselves." He said that looking to the polls Tuesday, "The work passes from my hands to yours." America reelected him on November 5, two weeks before Carolyn's birthday, while her family drove toward their new home. On the thirteenth, a grand jury chose not to indict Knight, and the city rioted again.

Carolyn had been born outside Houston, in a little town called Humble. "Now that's spelled h-u-m-b-l-e, like humble, but 'um-ble' is how it's pronounced," says Jim. The town is where Humble Oil started, which was part of what eventually became Exxon. Their red-brick housing development was in the suburb of Kingwood, bordered by inlets and forest. It had schools and a recreation center, cul-de-sacs and a trail system. It was an hour's drive from the space center where Susan's father had worked while she was growing up.

Susan was a first-grade Montessori teacher in Kingwood when she discovered she was pregnant with Carolyn. She and Jim had been trying to give Jenny a sibling and had failed a few times already. "Jenny was a baby, and then she grew up, and Carrie was the baby," says Susan. By the time Carolyn was born, Jenny was already in first grade. "I've always thought of Carrie as my baby, which I guess isn't that earth-shattering," Susan says.

For as long as Jenny could remember, she had prayed for a little sister. "Someone I could love forever," she would write in her victim-impact statement. "Not a baby doll, but a partner. And miracle of miracles, I got one." They were best friends from the start, despite their age difference. "People talk about how Carrie idolized me, but really, I idolized her. Her humor and intelligence and bravery were everything I wanted to be. She was born under the veil, and grew to believe in the stars, and with her in my life I was lucky."

Carolyn Hilton Bush was born on November 19, 1990. The moon was a waxing crescent on its path to conjunct with Saturn. A Scorpio, Carolyn's ruling planet was Pluto, but she was born in the third decan of the sign, so she was also blessed with the moon's influence. Pluto gave her power and determination. The moon made her sensitive, nurturing, and compassionate.

As a Scorpio, Carolyn was resilient and perceptive, daring and brave, creative and enterprising. She planned and strategized. She hated pretension.

"She has so much Sagittarius in her chart, though," says Pamela. Sagittarius is a fire sign. Carolyn's Venus and Mercury were both housed in it. "Mercury means playful, sparring in love and communication," she says. Venus rules love. "Mars in Gemini. Mars is how you fight. So, she fights with words."

Her element was water. "I'll bet she was a fish," says Jim. "As an infant, you'd blow on her face" to get her to shut her eyes, to wash her hair, "and she'd come out of the water with a big smile on her face." He and Susan separated for a short time when she was a toddler. One of his apartments had a pool where he remembers taking her for endless whale rides. "God, you couldn't get her out of that pool."

Jenny remembers, "When she was a child she spent so much time in the pool, she tore up her feet from dragging them along the bottom."

"As a small baby, she was a little bit colicky," says Jim. Jenny was sleeping through the night at two weeks, but it took almost eighteen months for Carolyn, who would scream and cry as soon as you put her down. "She didn't like going to bed." She never would, as long as she lived. "She was a night owl."

"Jim told you that Carolyn as a baby was colicky," Susan laughs. "My first reaction was, how the hell would he know? I recall her being the most low-maintenance kid I've ever met. She carried her own diaper bags."

"Always smiling," says her aunt Ann. "Even when she was really sick, she wouldn't complain."

She was named for Jim's sister Carolyn, but Susan likes to point out that the name is like Carol, her own sister's name.

"I wished that my name were Carolyn," says Carol—it's more melodic. They shared the middle name Hilton.

As a child, Jenny got a lot more attention, being the first. "Carrie was more independent," says Susan. "We lived in a house with a very long tile hallway, which Carrie believed to be her training ground for teaching herself to walk. She didn't want me watching her, so I'd be in the living room. Every time she'd fall, I'd rush to her side, and she'd jump to her feet and shake me off. As if to say, 'I have work to do! Leave me to it!'"

She was never into dolls. "She played with Legos, but she wasn't one to drag around a doll or a bunny," says Susan. She can picture her on a scooter. Carolyn also loved to climb trees and ride her tricycle.

"She never was one to let her mother or me comb her hair, or button her clothes, or tie her shoes," says Jim. "We had to get her Velcro shoes, because she didn't like to be messed with. She'd brush her own hair, but there'd be this big clump of tangles in the back.

"She was my rock 'n' roll boogie baby," says Jim. "That was how we nicknamed her. She was never afraid. She was always into things."

"One time I was on the phone, and she climbed up on the tank of the toilet, which was really dangerous," says Susan. "Maybe I didn't give her enough attention when she was a baby. These are all the things that go through your mind after your kid dies."

"I think I met Carrie for the first time when I found out how loud she was," says Jim's sister Robin. "She was two, going on three. She was riding a little tricycle around the kitchen and singing, and shouting. She was really cute." Robin had the reputation for being loud among her own siblings. "I think when you're a younger sibling it's natural to raise your voice. You get mean, you get heard."

Carolyn was also a lover of books from an early age. "I had one wall of Carrie's room completely covered with lowercase *a-b-c-d-e-f-g*," says Susan. "Although, Carrie was resistant to my desire to be a teacher with her. She would rather figure it out herself. She had her own ways of doing things."

"Gee, are you kidding?" says Jim. "She was very much a *Sesame Street* baby. We read all kinds of things." Some padded books, some plastic ones, the kind that babies can chew on. "I couldn't tell you when she began to read. It happened early. She was read to every night. I guess I read them *The Lord of the Rings* before she was six."

• • •

In Florida, the Bushes found a house on Eighty-Seventh Place, in Seminole, a mile from the sugar sands of the Gulf of Mexico. Susan still bemoans the state's backward educational system. She enrolled Carolyn in a Montessori school, where her teacher told Susan he wished he could have an entire room full of Carolyns. All of her teachers, all the way through school, would rave about her. "She's so imaginative," says Susan.

"She wrote millions of stories about candy," she says. "She liked every kind of candy. She wasn't really a chocoholic. She liked candy. Candy, candy, candy. She liked the idea of candy more than candy itself." When Sheryl Crow released her first hit single, "All I Wanna Do," Carrie adapted the lyrics: "All I wanna do is chew some gum."

In 1996, Jenny was entering the sixth grade at Seminole Middle School. Pamela's family also lived in Seminole, just a few blocks away from the Bushes. One day, Jenny and Susan came to a garage sale at Pamela's house and bought her childhood dollhouse. Pamela wasn't there at the time but her mom would later tell her that she remembered meeting Susan there. Pamela was also going into sixth grade at Seminole Middle School. She and Jenny met there and quickly became friends. The first time Pamela visited the Bushes' house, Jenny confessed to her that she, not Carolyn, had asked Susan to buy the dollhouse and that she was the only one who ever played with it; Carolyn had no interest.

"There's a way that our lives are obviously so intertwined that you have to believe in universal connection," says Pamela. "That's how my mom remembers meeting Susan. It's probably the only memory my mother has of her, seeing as Susan wasn't a mom who hung around."

"I was always hiding with my cigarettes," says Susan.

In elementary school, Jenny had a big group of friends that included Pamela. "Carolyn had fewer friends," Jim says. He and Susan argued a lot. "I think she wanted to escape that. Went to her room, closed the door. She liked having her space."

Carolyn found pleasure in spending time alone, with herself, reading and writing. "I think we encouraged her how to write well, but I can't remember sitting on my knees and her sharing her homework," says Jim. "She was very private, and very independent. It wasn't like she wanted a lot of help with her studies."

Her teachers praised and encouraged her and so did her parents. "She worked hard," says Jim. "Her end product was good, but it was often late. She wouldn't turn things in till they were perfect, in her mind."

"As an adolescent and young adult, I knew she wanted to be a writer," says Susan. "But now I look back and realize she was always a writer."

"That was her deal," says Jenny. "She expressed herself through writing. That was such a big part of who she was."

• • •

When Carolyn was eight, the family moved into a bigger house in Seminole, backing up to the Intracoastal Waterway. "This is the last nice house we lived in all together," says Susan. "It was a damn nice house." Carolyn's room had built-in bunk beds and bookshelves. "I thought it was so cool," says Susan. "The bookshelf was full." Carolyn's reading style was omnivorous, she would "go through one book, kind of peruse it, and pick out another one and peruse it."

One of the first times Pamela remembers seeing Carolyn, Susan had just come out of her bedroom and said to Jim, "We have to take Carrie shopping, because she feels a little chubby." She would have been six or seven at this time, and Pamela and Jenny were eleven or twelve.

"I'm not sure if she was shy or just kept to herself, but she wasn't one of these little sisters who was buzzing around, wanting to hang out with us," says Pamela. That would come later.

The way Jenny spoke about her baby sister impressed upon Pamela that she cared deeply about what was going on in Carolyn's life. "I never remember Jenny complaining about her sibling the way that other friends might. That never happened. There was a lot of unconditional love."

Their house wasn't a mansion, probably the same size as Pamela's middle-class parents' house, but it had a circular driveway and a split-level interior and was spread out, with more than one living area, and a tiny office. Pamela says, "Jim and Susan's room in my memory was this dark place where the lights were always off and you never went back there, and Susan was sleeping."

"We had a really big, deep pool in the back," says Jim. "When I'd come home every night, that's the first thing the girls wanted, was to go out and play in the pool. I never took the kids to the beach. It was always, we were swimming in a pool."

With the Intracoastal Waterway behind the house, you also could get into the family's boat. "I remember thinking that was kind of funny: water and water," says Pamela. "Everyone in suburban Florida had a pool. I'd seen kids move in from other places and think it was something special, to have a pool, but it wasn't that big of a deal. But not everyone lived off real water."

"We bought a little seventeen-foot, nothing fancy, a little seventeen bowrider," says Jim. "We spent a lot of time running up and down the ICW on that boat."

"Carrie had such high cheekbones that growing up in Florida, she would burn the shit out of the space under her eyes," says Jenny. "We couldn't put just regular sunscreen on her. We would have to paint on stripes, like an old-school lifeguard, with zinc, because she was such a water baby and she loved being at the pool, and she would get crunchy burnt on those beautiful high cheekbones that I don't have."

"Yeah, but the thing was that she'd burn twice, and then it'd turn into a tan," says Jim.

• • •

In 1965, Pinellas County submitted an initial plan to desegregate its schools, and in the 1980s, magnet programs for science, technology, medicine, architecture, and art opened across the county, encouraging voluntary bussing. By 1998, when Carolyn was in third grade, the Center for Gifted Studies had opened at Ridgecrest Elementary, and she tested into it. "They take a minority school like Ridgecrest

Elementary, and they put a gifted program in there, and that would bring in a population of middle-class white folk," says Jim. The school is named after the predominantly Black area in which it stands.

One of Carolyn's earliest friends was Paula de la Puente. Like Carolyn, she caught the bus to school from Madeira Beach Elementary, near both their houses, to Ridgecrest Elementary, seven and a half miles away. They became friends waiting in the bus circle on the first day of school. Their parents ended up becoming friends as well and would take turns picking the kids up from the bus stop after school.

"We spent a lot of time together," says Paula. "We used to just do stupid stuff like sneak out of the house to go to the gas station and buy drinks and microwave sandwiches. We were first starting to be independent."

Sometimes there would be miscommunication among their parents, and whoever was responsible for picking them up on a given afternoon would forget. Carolyn and Paula, with nothing else to do, would explore the swamp behind the school, making "sand balls" with sticky mud as the sun went down. That's when they really bonded. "We would be stuck at this empty school for hours," she says.

Eventually, they'd walk back to one of their houses, not wanting to split up. Paula lived on the beach, across the causeway bridge. She remembers their parents getting mad once because they had chosen to walk back there. It was far, along a busy road.

"Well, what the fuck were we supposed to do?" Paula says now. "You kind of didn't come get us and we didn't feel like staying outside any longer." She shakes her head. "Our parents were crazy."

"Carrie and Jenny were always very close," Paula says. "She loved her sister. She really looked up to her. Because she had an older sister, she got into all these things that kids our age didn't know about. Even though she was only a few months older than me, she was kind of like a big sister to me."

Jenny was already sixteen by then and would drive them home from school sometimes. "Carrie was super mature from being around her sister. That's probably the person she spent the most time with and had the most connection with out of her family," says Paula.

By the time they were ten, Carolyn was making Paula mix CDs with Dead Kennedys and The Bouncing Souls on them, CDs that she still has. "She's a big part of who I am as a person," she says. Carolyn was secure in her own interests and wasn't afraid to be different. She was interested in punk, astrology, cheerleading, and figure skating—she and Paula skated together—and didn't care if those things seemed contradictory. She embraced her contradictions.

. . .

When they were sixteen, Jenny was in an accident that totaled her car and she was left without a way to get to school. "I had my grandfather's old Plymouth," says Pamela. "I started giving her rides, and from there, we started hanging out more."

"We would hang out at John's Pass a lot," she says, referring to the boardwalk in Saint Petersburg, lined with shops and restaurants with live music. This was during the *Jackass* years, so an example of fun would have been stealing a grocery cart and pushing each other in it, maybe into a line of hedges or a pool.

They started hanging out with guys who were older punks. "Skate rats, really," says Pamela. "They were maybe nineteen or twenty, but we were sixteen or seventeen and it seemed like a big deal. That's when we started going downtown." They'd go to shows at the State Theatre or Jannus Landing or hang out at the Globe Coffee Lounge. "There was an anarchist bookstore on the south side called The Core. It always felt rebellious, going to the south side."

Jenny was well-read and would lend Pamela books. She remembers a novel, *American Skin* by Don De Grazia. It tells the story of a kid who joins a group of anti-Nazi skinheads in Chicago. A lot of people in the punk scene in Saint Petersburg were reading it then, since so-called Skinheads Against Racial Prejudice, or SHARPs, began multiplying alongside the outwardly racist skinheads around this time.

"I remember reading some books about grunge," says Pamela. She was learning about pop culture and counterculture through the books Jenny was loaning her. "Then it was natural that we would enter the punk scene." She admits they were outliers, though. "At best we were pop punk, maybe."

· · ·

Susan and Jim divorced when Carolyn was eleven, in the sixth grade, and Jenny was in her senior year of high school. The summer before, Susan had found a sleepaway camp for Carolyn in the Appalachian Mountains of North Carolina called Skyland Camp for Girls. It offered "swimming, rafting, archery, team sports, arts and drama," according to the ad she found in the paper, "with a focus on riding, tennis," and "excursion trips both camping and cultural." It wasn't cheap, but Susan wanted to protect Carolyn from the worst moments of their breakup.

Paula remembers when Carolyn told her about her parents' divorce. They were at cheer practice, after school. Carolyn had blue hair and Paula was in her emo-goth phase. "We still liked cheerleading, we just hated everyone else on the team," she says. "They thought we were weird." They were waiting in line by the mats to tumble.

"My parents are getting divorced," said Carolyn.

Paula said she was sorry.

"Honestly," Carolyn answered, "I'm happy about it. It's not a sad thing. It's for the best."

Susan and Jim had had their fair share of problems over the years. They'd split a few times then reconciled. "I stayed for the kids," Susan says. "I thought I was doing the right thing. That's the big thing we had in common, Jim and I: commitment to marriage, the big *M*." They thought they were stuck together, "And we were, in a way."

Susan was the first in her family to divorce, and she fears that Carolyn knew too much about the end of the relationship, but she had to explain to the girls what was happening and why. They were supportive.

"You had no choice," they told their mother. "You did the right thing."

The arrangement was that Jenny would live with Susan after the divorce, and Carolyn with her dad, in another house in Seminole. When Paula and her mom moved into a house across the street from Jim's, Paula was excited, hoping this move would mean she'd see Carolyn more. But often, when she would go looking for her friend across the street, she wouldn't be there.

"Hey, where are you?" she'd ask, when she next saw Carolyn at school.

"Oh, I'm staying at my mom's right now," she'd say.

"She just went between, whenever she wanted," says Paula. "Whatever she needed at the time, I guess, mentally."

Carolyn's maternal aunt Carol thinks that her niece's bold personality might have developed in response to the hurt of her parents' breakup. She always seemed strong, not easily upset, with a "you can't hurt me" sort of attitude. She was blunt and to the point. "Carrie was the least emotionally volatile of any of her family members," says Carol. "In huge contrast to Jenny, who is a very vulnerable, heart-on-her-sleeve kind of person."

* * *

From Paula's perspective, Carolyn was more introspective than other kids her age and liked to be by herself. As she aged into middle school, she became more aloof and "punked the fuck out." Unlike many of her peers, who were hyper-fixated on fitting in, Carolyn didn't seek validation. She sought to discover her own interests. Paula did too, but Paula was more boy crazy than Carolyn, who might have viewed

Paula as more of a little sister than a friend. Like siblings, they some-times argued. "When she found other people that looked up to her, or found other people who she bonded with more, I would be out of the picture," says Paula.

They grew close again, "because we started smoking weed," says Paula. Susan lived close to the Pinellas Trail, a bike path that bisects the county north and south along the course of some disused train tracks, where people go to walk, jog, and ride their horses. Paula and Carolyn would bike around and lie on the trail's benches, smoking weed they'd bought with allowance money, and stare up into the greenery. Then they'd wander through the woods to an abandoned house they'd found, to explore.

Samantha Mancino transferred to Seminole Middle School, which Carolyn attended, in the eighth grade. "It was the least diverse school I've ever gone to," says Sam. Very "repressed and Christian." Kids rebelled against their parents' restrictions, "finding ways to escape through drugs or the military." It's probably like that in a lot of places, but Seminole is deceptively "sleepy," she says. "Everyone there has the facade of being normal and well-off, even though that's not the case." Her friends from Seminole would begin dying when they were still teenagers.

Sam lived close enough to Carolyn that they could walk to each other's houses. Carolyn's room at her mom's house was small and "kind of messy," with beige carpet, band posters, snapshots on the walls, and records everywhere. She remembers getting ready in Carolyn's room one night with another friend and the three of them walking to a carnival. They got stoned on the way. "It was super dis-orienting," she says. This memory stands out because it's not what she and Carolyn would usually do together. There weren't many punk kids in Seminole, so they'd usually take the public bus to downtown Saint Pete, to find other kids loitering there.

"We would find ways to get alcohol and just drink at the shuffle-board courts behind the Coliseum Apartments, or in an alley, or on a rooftop." They'd go to punk shows at The State, where they saw bands like Subhumans. Another venue they frequented was actually "a strip club in Pinellas Park, where there were also punk shows." Other punks would buy cheap houses downtown and have shows in them. That was the thing to look forward to every week.

"She was so much more evolved than most people," says Sam. "You just don't meet many people like that, especially growing up in Florida." There's a lot of misogyny in Southern culture, and it was concentrated in the punk scene. "She was one of the only girls I remember who saw it too," says Sam. "I didn't realize until I moved away how poorly they treated the girls around them, or people who didn't look like them."

. . .

"Lots of music," says Jim. "We really loved music." At one point, he and Carolyn took guitar lessons together. "Our tastes were after the '60s and the '70s," and though he didn't always share his daughters' taste in music, he appreciated it. Jenny encouraged her sister to seek out new music, and so did Susan. "I used to make dozens and dozens of mixtapes," says Susan. Carolyn did too, and she liked to give them as gifts. Jim remembers her always looking for the right songs, poring over them, forming her own ideas about each one.

"Her mother is a feminist," says Jim. Jenny also is a "very adamant feminist." Jim considers himself, for his time, "supportive of the feminist idea. I'm not really about traditional roles," he says. He does the cooking in his house and helps with domestic chores. From a young age, he treated his daughters as grown-ups and expected them to be responsible for household duties. He enjoyed cooking with them and teaching them how to be helpful in the kitchen.

"Dinner was always a very big deal with Jim," Pamela remembers. "You got the impression it wasn't an option, to not love food. He'd take it personally. Sharing meals together at the Bushes seemed a little like how my parents felt about church. That was their bonding time. Not just the eating part, but the ritual of cooking and then afterward, we'd do the dishes."

• • •

Jim sold the family's house on the Intracoastal when Carolyn was halfway through eighth grade, and they moved to Saint Petersburg, which meant she had to change schools once again. The new house was on the corner of two brick roads, with a fenced-in yard and a courtyard garden, with bougainvillea and birds of paradise, across the street from an abandoned church. A sliding glass door led to the court-yard. "We weren't allowed out there, really," says Callie Kocemba, who met Carolyn on her first day at Riviera Middle School. Carolyn had tested into the gifted program there. "That was her dad's area," which didn't stop her and Carolyn from sharing half a glass of his wine there, "pretending to be adults" after long days.

"We had a lot of white supremacists in town, for a really long time," says Callie. "I was sort of ignorant to it." She naively went on a date with one of them around this time. He had a tattoo of a lightning bolt. He would carve *SS* into various surfaces and wear steel-toed boots with white shoelaces and a tucked-in white under-shirt. "You know he's a white supremacist, right?" Carolyn had informed her.

That year, 2004, the Southern Poverty Law Center estimated there were forty-three active hate groups in Florida, second only to South Carolina in terms of density. Jim's house was in a Black neighbor-hood; everything around Dr. Martin Luther King Jr. Street in Saint Pete traditionally had been.

The new house was a few blocks from the Flamingo Bar, where Jack Kerouac, in the 1950s, had raced toward death in a bottle; he died of liver failure at St. Anthony's Hospital, around the corner. "Carrie expressed wanting to go to the Flamingo Bar," says Callie. "I don't know if this is true, but this is what I've heard, that she is related to [Kerouac] somehow. That's the rumor."

"What a great rumor," says Susan, sarcastically.

"She probably felt an affinity with him and wanted to show off because she was insecure, as a twelve-year-old," says Jim.

"That was her author boyfriend at the time," says Callie. "We read Kerouac and Bukowski and the guy who wrote *Naked Lunch*. Books upon books upon books, and they're all folded in half, and she's got notes everywhere, and they're highlighted, and half-lost, the cover's missing, just everywhere. Notebooks everywhere. Legal pads with nonsense."

"What is that?" Callie would ask her, pointing to a scrawl in her bedroom.

"That's a haiku," Carolyn would say.

A what? she would think.

Carolyn's room was coral pink. "To match the coral pink necklace and the coral pink cardigan that was her favorite at the time," says Callie. She had a vintage vanity with drawers stuffed with scarves, fake pearls, clip-on earrings, a drawer for cigarettes smuggled from Jim's pack, and an overflowing closet.

Once she moved with Jim to Saint Pete, Carolyn bought all her clothes at Thrift City USA and Sunshine Thrift and invariably they wouldn't fit, and everything was safety pinned. "She always had this thing about secondhand clothing," says Jim. "Thrift stores and con-signment stores. She'd rip the sleeves off and cut the length off. Her ass would be hanging out all the time." With Doc Martens, which Jim remembers she was very proud of.

Carolyn's hair was bleached blonde, then dyed pink with Kool-Aid, then jet-black. "Baby bangs straight across, no layers, nothing, so blunt," says Callie. "She taught me how to tease my hair. You put baby powder in there to soak up the grease and the excess hair spray, so you can put more hair spray in. She taught me how to do winged eyeliner before liquid eyeliner was the big trend." Sharpen a red

Maybelline eyebrow pencil to a point, then soften it over a candle. Pair it with bright-red lipstick.

Make your own shirt out of a pillowcase. "Find a nice silky one," says Callie. Something with a little scalloping at the bottom. Cut the seam end off so it's a tube. "Fold it over, and then sew that fold so it's like a cowl-neck. Put it on inside-out. She'd use just any old highlighters, markers she had lying around, and just draw where the armholes are, cut a hole in the side. Sew a seam, or, fuck it, tuck it in with a safety pin. Just make it up as you go along." Carolyn had a leopard-print one and a pink one.

"Same thing with skinny jeans," says Callie. They weren't a thing then. "You couldn't buy skinny jeans at Forever 21 or Express. Everyone had bell-bottom hip-huggers. She would buy regular jeans and make them all into skinny jeans for me." Leggings too, when those became popular. "You couldn't buy leggings. You had to buy pantyhose and cut the feet off."

"She taught me how to ride the bus," says Callie. Next was teaching Callie how to shoplift. Go to, say, Walmart. "Go in with no purse, no sunglasses, and your shittiest pair of flip-flops, and just change into a new pair of shoes. Put on a pair of sunglasses. Get a new purse, fill it with some shit. Buy one thing, like a can of corn." As you're walking out the door past the security guard, "Take that receipt and put it in your mouth, because your hands are full. They're not going to touch that spitty, nasty receipt."

They were never caught. Of course, then, they were innocent looking. And they were white. They'd get ready at Jim's listening to Bratmobile, Sleater-Kinney, L7, and Gravy Train, then take the bus to the mall. Steal some shoes from Payless, take the bus over to Susan's in Seminole. "Go to Paula's house," since she lived by the coast, "go to the beach." Rinse, repeat.

· · ·

Within a year of moving to Ybor City, the party district of Tampa, Jenny ended up moving back to Saint Pete, to live with Jim again. Her bedroom was off the living room, next to Carolyn's, which was slightly bigger, a fact Jenny was trying to stay positive about. Carolyn had lived in the house first and would live there more permanently than her, so Carolyn got the first pick.

"Jenny would always think that we were going in her room and touching all her stuff, which we weren't doing until after she accused us of doing it so many times," says Callie. Then they would go in there and move stuff around, "just to fuck with her." This would get her screaming. Between the two sisters, Jenny got 100 percent of the teen angst.

"I'm the big sister too, at my house, so I get it," says Callie.

"Don't! Touch! My! Shit!" Callie would yell at her own sister.

But Carolyn took it in stride. "You wouldn't catch Carrie fist-fighting her sister, the way I would," says Callie. "I'll fight my sister. She wouldn't. I never felt tension between them like that, even when they were screaming at each other."

They shared a bathroom on the far side of the house from Jim's room, which was easy to sneak out of—right into the front yard, overgrown with bougainvillea. When Carolyn and Callie snuck out, they would have to negotiate the spiny vines and scale the chain-link fence without making a sound.

Then they'd walk to the Dairy Inn, across the street from the Flamingo Bar, to get hot dogs and ice cream. Then wander over to Crescent Lake Park, where they'd sit beneath the banyan trees and watch the moon on the water. Sometimes they'd meet up with Callie's "stupid boyfriend," as Carolyn referred to him. Then they'd sneak back into Jim's just as quietly.

Back inside, they would eavesdrop on Jenny and Pamela's conversation in the living room. *What are the older kids talking about?* And they would be greeted warmly. *Your sister's not scratching your eyes out like mine does*, Callie would think.

One night, Jenny was walking past Jim's computer as he was chatting with someone on Match.com. She peeked over his shoulder.

"Wow, that looks like a great match," she told him.

He had been looking for someone who played tennis and he wasn't finding anyone in the surrounding area, so, for fun, he had broadened his search to 2,500 square miles and matched with a woman in Charlotte, North Carolina.

"I thought she was going to be my pen pal," Jim says. "There was none of that pressure about dating."

"All the games people play," says Cindy.

"We established this friendship, this relationship because there was a distance."

"And I was never going to leave Charlotte," says Cindy. "Never."

After taking in Jenny's observation, Jim invited Cindy to come visit Florida, just to see if she liked it. A little while later, she took a leave of absence from the engineering firm where she was an accounts receiver. "And she never went home," says Jim.

"I feel proud that, at least from the time that Carrie was twelve on, she lived with me," he says. "I was able to show her what a normal relationship was, without that roller coaster," he says.

• • •

When Carolyn was thirteen, she spent most of her free time at The Globe Coffee Lounge, downtown's favorite all-ages hangout. It was a short bus ride away from Jim's and was where Saint Pete's wayward youth gathered to smoke inside over stale nachos, play Scrabble games with missing tiles, suck down endless cups for $1.50 on vintage velvet furniture late into the night, and sometimes see a local band or an open mic. An assortment of globes decorated the café's hand-painted front window beside an egg chair that people treated like a throne. The walls were painted mustard yellow and chocolate brown and featured magnetic poetry and work by local artists, and the baristas were crush-worthy and remembered your name. The Globe was *Friends* meets Harmony Korine's *Spring Breakers* (filmed in Saint Petersburg ten years later) meets CBGB, and it was a town square for downtown culture. Jim thinks that Carolyn's years at The Globe were one of the main reasons she was later so into Wendy's Subway. "Can you see the similarity?" he asks.

The Globe hosted Food Not Bombs meetings, zine fests, live music, queer kids avoiding their parents, art kids from the magnet school, sheltered kids from the suburbs, locals from the neighborhoods around downtown, bands in town for a night, activists, crust punks, train hoppers, and squatters—as well as some SHARPs and drunk racist skinheads brawling outside the skate shop next door or on the patio out back.

"Saint Pete was gritty as fuck back then," says Pamela. "It definitely felt like there were no rules. I was never worried about getting arrested downtown. If you had to be worried about anything, you had to be worried about other people in the scene."

The Globe shared a brick alley with The State and its neighboring restaurants on Central Avenue, where you could buy weed or coke from kitchen workers and meet your favorite bands. The coffee shop served alcohol, but not to its underage clientele. If you were getting drunk, it's because you were in the alley, and somebody had brought it to you.

To that point, Jenny was worried to find out that Carolyn was already partying, only she was doing it with other kids her age, who were as inexperienced as she was. "That's so young," she and Pamela said. They decided, "She might as well do it with us where it's safe."

They started letting Carolyn tag along with them. "We also were not of age," says Pamela; only nineteen. "At The Emerald, you just had to behave yourself. So even though we were underage, it seemed like it was fine." Jim started letting Carolyn go with them to shows at The State, since she was sneaking in without his permission anyway. He'd already had to march in on two occasions and pull her out of the mosh pit. Pamela remembers thinking that Carolyn didn't seem at all like a thirteen-year-old, then being suddenly reminded of that fact—at Carolyn's age, Jenny was still playing with Pamela's old dollhouse.

Around this time, Jenny moved out of Jim's again and into her own apartment on the south side. Gentrification was creeping through the historic houses, and rent was cheap. "It was one of those buildings that had been converted to be cool," says Pamela. Other people in their circle moved in and out of various units in the building over the two years Jenny lived there. Since Jenny lived alone, she could have friends over whenever she wanted. Carolyn was there all the time. "Isn't it cool that Carrie gets to grow up closer to downtown?" Jenny and Pamela would say.

"I mean, that's an inherently cooler place to grow up," says Pamela. "We'd always harbored some shame, growing up in the suburbs. Seminole was not cool."

• • •

"I decided that I wanted to buy a house," says Pamela. "I had heard real estate's a really good investment and my grandfather had given me ten grand." She had a scholarship for college and a good job. It was early 2004. She knew the house would have to be under $100,000 and went real estate shopping. She finally found a pink cottage with dollhouse trim, a screened-in back porch, a chain-link backyard that she never once mowed until the city threatened to fine her, and a garage facing the alley, all for $89,000. "I had done the math and figured that it would be less than renting," she says. She would live there until she moved to New York, five years all told, and it would, in a way, become everyone's venue, private bar, and second home, including Carolyn's. "I was trying to be an adult," she says. "That was all an exercise in trying to make my parents proud while, on the side, doing things that I knew would not make them proud." Like: not being a Christian, drinking, having sex, and hanging around with rock stars.

That summer, The Bouncing Souls were on the Warped Tour, and Pamela and Jenny drove down to Miami for it. They were drinking with the bassist in a truck bed backstage, cheap whiskey, mixing it with Monster Energy drink, a festival sponsor.

"My little sister would really have been so stoked to be here, and she's not here," Jenny said to him. "Will you sign something for her?" He signed a ticket stub, *Stay gold, Carrie.*

They drove home with nine stolen crates of Monster weighing down Jenny's car. "I had that shit for years in my garage," says Pamela. "When I drink it now, I still taste whiskey."

Carolyn kept the ticket stub, "even though she had much cooler taste than us," says Pamela. "She probably didn't like The Bouncing Souls that much." Pamela came across the stub years later in Carolyn's room. *So sweet that she kept it*, she thought. *And so sweet that Jenny was always thinking about her sister.*

. . .

"We had a friend, Sarah, who had a car," says Paula.

"We want to go to Cocoa Beach to watch the sunrise!" Paula and Carolyn said to her.

Saint Pete is on the west coast; Cocoa Beach is on the east coast. If they wanted to watch the sunrise, they'd have to drive across the state and beat it.

They summoned a guy they knew who sold weed and paid him with a bag of loose change. He gave them the weed in a red Solo cup.

Sarah drove and another friend came. They brought a disposable camera.

"Two and a half hours, and slept on the beach, although we didn't sleep a lot, on the sand," says Paula. "My blanket from my old bed. Probably some old gummies. Someone took a picture of a piece of seaweed. And we just hung out, and in the morning, we watched the sunrise as we intended to do."

Then they were hungry. They wandered into a beachside hotel's continental breakfast, sweaty and sandy. "We all sat down and ate the free food and left. The idea was probably mine, to be quite honest. If you've met my mother, she's always taught me to take advantage of whatever free thing I can get."

"Wait, Paula and her did that?" says Pamela. "Are you serious? Jenny, Corinne, and I did that when we were seventeen. There's no way that Carrie would have done that if . . . there's no way she hadn't heard that story."

"Being seventeen in Saint Pete, it was just a really magical time," Pamela says. "There wasn't texting, or social media, or any of that stuff. I didn't have a cell phone until I was older. Jenny didn't have a cell phone until she was twenty-one. She had a landline at her apartment. You were at an IHOP drinking coffee with your friends. You were at The Globe all night." You were racing against the dawn.

12.

Meeting with Hughes

Pamela calls when she gets off the train that Friday, after her meeting with ADA Hughes. "I do think that we have to be aware of the fact that he has to disclose anything we share," she says. By this time I'd found Render's Reddit and sent it with her to the meeting. Most alarming about it was the fact that Render had posted a picture of the murder weapon exactly one month before using it. Second was the listing for sale of his restored vintage motorcycle six weeks before the murder. I'd read through the rest of his posts and comments and had noted his general interest in guns and military history, as well as (and I'd hoped I didn't sound too uptight) a taste for violent movies. Sharing the Reddit with Hughes meant that, by law, he had to share it with Render's defense team.

"He doesn't know which direction the defense is going in, but if they do go for the fact that Render had an underlying psychological disorder that was exacerbated by marijuana, he could end up in a psychiatric facility under watch for a longer period," she says. "If they go in the direction of this incident just being a one-off"—temporary insanity—then, she says, that could potentially be disputed by someone who could testify to Render's past aggression or violence, and the defense might not want to risk that. However, so far, no such person had been found. "Hughes really needs help trying to figure out if Render does have this history," she says. "Who can tell those stories?"

"Because here's the other thing," she continues. "Carolyn was Airbnb'ing her apartment that weekend. So where was she staying? I mean, she could have stayed in her little nook area, but she could have used that as an excuse to go visit a boyfriend."

Carolyn's autopsy suggested she'd slept with someone within forty-eight hours of the murder. By then, that person's DNA had degraded too much to be identifiable. Chris Prioleau had seen her the Sunday prior, and the murder was Wednesday night. She might have been seeing other people. So far none, if they existed, had come forward.

"There's a theory there that I think Brian was chasing," says Pamela. "Which is: 'Did Render kill her because they slept together, and he got upset for some reason?' Certainly, you could imagine a situation where they hooked up and then he's getting back with his girlfriend and is overcome with emotion, and he killed her. Do I think that happened? I don't think so. Could it have happened? Sure. Will we ever know? No.

"It does seem like Hughes put together the information from text messages," she says, "about the Airbnb tension between the two of them. But that was back a few months. It seems like it had been resolved. They seemed to have a cordial relationship.

"He said that Render fancied himself an outdoorsman," she says, "and the psych defense is probably going to say that the murder is contingent on marijuana. He's claiming that he smoked pot sporadically, but apparently at one point he said that this was only the second time he smoked pot. Maybe he realized people could poke holes in that."

"I just feel like this is some country-club, boys' club bullshit," she says, "I think they're protecting him. 'Let's just cover it up and get on with our lives.'"

13.

Cleaning Clearing

Leaning Learning

"**I** hate talking about this," says Max Agrio. "The company that did the cleanup used her blood as a demonstration video for their services." Before Carolyn's family and friends were allowed into her apartment, the state recommended that Jim hire a biohazard-cleanup company called the National Crime Scene Cleanup Association (NCSCA) to sanitize 1861 Stanhope Street. Six months earlier, unbeknownst to Jim, the NCSCA had announced it was branching out into educational media with virtual reality training videos and 360-degree responsive live-action videos of their crime scene–cleanup crews.

The video of Carolyn and Render's apartment, "shot using state-of-the-art 360-degree camera technology, shows the teams working inside a New York City house that played host to a shocking murder late last year," the *Daily Star* reported, linking to the NCSCA's recently posted YouTube video—their first and only one documenting a crime scene cleanup. It quickly accumulated hundreds of views. "Blood stains cover the floor in almost every room of the house," writes George Mills, the *Star*'s reporter, "painting the staircase and hallway in a chilling dark red carpet. Men dressed in yellow biohazard suits package up items left in the rooms to be disposed of, before moving on to the next to begin the arduous task of cleaning."

I'd found the video googling Render's name, because the *Daily Star* article named him and Carolyn. "In one of the final shots included in the video, the camera is positioned inside the bedroom of the victim showing the horror of the scene that unfolded," writes Mills, as though the victim were not a real person in the world, with a name that, when published, becomes searchable. The video is two minutes long and could be played from the *Daily Star*'s website. By clicking on it and dragging, the viewer was able to move the camera to look at any area of the crime scene they wished to see, from ceiling to floor. It begins with white text on a black screen: "Warning: The following footage contains graphic content that viewers may find distressing."

The footage opens outside on the sidewalk, looking across the gated entryway of 1861 Stanhope, southwest toward the door that Joshua Cruz closed against Render to call the police, and toward Onderdonk farther on. We turn to the right and are inside the building. The stairs are stained with Render's bloody footprints. A burly man in jeans and a flannel shirt, one of the cleanup crew, enters the frame on the top landing, carrying a heavy-duty trash can.

"Nasty," he jokes, imitating Janet Jackson. "Nasty boy."

He passes a rack of coats and a black sunhat and enters the main apartment. The camera pans left across the floor, stained with more footprints, leading from the stairs into Render's bedroom. His room is spare: a simple metal bed frame, white sheets, and bare walls. More bloodstains on his bed and on the floor. A pile of clothes.

The video cuts to inside the room, pointing back at the door, focused on a man in a yellow hazmat suit bent away from the camera. Behind him is an open closet with a small black filing cabinet for flat document storage, beside a narrow shelf on which are stored books instead of clothes. There's a white towel hanging on the corner of the open closet door. The camera pans right, down at the bed spotted with blood, and back up and ahead, at the door to the hallway stairs. Beside the door is a simple wooden desk, on which Render's closed Apple laptop sits on a riser, and, farther on, an empty full-length easel resembling an electric chair.

The man in the hazmat suit stands with a baseball bat in his hand. He uses it to compress garbage in a large trash can. He leaves the bat inside. He strips the bed while the camera watches. Beyond it, Render's few clothes rest on shelves of a waist-high wire rack. His leather boots sit at an angle below it, amid crumpled clothes and debris.

We cut to the threshold of Carolyn's room. Outside it, a wooden stool sits beneath a shoulder-high shelf holding a motionless spiral wind ornament. A vine is sorely thirsty but still green. On the other side of the doorframe hangs a collection of scarves, gray, black, and burgundy, on nails. Beyond them is a bloodstained hallway and the kitchen.

Inside the bedroom, we see another clothing rack and her unmade bed, with blue sheets and a white down comforter. Her laptop sits open on it, the screen black. Below her bed is a lake of dried blood. The stain spreads to our feet, at the doorframe.

The camera spins and shows us a brief view of the living room, furnished in a brown leather couch, a brocade chair, and a glass table. A metal mid-century standing lamp. And an artwork framed in gold, beneath a window leading to the kitchen. The window holds a wooden palette used as a wall, or as another shelf.

We cut to Carolyn's bedroom, facing her freestanding clothing rack on wheels, the one she rolled into the hallway closet adjacent to Render's bedroom when she Airbnb'ed her own. We spin to face her laptop, still open on the bed. Spin again to look directly down at the blood on the floor, an irregular, mottled form—on one side, her oversize purse, on the other, her free weights, purple and black, below her bookshelf and dresser.

The video fades to a close-up of an orange Shop-Vac, which has appeared inside her room. A man in a white hazmat suit steps into the frame and bends down to pry some blood off the floor, which has hardened into a sock or a pair of underwear. He tosses it into a tall trash can lined with a red biohazard bag, next to her bed.

We angle up to her dresser, now seeing how she's turned it into a vanity: dried branches in a glass bottle, an empty window frame on the wall above it, holding small vials of scented oils, beaded necklaces on the wall. A full-length mirror holding a black blazer on its corner.

"Every aspect of promotion and advertising we do is based on the internet and technology," NCSCA's marketing and media manager said in the company's press release. "As new tech comes out, we want to be the first company in our industry to use it to our advantage."

"Shorts like this will produce awareness and insight into our industry and what our men and women go through when we go out to help families in need," says the CEO of NCSCA. "All of the 360 content will appear on our YouTube page within the coming months, and shall be shared out on all of our social media, and website."

"The popularity of TV shows such as *NCIS* and *CSI* shows the public fascination with this type of work," *Good Morning Web 3* reported, covering NCSCA's video initiative.

"I threw up," says Max of his own viewing of the video. *This is the worst thing I've ever seen, that my friend's death is PR*, he thought.

"I would always search her name randomly," says Iggy Isaacson, Carolyn's freshman roommate from Bard. One day, when googling "Carolyn Bush," she found the video. She left a comment on YouTube saying, "This is completely despicable that you would post this on the internet, and that when I search someone, I can find this."

"It's now a private video," she says. "There must have been a lot of outrage." One friend of Carolyn's told me she emailed the company every day to demand it be taken down.

"I don't understand why Carolyn's death can't be let alone in this weird way," says Max. "I don't want to forget about it. But it is continually exploited."

• • •

December 10 was the day that Carolyn's dad, stepmom, and friends were finally granted access to her apartment. "It took so long," says Adjua. "The bureaucracy of a crime scene. It needed to stay undisturbed for some amount of time. Her dad was just trying to get her stuff. He thought it was going to be in October, but it wasn't until December."

Susan wasn't able to make the trip. "I'm ashamed to say I have never seen her house in New York," she tells me on the phone. We talk at random times, for hours, sharing memories of Carolyn's childhood and of the weeks and months after the murder. She tells me she demanded that the district attorney describe Carolyn's wounds and tell her exactly how long she suffered.

"Susan didn't know so much of who Carrie was as an adult," says Pamela. "That has a lot to do with how twenty-five-year-olds are. Also, Carrie was not that kind of person. She's not talking to everyone about her day-to-day life."

"I was her mother," says Susan.

Pamela remembers showing Susan pictures of Carolyn's apartment. "I can't believe she had such an adult-looking apartment and that she's so clean," Susan responded.

It wasn't until Jim and Cindy were standing inside it for the first time that they realized Carolyn had been running an Airbnb out of it. "We kind of figured it out," says Cindy. "We saw her clothes were on a roll-around."

"There was a hallway that she had a bunk bed in," Jim explains. "I think that's where she slept when she had other people that were using her room."

"Well, we were just guessing because we didn't know," says Cindy.

Kevin remembers witnessing Carolyn's parents learning about her life, in its aftermath. The experience of "sort of filling in her father of what his daughter was. Everything was a surprise that he didn't know."

Carolyn's room "seemed like she did a lot of work in there," says Kevin. "Her furniture, books, jewelry, everything."

There was a mirror hanging above Carolyn's bed, far too high for anyone to see into. "I actually have that mirror," says Pamela. "She wanted to have it in a place where you couldn't see yourself in it on purpose, because she thought it was funny. I remember her saying to me . . . how did she word it?"

"I love an irrational mirror," was what she said.

Taylor Lambert helped with the cleanup too. He had lived with the owner of one of Carolyn's favorite coffee shops in Saint Petersburg, back when she'd frequented its weekly open mic nights. He moved in with Pamela just days after Carolyn's murder. "Pam wanted to save everything," says Taylor. "Everything. Shampoo, conditioner—Pam felt an attachment to it because it was Carrie's and she didn't want to see it get thrown away."

"I just like the idea of using things she used, holding the stuff she once held," says Pamela.

It got to the point that even Jim was saying, "Are you sure you want to take all this stuff? You don't need that."

"Yes," she would say.

"It's not going to fit in your apartment," he'd say.

"It will."

"I think Pam and I can kind of laugh a little bit now," says Taylor. After the cleanup, her apartment was "floor-to-the-ceiling, window-in-the-front-to-the-window-in-the-back, full of Carrie's stuff." Chairs, lamps, plants. "We all cope differently," he says. "She didn't want to see her friend's stuff go to waste."

"I actually still am using soap from her apartment, five years later," says Pamela. She realized it one day as she was refilling the dispenser. *Where did this organic soap come from?*

Taylor regrets that he only got to meet Jim and Cindy on this one horrible day. "What I can say is, really nice guy," he says about Jim. "Very typical sensible father from Florida. I could tell there was an attitude of kicking himself for letting his daughter live in the big city.

"He talked about donating a lot of money to Wendy's Subway and that being what Carrie would want to happen," he says. "He was still able to joke and have fun cleaning. They talked about Carrie as if she wasn't gone, because they were in her house."

"Carrie said this or that," or, "Carrie always does this."

"How come there's so much Himalayan salt in this house?" Cindy asked at one point.

"Everything in bulk. Carrie was definitely preparing for the end of the world," Taylor says. "Toilet paper and more toilet paper, more toilet paper than anybody had in New York City." They laughed about it. "Why do you need twelve toothbrushes? So many tooth-brushes, still in the package."

. . .

The most disconcerting part of the experience for Taylor was when Jim pulled him into Render's bedroom. "All his shit was still in there." Jim was obviously going through something, standing in the space alone. Having to clean it out.

"Fucking asshole," he'd say occasionally, looking through Render's belongings. He encouraged Taylor to take things if he wanted them.

"I don't want this guy's stuff," Taylor said. Finally, unsure what else to do, he rummaged through Render's closet. "I was curious," he says. In it, he found "a collection of bullets."

"I think it was Jim who told me they were vintage, so I never even considered how they might be something like evidence of his vio-lence," says Pamela. "I wish I had." She's surprised police didn't take them into evidence. Pamela has them now, but she's sure, because they tore apart that entire apartment, that there wasn't a gun to be found. "It's two different kinds," says Pamela, both for a handgun. "Win. 9mm Luger and PMC 45 automatic."

Render was interested in guns. Moira Donegan remembers taking a class with him at Bard called Literature of Louisiana. "I took a lot of classes with him," Moira says. "I heard him say maybe three words in four years. Just silent. It was like Jay and Silent Bob but not funny. He seemed unobjectionable. But since this murder happened, I've had this memory I can't get rid of. We're sitting in this Literature of Louisiana class, and he's got his little Moleskine notebook open, and he's very meticulously and carefully drawing a revolver in blue ink."

On June 27, 2016, three months before the murder, Render commented on a post on the /r/MilitaryPorn subreddit. The original post linked to a picture of a white man in full military fatigues and armor, standing on a winter mountaintop in snowshoes, holding what commenters identify as an SR-16 assault rifle, and smiling. The title of the post is "Jason Everman, ex-Nirvana guitarist and ex-Soundgarden bassist, went on to become a Ranger and a Green Beret in the US Army Special Forces."

Following a thread of people talking about the provenance of the SR-16 and its quality compared to other assault rifles, Render responds. "IIRC, Knights Armament Company worked with Eugene Stoner (designer of the AR-15/M16 rifle) before his death to tweak the design while retaining the original direct impingement system, which offers slightly better accuracy than piston-driven designs," he says. "So, according to some, the SR-16 is (or perhaps was, at the time) essentially the most refined iteration of the AR-15 to retain the original operating mechanism, with the added bonus that Stoner himself had a hand in the process."

Render also haunted the /r/guns subreddit. On October 23, 2014, he authored a post. "Shot some very pretty rifles in upstate New York this weekend," he writes. "Went up the mountain with a buddy to check the zero on three of his rifles and try out a pair of new binoculars, had a great afternoon. First time shooting a .308 and a .44-40—very happy with the groups I got with the Sako by the end of the day. The Lightning was hitting roughly a foot right and a few inches low of our POA at 100 yards, but I managed to vaporize a 4" clay with a very lucky offhand shot." He names what we're seeing.

"C. Sharps Model 1874 in .45-70."

"USFA Lightning Rifle in .44-40."

"Sako 85 Laminated Stainless in .308, Zeiss Conquest 3-9x40mm."

He links to an album with three photos. The guns are laid out on a long folding table in the woods, draped in a padded moving blanket. A red denim shirt lies folded over itself between them, complimenting a burgundy fabric sheath for one of the guns, amid three boxes of bullets, their contents spilling out; a large box of Bostitch coil nails; and a pair of binoculars. A disturbing still life.

Taylor stayed in the room with Jim as long as he could, but at some point it became too much and he had to leave. Pamela came in. "Screw this guy," she said. "I'm taking his shit."

She took some of Render's camping gear and a military duffel bag. "Everything was kind of in its place," she says. "It didn't strike me as weird but it was minimal for sure. He had nice things. His journals were Moleskine. He had nice coats. It just seemed very selected. It might only be one of each thing, but it was all expensive." She got the impression he came from money.

She remembers he had few books. One by Kafka. Herman Melville's novel *Moby-Dick*. Truman Capote's nonfiction novel and true crime classic, *In Cold Blood*. Robert Pirsig's fictionalized memoir and philosophical treatise on the subject of Quality, *Zen and the Art of Motorcycle Maintenance*. She took the latter three.

Published in 1974, *Zen and the Art of Motorcycle Maintenance* tells of the author's experience of psychosis, his electroconvulsive treatment, and his quest to recover his memory and identity. It follows a fictionalized seventeen-day motorcycle trip Pirsig took with his son and two friends, punctuated by recollections of the author's past and musings on the history of philosophy, especially the Greeks; the philosophy of science; epistemology, the nature of truth and knowledge; and the nature of the self.

The narrator refers to himself in the past as Phaedrus. Like Pirsig, Phaedrus was an unusually bright child. Pirsig graduated high school at fourteen and entered college at fifteen. Two years later, he enlisted in the Army and went abroad, where he studied Eastern religions and philosophy. He earned his master's degree in journalism. He taught briefly before starting a philosophy PhD at the University of Chicago, which is also Bard College's president Leon Botstein's alma mater.

Render's copy of *Zen and the Art of Motorcycle Maintenance* has an unbroken spine. There are no dog-eared corners, no notes or underlines, no wear and tear on the trim. It's possible he never read it, only kept it for Sofia's inscription. It reads, "This novel is a classic, it explores fundamental life questions and all takes place during a summer motorcycle trip across America. I think you might like this. You're inspiring & amazing. I love you. Sofia."

"Cindy found love letters, but I didn't read them," says Pamela. "She had found letters that he was saving, from a girl. She said that they were from somebody who was very much in love with him."

"Now that I'm thinking back," she says, "I wish I had looked more for information about his state of mind. There wasn't anything in a journal, just notes about some work thing, nothing personal. The journals were up in his closet."

She doesn't remember Render having a chair or anything to sit on in his room, aside from his bed. Since he was never seen in the living room, this seemed odd, not to have anywhere to sit. She says, "I mean, that could have been how it was always presented to him: that that was her apartment," meaning Carolyn's.

· · ·

The people from Wendy's didn't take much. "We took our couch, which is there," at Wendy's, says Matt, "leather Ikea. We took her books and this rickety coatrack."

"She was so proud of those books," says Jenny, "and had built her apartment around those books, and it's good that they're preserved."

"I took all those journals, and all of her work, and I gave it to Jennifer," says Jim. He thought that was most appropriate. "It's not something that I think her parents should have gone through in detail." He admits he's curious, as one of his true regrets is that he and Carolyn never moved beyond a parent-child relationship. "I wish we had developed a true friendship," the kind that can blossom once a child becomes an adult and sees her parent as an equal. "But I get it. You get a shit sandwich, you get a shit sandwich."

"I have all my sister's journals under my guest bed," Jenny says. "I sorted the clothes, and I shoved all the journals, and all the photographs, all of the really personal things, into a couple of those Rubbermaid totes, shoved them under the guest bed, and haven't seen them since."

"I did look at one of them," Cindy says. "I just read one little thing. I thought, you know what? I felt like I was invading. I could not do it. So, I don't know. You never know. Jenny might, but I just thought—"

"I flipped through them too," says Jim. "There was some personal stuff."

Wendy's Subway intends to compile Carolyn's writing into a book. This will include going through her journals. "The one thing that we can do, and want to do, and will do, is to collect her writing, and publish it," says Rachel. "I've talked to Jenny about it. She knows; we're all on the same page." Jenny told her that she wasn't ready to look at the journals. "They can sit there for a while before she can open them. Before we can open them. I need help gathering it, talking to people, and helping them understand that that's something that's also in the works."

"I think at some point we'll be able to see them all and read them all and try to see if there are drafts of poems in them that we want to put together," Gabe says. "Some kind of collection for her. But it's at this point unknowable how much work she actually produced."

. . .

"I don't think it was until I had all her shit in my house that I just broke down and cried," says Pamela. "I mean, I cried at the memorial. Everyone did. But I'm talking about it didn't really . . . I didn't have a moment to just be . . . overwhelmed. I remember sitting in my kitchen and having so much furniture around me. I remember my friend came over, and I was a complete wreck. They brought me a pizza and beer. I just cried in the bathtub. I mean, body aching, crying. It was just a visceral thing, being totally surrounded by her."

14.

Day Three

In December, Hughes calls Dr. Sean Kelly to the stand. Kelly performed Carolyn's autopsy. He testifies that he first examined the external condition of Carolyn's body, noting her clothing (pajamas). Whether Carolyn had any medical interventions, and her height (five feet seven inches), weight (137 pounds), scars, birthmarks, and other aspects of her general body habitus. She was X-rayed. Then her major organs were each removed and examined for signs of natural disease or injury, and specimens were collected for toxicology, cultures, and other testing. "When all of those results are collected, they're reviewed and a final determination on the cause of death and manner of death are rendered," he says. She had suffered internal and external blunt injuries. She had suffered six stab wounds and an incised wound on her arm.

Her blunt-force injuries included approximately twenty three on her lower extremities, a variety of colors and shapes indicating some were recent while others were healing. Her more severe blunt-force injuries may have been caused by weaponized objects or while she was defending herself or falling to the ground or against furniture. There were surface abrasions and bruises, internal hematomas and contusions, and three broken ribs, all on the right side, as well as a half-inch contusion on the inside back left of her scalp.

Render had stabbed her through her upper left arm, nicking her humerus. He left the incised wound on her left forearm. The stab wounds he'd inflicted to her neck and upper back, severing her carotid artery and her aorta and puncturing both her lungs, had probably happened first; they'd bled the most. Kelly measured almost a liter of blood inside Carolyn's chest cavity. The wounds Render had caused farther down, such as those to Carolyn's kidneys, ascending colon, and liver, had happened after the others.

It is collectively decided among Hughes, Justice Buchter, and the defense that the autopsy photographs and Carolyn's X-rays will not be displayed in open court, due to the "unique nature of the proceedings," as Hughes puts it. By which he means they will be too disturbing to the family members present. Instead, they will be shown by the witness to the judge, who is the finder of fact. Kelly clinically describes for Buchter the injuries of Carolyn's depicted in each exhibit.

Smallman cross-examines: "Would you agree with me, sir, that to a reasonable degree of scientific certainty the injuries that you are describing here today are consistent with an extremely violent attack?"

"Well, I think it resulted in her death," says Kelly.

"Would you agree with me on that?" says Smallman.

Buchter asks Kelly, "Did you form an opinion regarding the nature of the attack?"

"Well, I don't know what your definition of *violent* is," says Kelly. "All I can say is these wounds resulted in her death."

"What is your definition of *violent*?" asks Smallman.

Hughes objects. Buchter allows it.

"Well, in a forensic sense," says Kelly, "I would probably classify anything that is not a natural type of disease process as a—if the injury is being either self-inflicted or inflicted by another individual—as a violent type of injury." He clarifies, because the judge asks, that there is not a scale that he uses to quantify violence.

"Doctor, you described the knife wound that penetrated in a human to the extent of five inches?" asks Smallman.

"I'm sorry," says Kelly. "Which one are you speaking of? There are several wounds. They all have different depths."

"Did you describe a knife wound having a five-inch entry in your report?" says Smallman.

"Well, I described one of the wounds of the left neck, B, as having a depth of approximately five inches."

"Would you agree that is consistent with a violent act?"

Kelly says that five inches is just a measurement of the wound track.

Justice Buchter asks, "Some of the stab wounds caused fractures to the bone?"

"Some of them did," says Kelly.

"That would indicate to you the use of force?" says Buchter.

"Correct," says Kelly. "For the blade to go through various bony structures, a significant amount of force would have to be used."

15.

Secret Beach

"**W**e went to Northeast High School, which was not a good school," says Callie. "That's when we started to drift apart. She was in more honors classes than I was." Carolyn would often eat lunch in the library by herself, reading. Callie would go visit her there sometimes. But Carolyn wasn't having it. Very maturely and nicely, she would say, "Callie, I'm taking a moment. I would like to read in silence. Do you mind, dude?"

"I wasn't offended," says Callie. "People put on a show, there's masks we all wear. I don't think she has them. She was genuine. She didn't want to chitchat with me about boys." Carolyn wasn't boy crazy like Callie was. "I'm always boy crazy," says Callie. "I still don't know if she ever had a serious boyfriend."

"You don't need a man to do anything," Carolyn would say to her. "Why do we need to bring boys around? Your boyfriend is not coming with us to the mall."

"And put her foot down," says Callie, "and that, I appreciate. She knows her worth. She'd rather see your library than your dick pics. I could not invite boys anywhere." Callie understood it—Carolyn was bored with that game already. She was an old soul, "nothing was ever her first rodeo," and she thought, perhaps correctly, that a teenage boyfriend would hold her back.

"I think she wasn't having any of it to the point that even if she was interested in somebody, it would scare them off," says Callie. "She never saw the point, and no one ever lived up to her standards." Carolyn knew who she was and what she wanted her life to be.

That's why it was strange when Carolyn called Callie up one day out of the blue and said, "Let's go down to the skate park and see if we can flirt with some skaters."

"This is the one time she's ever suggested such a thing," says Callie. "I'm a complete ramp-tramp. I love watching skateboarders." They took the bus to St. Pete Skatepark. Met some guys there. Carolyn and Callie were fifteen but lied and said they were eighteen. "I think Don was about nineteen," says Callie. "Henry, I think, was thirty." Carolyn started talking to Henry because he had a beard and she liked beards. "I got stuck with Don because when there's two boys, you're like, 'All right, I'm taking the blond.' That's what happened." After a while with Henry, Carolyn gestured at Callie like, *Nah*, she wasn't into him.

Turns out, Don was living two streets away from Callie. They ended up going over to her house and hanging out until dawn. Then all weekend. Eventually they got married. "That's the same man I've been talking to now for fifteen years," Callie says. "We've been in a blood pact since 2015, but we've been bickering for fifteen years."

• • •

Carolyn's fierce independence was fueled by deep feeling and a rich interior life. "As a high school student," says Jim, "Carrie would often come home and go into her bedroom, and—"

"Close the door," says Cindy.

"Close the door," he says.

"And she'd emerge at dinner and—"

"Go back," says Jim.

Now in tenth grade, she was serious about her studies. She was taking her needed alone time. She was also hungry for her real, raw life to begin. She was writing and was secretive about some of it; she wouldn't show Callie or Paula what was in her notebooks, but on the family's computer, she catalogued Kerouacian odysseys on her LiveJournal.

In one post, she described waking up after studying for final exams with textbooks still open on her lap from the night before, the same clothes from yesterday, lying on balls of paper, with pencil shavings in her hair. Bleary-eyed, she picked up the candle she had left burning all night, and accidentally poured hot wax down her chest. She was mostly upset about her favorite sheets, but at least now she smelled like strawberry.

Exams were officially over and she had pulled off all As and Bs. "The dug hole has been filled," she wrote. She was driving to Fort Lauderdale that weekend with a friend, to see the band Lucero, and release the pressure. It was a four-hour drive south in her friend's car. Fort Lauderdale looked just like Saint Petersburg, except cleaner. They spent the afternoon in Miami, a city of "neon gas, tinted glass and modern architecture." Carolyn hated a city without ghosts.

She danced at the show because she wasn't allowed to smoke. She delighted in how alone she felt in the crowd.

The whole ride home while they listened to Syd Barrett, Carolyn tried to sleep. Arriving at two in the morning, a stoned Jenny convinced her she was God and "the messiah would come with the liberation of women and gays."

Today, she had a lot to be happy about—primarily that she'd been accepted into St. Petersburg Collegiate High School. She felt elated and relieved at the prospect of escaping Northeast High for a school that would intellectually challenge her on the campus of St. Petersburg College (SPC). She would even be able to take college classes and work toward an associate's degree. She would start there the following school year. She only had one semester left at Northeast.

· · ·

It was 2006, a precious short sliver of time in the life of LiveJournal, its peak. Part diary, part blog, part feed, all pure experimentation with writing, it was a new form of addressing one another directly, and everyone at once, and ourselves. Anyone could participate and possibly be discovered as the next Anaïs Nin or Henry Miller; they could even meet each other online, write their story together. Those already linked in the real world signaled it in their posts. For the first time, plans, hangouts, hookups, and breakups happened publicly. We romanticized our friendships, turning ourselves into characters in our memoirs being written in real time.

Friends claimed each other. Callie announced at the end of a long post that reads like a stream-of-consciousness body horror experimental fiction that she would be waking Carolyn up at nine the following morning. Carolyn responded wishing her luck, since she might "resort to violence when I see you that early." The back door of the house should be unlocked. If it was locked, Callie could "have a blast" on Carolyn's window.

"I took it very seriously sometimes," says Callie. "Then she would just roast me and make fun of me. 'What is this, you dork?' Editing my middle-school poetry."

"There was one post I did," says Allyson Erwin, who had met Carolyn in middle school and whose boyfriend would become her classmate at St. Pete Collegiate. "I was like, 'Comment anonymously with a secret,'" she says.

Carolyn, "not anonymously," wrote, "I have this giant disgusting boil on my ass right now." Then she responded to herself and said, "Whoops, not private."

"She was fucking hilarious," says Allyson.

Still, Carolyn was a typical adolescent saturated in hormones, with unfamiliar and overwhelming emotions. For the first half of her spring break, she had been "in a fetal position not answering the phone," she wrote. "Loneliness is the human condition and damn," she wrote, she had relished and hated it, but had known it before she was a teenager.

. . .

Carolyn loved going to the Wagon Wheel Flea Market with her friends. You had to get there early, before the day got hot and everything was picked over. Adrienne Tish remembers of the Wagon Wheel, "I wanted to get a tarantula. I think Carrie might've talked me out of a tarantula once or twice, or maybe into a tarantula, because I eventually did get one."

Once they had walked the miles of Civil War memorabilia, vintage movie posters, antique tools, tarnished jewelry, family photographs, reptiles, bulk products, Chinese imports, unopened 1990s VHS tapes, used books, cassettes, CDs, vinyls, vintage clothing, garden-fresh tropical produce, hot dogs, pupusas, nachos, burgers, and soft drinks, then they'd pile back into cars and go to Global Thrift and the Salvation Army and get wine and go to the docks downtown, or to Demens Landing Park, near the southernmost tip of the peninsula, where they'd climb out onto the rocks and look out at the water.

"It was never really planned stuff," says Wolf Willette, who met Carolyn through his then-girlfriend, Devon Lopez. Sometimes a group would convene at his house, down the road from Fossil Park, where they'd sit in the backyard and drink cheap beers and talk politics and philosophy. Devon was turning seventeen soon, and she and Wolf were talking about getting married.

On warm nights, they'd go to Secret Beach. "It's not really a secret per se, but it's private property," says Wolf. On Sunset Beach, next to Woody's Waterfront Café and Beach Bar, on the barrier islands, there was a public parking area for people who wanted to go jogging or fishing off the boardwalk. If you kept the Gulf on your right and kept walking south along the boardwalk, past the signs that said "No Trespassing," it would lead you around some tall condos and right up to a wave-break of boulders that hid the sand below. You could sit on the rocks that would shield you from anyone who might see you there, not that they would likely care—most of what went on at Secret Beach was some light underage drinking, maybe puffing a joint.

"Carrie always made it fun," says Devon. "She was special, sharp, sarcastic. Real." One night at Secret Beach with Carolyn and Adrienne, they went skinny dipping like witches in the moonlight.

• • •

Carolyn and Jim were moving into a larger house without all the quirks of the one by Flamingo Bar. Carolyn wrote that she was excited to purge all her shit. Reassess herself in a new space. Live in a house without palmetto bugs assailing her during her bubble baths. Her new room won't have pink paint on the walls that she admits now was a mistake to begin with. She can dispose of the thrifted garments she never got around to sewing into the masterpieces she intended. In her new room, her antique yellow vanity, once her favorite piece of furniture, looked out of place. Her own skin looked unfamiliar in the lighting. She was not allowed to smoke inside. She reassured herself she would be fine.

She was planning a road trip for her and Susan that summer, up to Asheville, where she hoped to visit the Skyland Camp for Young Girls, which she remembered fondly. "Everything was designed for me, something I would enjoy," says Susan of their journey north. She wonders if Carolyn felt guilty for choosing to go to high school in Saint Petersburg instead of Seminole, which meant she would continue living with Jim instead of with her. On their way to Asheville, Carolyn arranged for them to visit the park in Savannah where *Forrest Gump* was filmed. Sitting on the famous bench, Susan told Carolyn about how, in 1978, while she was in Savannah, some of her friends invited her to the movies. They all stood in line. She overheard some people talking about the feature they were about to see. "I had never heard of *The Rocky Horror Picture Show*," says Susan. "It was tremendous! The audience was well rehearsed." She told Carolyn, "The old woman in that cosmetics commercial? It's the same girl who played 'Dammit Janet.'" Carolyn was amazed. They talked in the car all the way to Asheville.

"She often asked me questions," says Susan. Like, how did you pronounce *irreparably*? "I pronounced it in some pretentious way, as my own mother would," says Susan. They were reading the same book, and she told Carolyn that a "half nelson" is a wrestling term.

"Oh," Carolyn said. "I'm really glad you told me that."

• • •

"Two young skinny-jeaned females with two very well-behaved kitties seek two bedroom apartment," Jenny wrote on her LiveJournal. She and her friend wore the skinny jeans, and every apartment they had looked at so far said no drugs, no smoking, and no pets. What were they to do? They accepted no less than perfection. Their apartment must have hardwood floors. Big closets to store grandma clothes, a claw-foot tub for stoned readings of Tom Wolfe novels, a "seen-better-days kitchen" able to accommodate a lot of pad thai and chicken-salad sandwiches, and "a fridge big enough to store endless Coors Light and bottled water."

Finally, they found one on Crescent Lake, with "Decent low-pile carpet throughout, ceramic in the bathroom and kitchen. Dishwasher!" Since her friend was often at her boyfriend's house, it was practically Jenny's apartment. Carolyn was always there.

Jenny's twenty-first birthday had come and gone, and yet another year passed, and she had finally managed to register for classes at SPC—no thanks to the school admin, fuck its bureaucracy and endless lines, she said. She felt like she was moving forward, "a triumph no matter how slow the progress."

• • •

"Then Carrie went to the program at SPC," says Jenny. She would spend her junior and senior years of high school there. "It's a charter school, and they say it's a lottery system," says Alexis Novak, who was her English teacher that first year. "I don't believe that, because it's always kids that have higher standardized test scores, usually honors students." High school classes were in portable buildings. Some of the chairs were upholstered with peace signs, heads of Elvis, yin-yang symbols, Route 66 signs, wings, and the phrase "Everybody Let's Rock!" When she wasn't in high school classes, Carolyn was taking college courses.

"She was just a character," says Alexis. "It would almost be easier to imitate Carrie than to describe her. She was always five minutes late to class with a Starbucks. She always had these ginormous sunglasses, Brigitte Bardot hair kind of a hot mess, always up but disheveled, and those long bangs, her skinny jeans. She always looked chic."

She would come in and mouth to Alexis, "Sorry, sorry," slip into her seat.

"I couldn't be mad at her," she says. "She was such a good student; everybody sort of accepted that about her." She was funny and well liked. "I think she was a leader, but she didn't want to lead. I think that she wanted to always do her own thing."

Before Alexis was Carolyn's teacher, she had been Jenny's. She was the only teacher they had in common. Before she was Jenny's teacher, she'd taken classes with Pamela at the University of South Florida. It was funny to Alexis, to have students now who were friends with her friends, but she didn't think of it as weird. Carolyn didn't seem like a teenager. "She was so unselfconscious as a writer, really funny and self-deprecating," she says. "She opened herself all the way up on the page in a courageous way that teenagers usually don't do."

Growing closer, Carolyn and Alexis would talk about their step-moms. Like Carolyn's parents, Alexis's had seemed to hate each other for a while after they divorced—they didn't talk for years.

"She explained to me that she had some complicated family relationships," says Alexis. She assured Carolyn that was normal. "I've been down that road," she told her. "You're going to survive all of this."

• • •

Since switching schools, Carolyn's friend group had shifted. She grew closer to Devon, who was also at SPC, and to Sarah, Devon's cousin, and Callie was mildly annoyed by this change. Callie too had left Northeast High, because of gun violence. "We had drifted apart a little bit," she says. "Sarah was a little bit older than us," which appealed to Carolyn. Quietly, Callie would exact revenge on Sarah by stealing books out of her car, which chauffeured everyone around.

Adrienne was a year ahead of Carolyn at a different school, a senior. "We really started to smush together," she says. Carolyn seemed to be coming into herself more and mellowing out a bit as she aged. "She was more of an intellectual," says Adrienne, less of the punk who had flashed everyone in the State Theatre bathroom when she was fourteen.

Adrienne remembers Carolyn's purses were massive and contained anything you needed inside: rose balm, a bobby pin, an essential oil or two, tobacco (she always looked classy and sort of French with a cigarette in her hand), ChapStick, dry shampoo, baby powder, a flask. "We're sixteen," says Adrienne, laughing. "Who has a flask?"

Carolyn also always had a deck of tarot cards. "She was one of the first people who showed me that the cards can be your intuition talking to you," Adrienne says. You can use them to read into your own subconscious; the reader doesn't have to be some stranger in a storefront. She also, always, had a book in her bag. Adrienne remembers when Carrie started at SPC, she said, "I've already read all these books."

• • •

Jenny was now talking about moving to Portland, Oregon. "The website for Portland State University got me really excited," she wrote on her LiveJournal. "Butterflies in my gut, this feeling like I may be onto something. New York never made me feel that way. PSU describes itself as an 'urban university' which is exactly what I want." Portland urban isn't New York urban, she says: her apartment will be spacious and beautiful, yet she'll still be able to afford to eat.

"Been friends with the same girls since the seventh grade," she adds, "never had to work to find more." Now she'll be forced to grow her social circle. That's part of what college is for.

Furthermore, Saint Petersburg was killing her. Was Portland a light at the end of the tunnel? A chance to find herself without the preconceptions always following her in her hometown? "A reason to spend my day in the library surrounded by idiots? The knowledge that I'm doing something to make this all better? A real school? A real campus?"

• • •

Jim and Cindy were engaged. That Thanksgiving, Carolyn was going with her dad and soon-to-be stepmom to New York, to visit Cindy's family on Long Island. Paula had moved to Poughkeepsie the year prior. Carolyn knew she had to see her old best friend and coconspirator. Paula would take the train down to meet her in New York City and they would celebrate Carolyn's birthday a few days late—she was turning sixteen on November 19. It would be her first time seeing the Big Apple.

She listened to Devendra Banhart's "Roots (If the Sky Were a Stone)," looking down on Earth from the airplane. She noted how, from thousands of feet in the air, civilization was "asymmetrical," as if mocking humanity's efforts to delineate boundaries and organize everything into neat right angles, and thus were her "design skills on The Sims forgiven," she wrote. Her Avant-Guide book told her to look out for ghosts in the city. As Manhattan Island came into view, "the landscape aligns itself to closer grid patterns," she says, but "in the same wash of faded brown."

The trees looked so "New England." Not a date palm in sight. It was freezing, but she looked hot in her new coat and scarves, and the air was cold. It felt clean.

She was not looking forward to Thanksgiving, as she was staying in Cindy's mother's house, a woman who seemed to hate food. Making a ham-and-cheese sandwich turned out to be painful. "No fucking onions?"

The next day, she saw Paula, her best friend of eight years, and they slipped amaretto into their coffee to stay warm while ice skating at Rockefeller Plaza. Then, "We roamed the city by ourselves," says Paula. Around the area of Rockefeller Plaza, there was Radio City Music Hall, Times Square, Bryant Park, Grand Central Station, the Museum of Modern Art, the Empire State Building, and all the famous avenues Carolyn had read about: Fifth Avenue, Madison Avenue, Park Avenue, and Lexington; then there was Central Park. She and Paula took pictures of each other to document this pivotal moment, in which they both felt suddenly like adults, coming full circle on their journey together in this life.

Home, Carolyn was listening to CocoRosie, "Terrible Angels." She wrote on her LiveJournal of her conception of herself, one year ago. On the outside, she looked much the same: same hair, same style, same brand of deodorant (she smelled the same). She listened to the same music, was also single. Same goals, insecurities, frustrations, questions. But, as she quotes Robert Frost, "Nothing gold can stay."

· · ·

Carolyn was shedding and finding deeper parts of herself as she finished her first semester at SPC. Exams were a marathon and a sprint at the same time. The days blurred together and she was creating new run-on sentences while fixing old ones. She didn't even have time to breathe, let alone bathe. She was embarrassed to pause, even to write this post. She had lost herself entirely and it felt "fucking amazing."

Later, she wrote to her future self—the one lurking her own LiveJournal, soul-seeking or feeling nostalgic, or just bored. She wanted to remember that today she was happy, tonight she was content, and how she felt like herself for the first time in a long time. She wanted to remember this feeling. "It's ebb and flow, baby girl."

16.

Day Four (Part One)

Joshua Cruz is the only witness testifying on December 10, 2019. He is thirty-three. He has moved to Florida since the murder. To Sarasota, in fact, just an hour south of Saint Petersburg. He's now working in a shipping warehouse. Previously he had been a security guard in Queens, doing "security for a couple of different companies," living off and on with his mother in the basement of 1861 Stanhope for nine years. He'd met Carolyn only once, when he'd accidentally grabbed some of her mail and returned it to her face-to-face. He "vaguely" remembers what she looked like.

Hughes plays the video-surveillance footage from the night of the murder showing Cruz standing in the middle of Stanhope to flag down police.

"Had you ever seen him before?" Smallman asks him of Render, on cross-exam. No. "When you saw him come out of 1861 Stanhope, that was the first time that you saw that individual?" Yes. "How about hearing his voice? Have you ever heard his voice before?" No. "I assume then that there wasn't anything that you would have ever heard regarding any of these people that would have disturbed that peace; right?" Yes. He asks what Cruz's purpose was in exiting the alleyway, after hearing a woman scream.

"To proceed on doing my laundry," he says. Then he saw Render exit the building.

"What was your impression of when you saw him exit the building?"

"Not a good one," he says, "I—pretty much was trying to figure out why he was outside in boxers, as it was cold."

"Eleven thirty at night on a fairly cool evening, you were not expecting to see someone in their boxers, fair to say?" Yes. "And then what, what did you do next?"

"That's when I seen the defendant proceed to do what he was doing on the video, and I backed into the doorway."

"I think you described it, his behavior as being somewhat aggressive; is that fair to say?" Yes. "How about irrational?"

Hughes objects. Buchter sustains it.

"Well, did you see anybody else on the street that evening behaving that way?" No. "And his behavior caused you to withdraw to an area where you felt a little more safe; right?" Correct. "You were not interested at all in confronting him; right?" Correct. "Were you able to look at his face at that point?" Correct. "Can you describe his eyes?"

"Blue."

"Pardon?"

"Blue," says Buchter.

"Blue," Cruz repeats.

"Did they look in a normal type of gaze to you?"

Hughes objects. Buchter sustains.

Smallman pivots and asks Cruz about his work in security. "Building security, bodyguard, pretty much, uh, reception as well, all types of events," says Cruz.

"Any musical events?" Yes. "You did security for music events, like concerts and shows and things of that nature?" Yes. "And part of your security detail would have been clearly observing people; right?" Correct. "Have you ever seen people at such an event that you believed to be under the influence of either alcohol or some other drug, let's say?" Yes. "So you're capable of making that observation and arriving at that conclusion; right?" Cruz believes so. "What observations did you make of Mr. Stetson-Shanahan that evening?"

"Just normal, just making regular movements. Didn't seem like he was under the influence of anything," says Cruz.

"Are you saying to this Court that his behavior was normal as you observed him that night?" says Smallman.

"No, it was . . ."

"Well, what would you describe it to be?"

"You didn't see him staggering or smelling of alcohol, nothing of that nature?" says Buchter.

"Nothing of that nature, no," says Cruz.

"What would you describe, what was your impression of his behavior?" says Smallman.

Hughes objects.

"I'll allow the question," says Buchter. "Don't tell us what he's thinking. What was your impression of his behavior?"

"He was just aggressive, hostile," says Cruz.

"Aggressive and hostile," says Smallman. "Nothing else?"

"That's it."

"Even though he was dressed in his underwear?"

Objection. Overruled.

"Taking into account that he was standing there dressed in his underwear on a chilly night, was there anything else you would add to that description?" No. "At any point did you tell the 911 operator or the responding police officers that you thought his behavior was crazy?"

Objection.

"This is a prior inconsistent statement," says Buchter. "I'll allow the question. Did you tell that to the police officers?"

"I don't recall."

"You may have—"

"He said he couldn't recall," says Buchter.

"I said, 'But you may have,'" says Smallman.

"I cannot recall," says Cruz.

"How was his tone of voice?" says Smallman.

"Normal, normal tone of voice," says Cruz.

"As he threatened you, it was in a measured, even tone of voice?" says Smallman.

"Yes, an even tone of voice," says Cruz.

Smallman asks him to imitate it. He does. "Just like that?" says Smallman. Yes. "No further threats?" No. "He didn't say he was going to stab you?" No. "Anything like that?" No. "Do you recall talking to a reporter shortly after this incident and saying that he tried to stab you but you blocked his thrust?"

Objection. Overruled.

"I don't recall."

"You don't recall," says Smallman. "Do you recall what reporters you spoke to?"

"None, to my knowledge," he says.

"You don't recall talking to any reporters?" says Smallman.

"I remember speaking to officers or people that was with officers," says Cruz.

"But as you sit here today, you don't recall having any contact with any members of the news media?" No. "*New York Post*, *Daily News*, *Daily Mail*, TV stations, none of those?" No. "Do you recall testifying in the grand jury in this case?" Yes. "Did you know my client's first name at that point in time?" Yes. "How did you find that out?"

"Through one of the officers that had took me to the precinct," says Cruz.

Smallman asks how many people Cruz saw Render confront that night, at the precinct.

"Confronted, just [a] whole bunch of cops that was there, confronted multiple people," says Cruz. "In front of the building at the precinct."

What was he saying?

"Asking questions," says Cruz. "The matter that currently took place."

17.

What to Do with

Shitty Men

In July 2017, I messaged Pamela on Facebook and asked her to meet with me. She suggested a bar in the West Village near NYU where she and Carolyn had often met. It had heavy wooden tables and served crepes. It was midafternoon. It was the first time we'd met one-on-one, eight years since first meeting in Saint Petersburg.

"I think I need to write about Carolyn," I told her. She said she'd suspected as much when she saw my message. The feeling had been following me for weeks. I knew others had written about her and dedicated poems and books to her. I had started collecting the works I knew about and saving the posts people were writing about her on Facebook, hoping to preserve her. I wanted to create an archive of the stories people were sharing and find more of them and gather them all into an indelible record of her impact. "I want to tell her life story," I told Pamela, "and I plan to attend the trial."

"If you do this, you have to include me in everything," she said. "I need to know everything." She felt protective of Carolyn and her family. I promised full inclusion and transparency. She put me in touch with Jenny and Jim, and we continued to meet up regularly.

· · ·

The following month, on August 12, I went to Governors Island to meet Finnegan. He was not expecting to meet me. In February 2016, his first album, *The Two Halves*, had been released along with eighteen intricate "dream map" illustrations by Render, which served as album art. In a free outdoor concert for the Rite of Spring Festival, the album was now being performed by Contemporaneous, the twenty-two-person new music ensemble Finn had cofounded at Bard.

Patrick and I lay on a blanket in some shade. I scanned the other picnickers. Four days earlier, Finn had removed any mention of Render from his Facebook posts about the album. I had just finished listening to Finn's interview on the *Talk Music Talk* podcast, where he discussed the performance we were about to see. The host asked about his family. "Creative family, definitely," he said. "I have a lot of artists in my family."

"Big family? Small family?"

"I mean, my immediate family is small," he said. "I have one brother, and my parents were both artists. My mother was a dancer, and my father is a cartoonist, and so I definitely grew up around artwork, and I have some other relatives who are painters and screen printers and songwriters and stuff like that."

After the performance, I asked Finn if we could talk. We sat on the grass, a small distance from the stage. I told him I had enjoyed his interview on *Talk Music Talk*. He thanked me. I handed him a copy of my book *Sunshine State*, with my contact information written inside it. I had also sent one to Render. I told Finn I was a friend of Carolyn's and planned to write about her. I said that I wanted to talk with him and his family. His blue eyes filled with tears. "There are things I want to tell you, but I can't," he said. He had been told by Render's lawyers, as everyone in the family had, not to talk to anyone. I saw his mother, Janet Stetson, pretty and blonde, sitting nearby on a blanket. He asked me not to approach her.

While researching Carolyn and Render, I had found Janet on Facebook and seen that on November 29, 2016, two months after the murder, she'd changed her profile picture to one of Render on a motorcycle, wearing sunglasses. Then on December 5, she changed it again to a graphite drawing of Camille Claudel, "Sculptress, model, muse of Rodin," she wrote in the caption. "Render drew this for my birthday during his first two months at Rikers. Pencil, approx. 4" × 5". Conditions far from conducive for drawing—no eraser, no table, and done after lights were out. December 2016."

Like her sons, Janet is a graduate of Bard, class of 1981. Since 1999, she had been the school's senior associate director of admissions. Then in January 2017, she was promoted to director of graduate admissions. I would hear from someone she supposedly told at the time that Bard's president, Leon Botstein, had planned, before the murder, to make her the new director of admissions, as the current director was leaving. Then Janet's son was jailed for murder, and she took a leave of absence; "Then she came back to a less stressful position," they told me. She returned to the position of director of graduate admissions. Graduate admissions, Janet had told them, was easier than undergraduate admissions, with fewer applications. Then she supposedly said, "Look, I know Leon has done some stupid things, and he can be mean. But he's been very, very kind to me. He helped me get a lawyer." Meaning, for Render.

I reached out to Leon to inquire into his relationship with Janet. "To the best of my recollection I did not 'help' Janet Stetson find a lawyer in any way," he responded. "My vague impression is that Janet has multiple family connections to the legal profession on which she relied." He said Janet was recommended for the position of director of graduate admissions by the current director of graduate studies, Norton Batkin, because the long-time director of admissions, Mary Backlund, was leaving the school, and the Office of Admissions was being "restructured." He did not mention that Norton was Janet's next-door neighbor for over twenty years, nor that Norton's wife, Rachel Cavell, a professor at Bard, is a close friend of Janet's. Rachel wrote a character witness statement for Render but Norton did not.

They declined my request for an interview.

In February 2017, Janet emailed her "dear friends and family." "The situation continues to be sobering," she told them. "Render is still housed at Rikers Island, not in general population or a cell but in a medical observation dorm. He is relatively safe, living in a room with 40 plus male detainees sleeping side by side on cots, with the *very* basics of food, clothing and hygiene.

"But our family has reason to be spirited," she said. "Render's courage is extremely heartening. The conditions in our jails are shamelessly uncompromising and demoralizing but he chooses to live affirmatively each day, reading, writing, reflecting, and offering support and compassion to inmates whose situations reveal hardship far greater than his." She and Danny talk to Render twice a day on the phone and visit him once or twice a week. "The hour-long visit rules allow us physical contact, which helps immeasurably. Please keep Render in your thoughts. His well-being and future are central to our family's essence."

When I ask Leon about a story I'd heard, he confirms that on the morning of September 29, 2016, he received a call sharing news of Carolyn's murder. It was very early. He was in his home when the phone rang. Leon tells me of the phone call, "The only person with me at that time was my wife."

A colleague claims they were there with him. "Have Finn call me," they remember him telling Janet. Finn had studied music at Bard, and Leon is the school's lead conductor. Finn called him, and Leon told him, "You're going to be alright. You're not alone."

Leon told me, "I don't recall having had such a call."

"In closing, as I noted at the outset of this correspondence, since I still do not quite grasp what my relevance to your subject is, I hope this will be the last of your questions," he wrote. "In our culture we have a bad collective habit of ascribing to colleges and universities undue influence beyond the narrow range of the acquisition of skills and knowledge. We therefore give unwarranted credit for triumphs and assign blame too readily for tragedies to institutions that occur well after students shed their status as students and enter an independent adult world."

. . .

Five days after the murder, October 3, 2016, Leon had emailed Jim Bush his condolences. Jim and Cindy would later share the emails with me. "He was very sympathetic," Cindy says. "He lost a child when he was a younger man." In 1981, Leon's youngest daughter, Abigail, was hit by a car while waiting for the school bus when she was a month from turning eight. She is buried in the Bard College Cemetery on campus, just a few steps from his house on Faculty Circle Road.

"So, well, you know Bard had asked her to leave," Jim says, meaning Carolyn. Cindy corrects him. "Twice," she says. "I think it was twice."

Leon's original email to Jim is lost. On October 15, 2016, Jim responded, thanking him for his condolences. He admitted the family was shattered and struggling to cope. He appreciated Leon offering his assistance. "After 'leaving' Bard College," Jim wrote to Leon, "Carolyn moved to New York City." He told Leon about Wendy's Subway and of the challenges facing any nonprofit. Rather than requesting a monetary donation from him or Bard, he instead asked that Leon "query his network" for any associates, colleges, or members of his community that may have a passion similar or complementary to the mission of Wendy's Subway. "Look into the board of Wendy's Subway and see if you can help with your contacts," Jim wrote. For him, it was most important to ensure a legacy for Carolyn.

Leon wrote back a day later, calling Jim's response "very touching" and "remarkable," praising its "wisdom." He alluded to Abigail's untimely death. "I perhaps know better than some how hard it is to 'cope' and confront the overwhelming emotions," he said. "Like you, I am a survivor of the now unnatural circumstance of surviving one's own child."

He writes that most of his own life and work are "linked to trying to rescue some good from my daughter's life and death, and cheat death of its finality." He says, "I can tell you that it is worth the effort" for Jim to make himself an "instrument" to share the "unique gift of life Carolyn can continue to offer" via Wendy's Subway. "If I have ever done anything of any value for others, it is because of my daughter's presence and her memory." He promises he will "ponder how best to proceed" and that he or another Bard representative would be in touch with Rachel Valinsky. He signs off with "warm regards, and in admiration."

Before Thanksgiving, Leon reached out again to Jim, to send his holiday greetings. Jim responded in thanks and told him that a Bard dean had been in touch with Rachel.

Erin Cannan is Bard's vice president for civic engagement and deputy director of the Bard Center for Civic Engagement. She had emailed Jim early in November. "Leon and I spoke about ways we might help, and he asked me in my capacity as the dean for civic engagement to reach out to Rachel Valinsky as you suggested to brainstorm," she wrote. "Rachel and I are now in touch and are working on scheduling a time to speak for next week."

Rachel and Matt talked to Erin on the phone. "She wanted to learn about us and expressed the possibility of doing something together down the line—some partnership," says Rachel. "There was no further follow-up on either end."

Jim had also noted in his Thanksgiving email to Leon that Wendy's Subway received a donation from the Resnick Foundation, which is funded by Bard's long-time board member Stewart Resnick and his wife, Lynda, billionaire owners of The Wonderful Company. Jim called the donation "very generous."

In fact, the Resnicks' granddaughter, Danielle Sinay, was a close friend of Carolyn's at Bard. The donation, for $1,250, had come from her. Her grandparents were unaware of it and so was Leon. "We didn't hear from anyone at the Resnick Foundation," says Rachel. "We simply received a check in the mail." It's unclear why Jim felt he should thank Leon for it, and Leon did not respond to correct him.

Then Jim, a Southern man, says to me, "You know the story about Southern men and how to your face they are very loving and caring?"

"Then you turn your back," says Cindy.

"Turn your back and they stab you in the back," says Jim. "And I mean, it's true."

In the spring of 2017, soon after Janet's promotion, and prior to Render's July indictment, along with the customary character witness statements sent by family, friends, and employers to the courts in support of a defendant, nine administrators and professors from Bard, including Janet and including Leon, sent such letters in Render's support, on Bard letterhead. Five of those people, including Leon, would send more letters in 2020, prior to his sentencing.

Leon's first letter says that he's been the president of Bard College since 1975 and that Janet is a Bard alum. He's known Render since he was nine, subsequent to the boy's family moving to Rhinebeck and his mother's employment at Bard. Leon had always taken an interest in Render's life, as the son of his employee, and later when he became a Bard student. "In all of the years I have known Render he has made a consistent impression of being kind, well-spoken, and polite, if somewhat shy," he writes. "He struck me always as a very appealing, well-mannered, well-groomed, and thoughtful person, with a very distinctive artistic talent, which I suspect he inherited from his father." Render was always "regarded as an exemplary citizen" at Bard. "He maintained a happy and stable relationship with a girlfriend who was also an undergraduate at the time." He graduated in good standing.

• • •

A few weeks after the Rite of Spring Festival, in September, I went to Ucross Foundation as an artist in residence. I arrived as one of ten artists on a forty-thousand-acre ranch in remote Wyoming. I was there for four weeks to write a novel, and I intended to begin in earnest my research into Carolyn's life by reaching out to more of her friends, since talking to Pamela. I continued to feel, more intensely since our conversation, that Carolyn was telling me to write about her. Wildfires raged in Washington, and some days the air was choked with smoke. Bald eagles circled above the creek outside my writing cabin, where artists went swimming in the clear sunlight and elk grazed.

A week after I arrived, a few of the artists left and others took their places. Among those who arrived was Dylan Mattingly, co-artistic director of Contemporaneous and a friend of Finn's. I could have sworn I'd just seen Dylan perform with Contemporaneous on Governors Island, but I would learn he hadn't been there, so I must have seen him online. I recognized him immediately by his hair, which is long, red, and very curly.

I did not know Dylan would be at Ucross. He did not yet know who I was, sitting across from him at the dinner table while he introduced himself. We went around in a circle, one by one describing our projects. A visual artist was making intricate drawings of rocks to draw attention to climate change. Dylan was writing the score for his six-hour opera, *Stranger Love*, Act I of which was due to premiere as an unstaged concert in Brooklyn in January. I told everyone I was writing a novel and had just started researching for a book about my friend Carolyn, who was murdered a few months prior in Queens. As I said this, I watched Dylan's eyes travel to his plate.

A few nights later, on September 20, one week before the anniversary of the murder, I interviewed Dylan in his studio. It was around ten o'clock. The group of artists had each taken turns with a studio visit or reading that evening. In his own, Dylan had played music from his earlier pieces, and then talked about his intentions for *Stranger Love*. I'd read from my novel around a bonfire.

Afterward, we smelled like smoke and the light in Dylan's studio was orange. Dylan told me he had always seen Render as very quiet and serious about his work as an artist. The brothers were good friends, and Finn seemed to look up to him. They came from a close family. "Especially his mom, everything she does is about her children," he says. "To a fault, she's the sort of person that's just, 'You don't need to be thinking about Finn in this moment.' She's just everywhere and all over her children."

He remembers eating at their house a few times. On one occasion, Danny made bacon-wrapped shrimp. "I met Render when he did some art that Contemporaneous had used," he says. "I had a phone call with him when he was at the printer.

"When I heard about it, I was on a family outing at Alcatraz," he says of the murder. Though Dylan is from the Bay Area, his family had never done the "touristy Alcatraz thing" before, which now strikes him as strange. "It'll be forever marred by this moment for me."

While waiting in line, he'd checked his email and found one from a Bard teacher who also knows Finn and his family quite well. He doesn't say so, but I would put together that this was Thomas Bartscherer, a classicist and philosophy professor who was then writing the libretto for *Stranger Love*. Bartscherer is on the board of directors of Contemporaneous and would write two letters of support for Render. His email was "ridiculously vague," says Dylan. "Something like, 'I'm sure by now you've heard the horrific news. I can't imagine how Finn is doing.'" Panicked, Dylan tried to call him, but there was no service on Alcatraz. He tried Google and was finally able to find an article that explained what had happened.

"Then because I run Contemporaneous, we always have scheduling emails going out," he says. There were several contracting emails to Finn, asking him to play on various days soon; he's one of the company's violinists. Dylan released him from any responsibility to the group for the foreseeable future. He tells me that he worries about Finn and hasn't seen him much since. I say that he had been very kind to me the month before, on Governors Island, considering how I approached him out of the blue.

"I'm not surprised," he says. "It's hard for me to know just how this has affected him, but I think it's really broken his parents." Seeing Janet in public even six months after the murder, Dylan remembers thinking she seemed on the verge of tears.

Dylan knew many of the same people as Carolyn from Bard, but he didn't know her personally. "I actually don't know that many people that knew Render," he says.

• • •

For most of 2017, a small contingent of Wendy's Subway members had made a point of getting together every Wednesday night in the wake of Carolyn's death, to write, play writing games, and talk about what they were collectively going through and what they needed to do to honor their friend. There was talk of cataloging her books, many of which were still in a storage unit. They wanted to get them out on the shelves where people could interact with them, "spend time with her in that way," says Gabe, who had published a poem dedicated to her, "Regression," in *The Brooklyn Rail*, in June. It incorporated lines from Carolyn's poem "A Magnificat." There was still talk of publishing a collection of her writings. Most of her writing was thought to be on her computer, though, which her father still couldn't log into, or in her journals, which Jenny still hadn't touched, in storage containers under her bed.

Wendy's Subway was changing as an organization. Before Carolyn died, "You could feel her presence in that room, and in a way that was guiding and very attentive and passionate," says Gabe. The board was still working together to get things done but it had been "harder to be together in an official way. It feels like a void, in terms of not having a meeting where everybody's there. A hole. Everybody's circling that space and what that would mean to all be together and make decisions together."

"On the anniversary of her murder we got together," Matt remembers. September 28, 2017. "We were talking about her on social media, and nobody in Wendy's had really done that. Everybody had felt super grave and quiet around it. We got together at Wendy's and laughed and had a really lovely time together. We talked about her in this joyful way and took this photograph of ourselves arm in arm." It was one of the first times since she died that they'd all been together as a collective, with everyone present. "Then, a month later, Kevin was gone, Chris was gone, Macgregor was gone."

• • •

Moira Donegan would later write for *The Cut* that in October 2017, "I created a Google spreadsheet called 'Shitty Media Men' that collected a range of rumors and allegations of sexual misconduct, much of it violent, by men in magazines and publishing." Such examples of misconduct included everything from creepy lunches to sexual harassment, to sex in the company offices, attempted rape, and rape. "The anonymous, crowdsourced document was a first attempt at solving what has seemed like an intractable problem: how women can protect ourselves from sexual harassment and assault," she wrote. Fundamentally, what she had created was a digital whisper network; the document was supposed to be kept private, among the people who had contributed names and accusations to it. "It was active for only a few hours, during which it spread much further and much faster than I ever anticipated, and in the end, the once-private document was made public."

It was soon revealed that Kevin's name was on the "Shitty Media Men" spreadsheet, listed alongside his affiliation with Wendy's Subway. "At this time Kevin had cut off, and he had gotten very private," says Macgregor. "Maybe he already knew that list was coming." Max had seen Kevin in this state as well, a few weeks earlier in Cooper Square, while passing him on the street. "He was debased," says Max. "He was so depressed. He was so grim." Max was caught off guard. He also thinks, "Kevin must've known that something was coming." When I asked Kevin about the list, he declined to talk about it.

"For me, that history is really bound up with the time when Wendy's was just starting out," says Gabe. "An experience we had when we were maybe four months old, really just starting to figure out who was a member, what being a member meant, how to participate as a collective. At that time, it was open to any member, anybody who paid. And still that invitation is there, but it just became clear that there had to be people who were holding down the fort in various ways, and those people became the board members."

At a Wendy's event early in their history, "Somebody drugged a couple of drinks," he says. "The people who were affected by that, and many other people in the poetry community, felt like Wendy's had a responsibility, which we also felt." An event at The Poetry Project called Enough is Enough engaged the community in a series of dialogues about sexual violence. Gabe feels like those conversations were "precursors to the Me Too movement.

"Carolyn was so present in the process of dealing with that and we spent hours upon hours trying to figure out how to talk about it, how to express the anger and frustration," says Gabe. He remembers there being about twelve members of Wendy's Subway sitting around the table at one point, including Carolyn, Matt, Macgregor, Adjua, Rachel, and Kevin. "It's important to me to talk about that just because it was so difficult and anxiety-inducing for everybody in the room," says Gabe. "One of the really, really sad things about that time for people was that Wendy's members were largely female."

Wendy's released a statement on Facebook. Carolyn was the first signer. "As a newly formed organization, we were saddened and daunted by this incident, and determined to consider proactive ways to respond to, and if possible, prevent such attacks on the safety, freedom, and well-being of our members, our guests, and our friends," it read. "To be clear, the members of Wendy's Subway do not and will not tolerate sexual violence or harassment, misogyny or discrimination of any kind.

"We understand that misogyny, sexual violence and misconduct are pervasive problems that will not simply disappear," it continued. "Yet as an organization we are involved in a constant engagement with and attempt to answer to these problems. We continue to believe that dialogue, awareness, care, and solidarity are our most powerful tools in this fight."

"That statement, and policies that we were implementing in terms of making sure people knew who they could talk to if there was a problem—all of these different protocols centered around how to create safer spaces, or spaces that felt supportive," says Gabe.

It was around this same time that Kevin had first told Gabe about his experience with the woman who would later put his name on the Shitty Media Men list. "He told me the story in very general terms, but he was afraid that this was something that would come up later in his life," he says. "Kevin was my roommate, so he might tell me things in a different way at a different time than he might tell somebody he worked with previously, or somebody like Matt or Macgregor."

When the Shitty Media Men list came out, Macgregor remembers that Adjua took to the Wendy's group text, to have an intervention with Kevin. He says she wanted to lead him to an understanding of what was wrong with how he'd been using the Wendy's space. "There were people that Kevin had brought in and had kind of promised all this stature, and accolades," says Macgregor. "He'd date them quickly and then break up with them, and suggested they shouldn't come back to the space." Others on the group text were adding their own thoughts. The incident that appeared on the list "was not, as Kevin was trying to paint it, this isolated misunderstanding," says Macgregor. "Adjua was getting him to see how these patterns played out in different ways, but always the same, group problem."

"There were probably multiple group texts with and without Kevin," says Adjua. A lot of Wendy's business was routinely conducted over text. She also remembers talking with him on the phone one-on-one, getting nowhere. "We were all immediately suspicious of Kevin after he showed up on that list," she says. "I know that at some point, I had everybody come over to my apartment because we needed to talk in person." Everyone was there except Kevin. She recalls that, during the meeting, he was texting various people in it, asking them to stick up for him.

"We were having conversations every single day for a week and a half trying to figure out what to do," Rachel says. "Trying to talk through this. Trying to model the right behavior." They were rediscovering and redefining together how Wendy's Subway, as an institution, should respond to male violence or the accusation of it. Rachel had also heard about the incident in question, which had taken place years earlier; many in Wendy's had, including Carolyn. Kevin was embarrassed by it and would obsess over how his actions on that night should be defined, what the incident meant about him as a person, as a man. He characterized it as a misunderstanding, or a breakdown in communication, between himself and the woman who had put his name on the list.

"I think he ended up maybe not telling Macgregor," says Gabe. "That was, I think, one of the big sticking points for Macgregor because it felt like other people were talking behind his back. Kevin was the one who kind of controlled the narrative."

Alarmed by what he was learning in meetings and over text, and what he perceived as others' inadequate response to it, Macgregor was soon advocating to shutter Wendy's. "I was so angry that they weren't taking this seriously," he says. "Then I quit in dramatic fashion."

"I biked in the rain from Crown Heights to Queens and spent, oh my God, a couple of hours chatting with Macgregor and just trying to process everything," says Gabe. "There were two kinds of actions that happened during that time, and some of those actions were highly driven by emotion and trauma and heartbreak and despair," especially in the shadow of Carolyn's death. "Other people felt like in part, I think to honor Carolyn, we needed to see this through in an institutional way. I'm sympathetic to both responses."

Matt had urged Kevin to resign. Now he pointed to Macgregor's quitting to show Kevin that if he didn't leave, the organization would not survive. He and Rachel later reached out to Moira to express their support for her.

"I never spoke to Matt or Rachel again, except in passing once," says Macgregor.

After Macgregor's resignation, Chris decided to leave too. "Kevin was the reason I was brought into the organization, and he was my closest friend out of everyone," he says. "I would also talk to him, check on him, see how things were going," throughout the friends' breakup.

"There was this one conversation," he remembers, "where someone who I care about was like, 'It almost feels violent to me, that you would even suggest that we should watch out for how he feels,'" meaning Kevin. Chris remembers the person saying, "I literally don't care if he lives or dies in this moment."

"Looking back on it, I can't judge anyone for feeling that way, or saying that," he says. But in the wake of Carolyn's death, he couldn't bear it. "Things were so fragile, and so precarious." *I can't open the door for this type of trauma*, he thought. He knew Kevin was in a horrible state. "Some of the lowest I've seen a person," he says. "Floating around," like someone already dead.

"It was a hard situation for everyone," he says. "Things got pulled into these extremes. Some of the reason why things are pulled into the extreme was these weird shadows of trauma sitting all over everything."

Chris tried to separate from the organization on good terms. "It was also really damaging," he says. "It was like its own loss."

Carolyn was a feminist and passionate about Wendy's as a political space and, according to Rachel, as "a space that's supposed to be founded on some notion of solidarity and care for others." But it's hard to imagine that her feelings about the situation wouldn't have been "complicated by her own relationship to Kevin and that history."

"There was a sexual component to their relationship," says Chris. "They hooked up once or twice," but her feelings for him were unrequited, and "he was being kind of a fuckboy." Carolyn and Chris would spend a lot of time "jokingly talking about it."

"Dude, you got to get over it," Chris would tell her. "He's not going to give you the things that you're after. You know that. This isn't a forever thing. You're just having stupid feelings that you don't even want to have. Time will let you get over that.

"Some people did see themselves as needing Kevin to face consequences, in the spirit of her," says Chris. "My understanding of what had happened between them wasn't anything close to some of the other stuff he was being accused of having done. It wasn't a happy equitable thing, but it also didn't necessarily seem, when she and I talked about it, like a lane of trauma. Because she's not here, you can bring her into the room for whatever purposes are going on with you, personally, and I wasn't into it.

"I don't know how she would have felt about the entire thing," he says. "I don't know how it would have caused her to reflect on what had happened between them. I don't know where she would have stood in the whole thing that ripped up her incarnation of Wendy's, and we'll never know."

"It's really hard," Rachel says. "That place feels marked with loss and pain in yet another way now."

"Many times, I've been ready to throw in the towel, but at this point, I think that'd be unfair to Rachel and other people who have actually invested something in there," Matt says. "Carolyn too. I think her dad's belief that she cared about that place and that it could be like a legacy of hers was real. She did care about it. She cared about it for the right reasons."

Today, Rachel is Wendy's Subway's artistic director. Matt and Gabe are still on the board but have stepped back from active leadership; Adjua has too. Wendy's is a nonprofit women-led organization, now with ten part-time employees and a position for an annual fellow. It has grown to have an international reputation in the worlds of art, publishing, activism, and academia. The mission reads, "We prioritize collaboration and horizontal decision-making in our work towards being a responsive and sustainable organization."

Wendy's Subway's publishing initiative releases upwards of ten titles per year, artist books, chapbooks, essays, poetry, and hybrid works, with one by the annual Carolyn Bush Award winner. The titles can be found in hundreds of bookstores and library collections at prestigious universities and museums across the US and worldwide. Wendy's residency programs help build strong relationships with organizations with similar missions, who operate as their neighbors in New York City, and in other neighborhoods across the world.

"In honoring Carolyn and continuing her legacy, we seek to acknowledge her fiercely particular approach to learning, writing, and collaborating," says the description for the Carolyn Bush Award. "Carolyn chose her own path and followed her own schedule. She was wary of formal education but sought out workshops, reading groups, and informal collectives where learning is enacted relationally, as a form of exchange and intimacy. She engaged mentors but was skeptical of received wisdom of any kind. Her library included poetry and fiction, mystical and religious texts, feminist theory and biography, and idiosyncratic curricula including a collection of texts on the limits of language itself. The poetry and essays she left us are densely allusive, hybrid in forms, galvanized by her concern with social and political justice, and alive with the curiosity and irreverence for which she was famous and beloved. She loved truth-tellers, and was one." The award goes to someone who writes in her spirit.

I visited Carolyn's library to photograph it, decipher her marginalia, look through her mind, what she was learning, fit titles into the timeline of her life, see if there was writing yet undiscovered, and what I found was her grandfather's bible. It was light and worn soft, with an inscription inside from her great-grandmother Ruth, identifying the bible's owner as "John McKinstry Balfe," dated 1935, when Mac was ten. She signed it "Mother."

I found books by Carolyn's friends and teachers, and her contemporaries in the communities she moved through. Chapbooks of many sizes and colors and textures. A zine from the Bard reading where she shared her work, with "A Magnificat" in it. A lavender zine called *Passion Fruit: Anti-Authoritarian (Con)Sensuous Games.*

Books by Renata Adler, Claude McKay, Rainer Maria Rilke, Jamieson Webster, Wayne Koestenbaum.

Homer, Hesiod, Plato, Sophocles, Parmenides, an anthology of Greek love poems.

Ovid. An anthology of love poems by women. *Plato on Love.*

Chaucer, Blake, Flaubert. Joyce, Jung, Melville.

So much philosophy, from Maurice Merleau-Ponty to Foucault to Derrida, Heidegger, Marx, Nietzsche, and Wittgenstein.

Books by women. Lisa Robertson, Leslie Scalapino, Rochelle Owens. Anaïs Nin, Toni Morrison, Clarice Lispector, Mary Karr, Luce Irigiray, Emily Dickinson, Virginia Woolf.

Poets from CAConrad to Dante. Three books by Joseph Campbell. Hilton Als's *White Girls*, which came out the year we met. "Like grand dance of capital," she wrote in the margin of Chris Kraus's *Where Art Belongs*, which we talked about in a book club that same year.

In July 2022, Wendy's Subway moved into the space next door to the one on Bushwick Avenue, where they had been for six years, and which Carolyn had helped furnish. The new space is larger, with more room for free public programs like readings, talks, screenings, performances, and sliding-scale workshops. It has more space now for the non-circulating library, which has grown to over three thousand titles, including the Carolyn Bush Collection, which has a dedicated bay of shelves and is now partially catalogued.

• • •

Chris and I met at a Mexican restaurant in Fort Greene, Brooklyn, two days before the end of 2017. It was freezing outside but warm in the close space that smelled spicy, and we ordered brunch and coffee. It was noon. Chris told me he was working around the corner at a non-profit that set up creative writing workshops in various places around the city. They had workshops on Rikers that needed staff, and Chris's name had come up as a person to staff them. "I can't do that," he'd told his bosses. "I absolutely will not do that."

"You know what?" he says. "Criminal justice, and the rights of prisoners, is something that I actually really give so much shit about. But after this, it's been difficult. It's like, do I think that that was temporary insanity?" he says of Render. "Maybe. Do I think that maybe he should be hospitalized? Maybe. But at the same time, I spent so much time fantasizing about a way to kill him myself."

I'd been attending Render's pretrial hearings. He wasn't always there but when he was, he wore prison tans and plastic prison-issue glasses. He'd grown some muscle and become substantial, like maybe he was working out. He had close-trimmed hair and a thick beard and soft white hands that would shake.

A week or so before my lunch with Chris, I had gone to one of the hearings and met the original prosecutor, ADA Jack Warsawsky. He was a veteran lawyer approaching retirement. We talked in the hall-way of the courthouse. He told me Render was now being assessed by psychiatrists on both sides. I asked Chris what he wanted to happen to Render.

"I want whatever her family wants," he says. He admitted that even what her family wanted, likely, would be complex, and not one unified thing. "I don't know what the truth is. I think so much about consequence. It would feel shitty for him to get off, without suffering the consequences that he should. At the same time, I don't know him. I've never met him. I will never meet him, hopefully. I don't know how I would function if, two years from now, he was out and around."

"It's also, sadly, something I almost expect," he says. "The system isn't set up to punish him. That's the thing, he's saying, 'Oh, he didn't mean to do it, he didn't mean to do it.' There's just so many things that I didn't mean to do and that I had to suffer the consequences of."

A few months prior, one of Chris's friends had dropped acid for the first time and "was gone for several months," he says. "Thought that God told him to give away all his possessions."

"He's back now," he says. "The things that he did when he was gone, he burned some bridges by being a dick to people. But that was always something that was inside of him. He's always been kind of a dick; you know what I mean?"

"The older that I get, the more I see, when people aren't taking care of themselves or when people go off some kind of a deep end, they just become a more intense version of some unlikable thing about themselves that they've already presented," he says.

That's the thing that's so scary about Render. "You get high for fifteen minutes and you straight up murder a woman?" he says. "That lives somewhere, it exists somewhere. That's going to show itself in other fucking ways, whether it be violence or whether it be a reckless disregard for the autonomy of a woman or the autonomy of other people. It's not something that's completely out of fucking character. It can't be."

18.

Day Four (Part Two)

A fter calling the EMT and paramedic, Hughes rests his case.

"All right," says Buchter. "Motions at the end of the People's case."

"At this time, Judge, the defense asks for a trial order of dismissal," says Smallman. "At the close of the People's case and the submission of all of their proof, that proof failing to meet the legal standard required to obtain a conviction under any count in the indictment or any lesser included count of the count existing in the indictment."

"Motion denied," says Buchter. "Do you wish to make an opening now at this point?"

"Yes, Your Honor."

Margulis-Ohnuma opens. The lawyer's mother, I would later discover, is the evolutionary theorist and cellular biologist Lynn Margulis, whom Donna Haraway writes about in *Staying with the Trouble*, a book Carolyn was reading when she died. "The core of Margulis's view of life is that new *kinds* of cells, tissues, organs, and species evolve primarily through the long-lasting intimacy of strangers," writes Haraway. "Margulis called this basic and mortal life-making process *symbiogenesis*." She helped James Lovelock develop Gaia Theory. For the "multileveled systemic processes of nonreductionist organization and maintenance that make earth itself and earth's living beings unique, Margulis coined the term *autopoiesis*," writes Haraway, who then in turn borrows another term from M. Beth Dempster: *sympoietic*. Creating, not each alone, but together.

"So, Your Honor, may it please the Court, at this point in the trial, what we've heard are the external circumstances, the horrible, awful events of the night of September 29, 2016," Margulis-Ohnuma begins. "And my heart and the heart of Render and his family and my cocounsel, Mr. Smallman, and everyone in this courtroom goes out to the victim of this terrible, terrible tragedy.

"What we haven't seen so far and will see as we present our case is the internal struggle and events inside the mind of Render Stetson, what was happening to him that caused him to engage in this conduct.

"The People haven't proven a motive and of course they can't because there was no motive. There was nothing rational about what happened that night." He says there are two reasons for that. "The first reason is that he had an underlying psychotic disorder that was triggered in the past by marijuana use." His father would testify to that momentarily. The second reason would be explained by the defense's expert, Dr. Alexander Bardey, when the trial reconvened in January.

"What Dr. Bardey will tell you is that the state that Render was in that night was far beyond intoxication, what it was, was an induced psychotic state, where he actually believed his altered perceptions were reality. So, he lost his grip on reality during the time period that he was affected by the triggering effect of the drug. So, it's a little bit different from intoxication and he'll explain that of course in more detail.

"In the end, stepping back from the technicalities of it for a moment, both the external evidence that we have already seen, these crazy pictures and crazy videos of him breaking windows for no apparent reason, lunging at someone for no apparent reason, stabbing himself for no reason, that external evidence as well as the internal evidence, that's what we're going to show in our own case, shows without a doubt that he was absolutely crazy when he wielded that knife so horribly against the victim." The best proof that Render didn't mean to do it is in the deep remorse he feels now, says Margulis-Ohnuma.

"At the end of the day, he was out of his mind when he did these things, and although of course he feels horribly responsible, the People ultimately cannot show that he did them intentionally because he was out of his mind at the time," says Margulis-Ohnuma. "Thanks very much."

With that, Smallman calls Danny Shanahan to the stand, who will be followed by Arun Saxena, to recount the following episode. In October 2007, Render and Arun were high school seniors. They saw each other throughout the school day, and after school one day, they went to Arun's house with two friends to smoke weed. One of them rolled a joint. "I think we had one joint at our house," says Arun. Compared to other marijuana Arun had smoked before and since, this was definitely "more intense." Granted, he says he hadn't smoked much by then.

Twenty or thirty minutes afterward, "Render started acting a little strange," says Arun. "We all thought he was joking. But it turned out to be a little bit more serious than we thought." He was talking with "I would say, an Old English accent. He started reciting what seemed like biblical verses to me." He kept saying he was going to die. "At one point, he went down on his two knees and seemed like he was looking up toward what seemed like God." He lay down on the couch, repeated that he was dying, and had Arun get a piece of paper and a pen and write out his will. "It was along the lines of his last wishes, [a] message to people close to him," says Arun. Render seemed really nervous. His voice had a "trembling quality."

Their other two friends had left after ten minutes or so of Render reciting bible verses. They both told Arun, "I don't know what's going on. I'm going to get out of here."

"After I was done writing, he continued resting on the couch, on his back," says Arun. "I went on the computer, trying to search for things to see if he was actually going to die from marijuana. Then I remember hearing his voice. I looked around and he was on the cell phone calling his father."

Danny testifies that Arun was the one to call him, saying Render needed to go to the hospital after smoking weed. "Well, when I got there, I parked and I started to go to the door and Arun and Render came out and I saw my son Render, and he was, he looked exhausted, he looked terrified," says Danny. "I did see his eyes, they just looked glassy and somewhat unfocused."

Danny loaded his seventeen-year-old boy into the car and drove toward the hospital, but since their house was on the way there, just a few minutes closer, he tried to talk Render into going home instead. "You don't need to go to the hospital," Danny told him. "You'll be okay, you just need to lie down, have some water."

Render told his dad he felt like his heart was going to beat out of his chest. He said he needed to go to the hospital.

"I thought that was something that I wasn't going to fool with," says Danny. They drove to the emergency room of the Northern Dutchess Hospital in Rhinebeck, where Danny explained the situation to the woman at the front desk. They were escorted into a triage room with a curtain, and Render was given a gown. A nurse came in and took Render's blood pressure and drew some blood for a toxicology panel. They gave him a blanket and some fluids. "After a few hours he was feeling better and it was that evening he was discharged," says Danny. "We left together."

Dr. Godfrey Pearlson is a professor of psychiatry and neuroscience at Yale University and director of the Olin Neuropsychiatry Research Center. He might categorize Render's reaction to marijuana as delirium. "Objectively, delirium is a brain state identified by a combination of symptoms that can occur acutely whenever our brain is compromised from a huge variety of factors originating from outside the brain itself," he writes in *Weed Science: Cannabis Controversies and Challenges*. These factors can include drug intoxication, drug withdrawal, fever, infections, liver failure, malnutrition, or sensory deprivation. "You've no idea what time it is, or how you got here, wherever here actually is, which seems distinctly open to question. It's very difficult to think straight."

Pearlson might also describe what Render experienced as short-term psychosis. However, he writes, "Four distinct psychosis-related syndromes can be provoked by acute and/or chronic cannabis use," neither of which applies in this case: Render didn't smoke much that night, and his use wasn't chronic. Pearlson describes cannabis psychosis as "Both an acute (i.e., hours-long) psychosis with prominent positive symptoms (e.g., hallucinations or delusional beliefs) and an acute delirium with disorientation, waxing, and waning levels of alertness (sleepy 1 minute, alert the next) accompanied by short-lived cognitive problems."

Danny testifies that by virtue of working from home, he was very involved in his sons' lives growing up. He was never once called to school for a behavior-related incident. He has never, in his entire relationship with Render, known him to engage in any type of violent behavior. He says this incident with Arun was only the second time Render had ever tried marijuana. He says Render has no psychiatric history and has never had any reason to be treated for any kind of assault.

"Mr. Shanahan, some of this is going to sound obvious," says Hughes, as he begins his cross-exam. "Just please bear with me. Render Stetson-Shanahan is your son?" Yes. "As he is your son, you care about him a great deal?" Yes, he does. "You love him?" Yes. "As a result of that, you don't want to see anything bad happen to him, right?" He doesn't. "You have supported your son, basically, his entire life, right?"

"Emotionally and financially, for some of it," he says. He's provided Render with guidance, has tried to keep him out of trouble whenever possible. Render lived with him most of his life. "That included into adulthood, right?" says Hughes. Yes. Danny says he did not help Render with rent at 1861 Stanhope, but he admits that he is funding his defense. As a result, he's conferring with Render's counsel and has spoken to them multiple times about the arguments they will make.

"They spoke to you today about your potential testimony?"

"Yes, briefly."

"Did they speak to you regarding the potential testimony of the expert that they are intending to call, Dr. Bardey?"

"A little bit, I guess. Dr. Bardey also interviewed me."

"That was the next question. In fact, you spoke to Mr. Bardey, right?" Yes.

"It is fair to say that, upon testifying here today, the defense that was being offered in your son's case was one of a marijuana-induced psychosis?"

"Yes, it would be fair to say that I knew that beforehand," says Danny. "I also knew that he would never do something like this."

Buchter tells Danny to answer only the questions asked. "The attorneys can ask additional questions on redirect."

Hughes asks Danny to confirm that he has been in court every day for the trial, has heard all of the proceedings, and that nothing that's happened so far in court has been surprising to him. Danny confirms this. "One of the questions that Mr. Smallman asked you was the type of individual that your son was in terms of his behavior. Do you remember him asking you that?" Yes. "You have never seen him act in any violent capacity you said, right?" Yes. "Of course, you are aware that your son recently got into a fight in jail?" Yes. "That he actually punched someone in the jaw?" No.

"You are not aware of that?"

"Well, I was aware that it was written down, that he punched someone."

"Were you aware that he was found guilty of a violent jail infraction?" Yes; they spoke about it. "Would you agree with me that punching someone, that is an act of violence, right?"

"Yes, it is," says Danny. "I don't believe he punched someone. He did hit someone, yes."

Hughes has him return in his memory to that day in 2007 when he took his son to the hospital. He asks if Danny was given discharge paperwork for Render. Danny says he's not sure, so Hughes shows him the discharge instructions in the hospital records Margulis-Ohnuma previously entered into evidence. Hughes has him confirm that in them, it states Render was given half a Xanax and told to follow up in two days. Danny testifies that he's not sure if they did follow up, or if the doctors explicitly told Render not to smoke weed again.

Hughes's questions collectively suggest the parents weren't all that concerned about Render's high school marijuana incident.

"Had you ever spoken to your son about Carolyn Bush?" Hughes asks.

"Not that I recall. No."

"So, I just want to clarify, for timeline purposes," says Hughes. "Prior to her death, did you ever speak to your son about Carolyn Bush?" No. "Did he ever tell you who he was living with?"

"Yes, he did," says Danny. "I am not quite sure how often we spoke. He might have mentioned that he was renting a place from someone that wasn't a Bard student."

"Never referred to her by name?"

"I don't remember if he did or my wife did. I might have heard her name before."

"Did he ever express any issues that he was having with her?" No. "Did he ever talk to you about her Airbnb, renting out the apartment?"

"He was amazed that other people would have a problem with that, but he never did."

"That is what he told you?" Yes.

When? "I don't recall when that was." Before or after the murder? "It might have been after or it might have been before."

"Well, if it was before then you had spoken to your son about Ms. Bush, obviously?"

"I guess so, if it was before," he says. "Yes. I don't remember if it was before or after."

"You are familiar with Sofia Bonami?" Yes. "That was your son's girlfriend?" Yes. "He had been dating her for an extended period of time?" Yes. "They were on again, off again?"

"At times, yes."

"Alright."

"At that time."

"Your perception of that relationship was that it was a serious one?" Yes. "Your son cared about her a great deal?" Yes. "And she him, the best you could tell?" Yes. "Are you aware of what the status of their relationship was in the last week of September 2016?"

"I think they were apart and planned on getting back together."

"So, your recollection was that leading up to this incident, he and Ms. Bonami were considering reconciling; is that right?" Yes. "Are you aware of the last time that he saw her?"

"I don't remember. I think it was—I don't remember exactly."

"Was it the morning of?"

"It was very close to," he says. "I am not sure. It was not long before."

When it is Arun's turn at the stand, Hughes asks him whether Render told him about any of the issues he was having with Sofia, leading up to the murder. Arun says no.

"Nothing at all?"

"No issue. No."

"Did he tell you whether or not they were together?" Yes. "Were they?"

"I believe so."

"You recall, leading up to September 28, 2016, he informed you that he was in a relationship with Sofia?"

Arun says yes.

"Would it surprise you to learn that they weren't?"

19.

A Place to Think

In August 2006, independent filmmaker Chris Fuller premiered his film *Loren Cass*, which told a fictional story of Saint Pete punk kids coming of age in the aftermath of the 1996 race riots. By 2007, it was making the rounds of festivals, and its success reinvigorated racial tensions among Saint Pete punks, or at least gave them a reason to brawl.

"Downtown Saint Pete used to be a mob of punk kids," says Ian Taylor, who met Carolyn through Adrienne. Friday and Saturday, they would congregate outside The State, or Star Booty, the punk rock hair salon and boutique, or Daddy Kool Records; then they'd spread in a mass down Central Avenue. "The Nazi kids would show up and somebody would get pepper sprayed or punched. Anybody who kind of didn't like you absolutely hated you back then." Saint Pete at that time was "a total *Lord of the Flies* situation."

Carolyn had been on the fringes of Ian's friend group. Then she started hanging around more, until it was just the two of them sometimes. "We never got super romantically involved," he says, but they liked each other. "She was independent and not wanting to be a girlfriend, but she wanted to be loved. She was very intelligent and quick-witted, loved to joke and would bust my balls. She would not shy away from a confrontation, which I liked about her."

Ian had been into street punk, then thrash, and metal, but by the time he was hanging out with Carolyn he was creeping toward shoegaze. He remembers lying around with her in his bedroom, listening to records. "She would play me stuff she'd found; I would play her stuff I found." Anything they could throw at each other: Sonic Youth, Swans, The Smiths, Black Rebel Motorcycle Club, The Brian Jonestown Massacre, Dig, Cocteau Twins, Pale Saints. He links his change of taste during this time to hanging out with her. Soon, he was making his own beats in a program called Reason and playing over them. "I didn't know what I was doing, but she thought it was cool. She knew it was early but still dug it."

Adrienne was in her last semester before moving to Orlando. "Fall 2007, I left for college," she says. "I left her in Ian's hands."

"Carolyn was in her own hands," says Ian.

• • •

On September 28, 2007, Jim and Cindy married. The next month Jenny moved to Portland for school. Her friends held a farewell dinner at Portofino and goodbye drinks at The Emerald, then a going-away party at Pamela's. The last few months before her departure, Jenny had been living at Pamela's, in the house she had bought with her inheritance from her grandfather. At the party, she gave Pamela the house key she'd been using and said, "Take care of my baby sister." Pamela walked the key over to Carolyn. She would turn seventeen in less than one month. "She would come in and out all the time. We were like family. I could say something cheesy like, 'I took her under my wing,' but we just became really good friends. It was a sisterly relationship."

It was around this time that she started telling people to call her Carolyn instead of Carrie. "Everyone else takes allowances when they start to nickname you," says Pamela. "They cut your name in half and add some sort of sophomoric ending."

Carolyn was serious about her studies at St. Pete Collegiate and had a new job as a volunteer teachers' assistant at a nonprofit that served immigrant and refugee families. She still liked to be alone. She wrote fondly in a LiveJournal comment of how one Saturday night was spent watching *Blades of Glory* and eating pad thai.

As the season turned, she noticed how cold made the stars look clearer. It reminded her of how "all that hot vapor" only chokes us and "obstructs our vision."

Jenny came home for Christmas and Pamela had a party in the backyard. A drunk friend toppled Carolyn onto the concrete sidewalk to the shed, and she stood with a bloody knee, in a waist-high jean skirt and jelly slip-ons, laughing and leaning on Jenny in a Christmas-light headband. "I think you can kinda tell I sidestepped the hurling bodies just before they hit the ground," Jenny wrote. "I just prevented further bodily injuries to the people standing next to me by halting the domino effect."

At midnight on New Year's Eve, Carolyn responded to her sister. Jenny was back in Portland and she still had two hours left until midnight. "Here's (holding nothing—didn't drink tonight) to having one that might not suck as much as last year," or the ones before it, wrote Carolyn. And even if 2008 does suck, it'll still rule. "I betcha-I betcha. 'specially for you, missy."

· · ·

"We had matching bikes and not on purpose," says Pamela. The fixed-gear scene was gaining heat among Saint Petersburg punks. Green anarchist ideology, veganism, and DIY culture were trending. Pamela asked around for what the right bike would be for her.

A person in the know recommended the female version of a certain blue Nishiki. Unbeknownst, Carolyn had already been given the male version of the exact same bike, same color and everything. "We did our conversions at the same time," says Pamela, turning them into fixed-gears, so they could compete in the races flaring up downtown.

"The fact that Carrie was already doing it, she was kind of my excuse to feel more comfortable," says Pamela. "I would have somebody to ride with." With the matching bikes, "Everyone thought we were sisters."

They started organizing Sunday bike rides with vegan brunch after. Soon, the rides and brunches became fundraisers. "They evolved into, 'Let's make cupcakes and go to the races,'" says Pamela. Then they would donate the money from selling the cupcakes to charity.

The brunch rides weren't officially girl-only, but it happened organically that they tended to be mostly girls—and a lot of them. Finally, another girl said to Pamela, "We should start an all-girl group." Make what they were doing with bikes official and give it a name. The conversations started, and soon Pamela was introducing the St. Pete Skirts. "Listen up! There are some girls in Saint Pete, and they are riding some bikes," she wrote on the new Blogspot. "To boot, they are getting some other girls to ride bikes, and raising some money for charity. Expect workshops, fundraisers, cupcakes, high fives, bike rides, festivities, sugar, spice, and other toing and froing. Details to come." The headquarters were Pamela's garage. She was president. Carolyn initially was "internet consultant" but soon volunteered as vice president.

"It was supposed to be a safe place where women and girls felt comfortable riding with a group," said Erin Hart-Parke, an early board member. She hadn't been on a bike in seven years when she joined. "Where it wasn't a competition. A place where they could ask questions, where they could learn how to take care of their bikes, and where they could train, or just ride for fun. One of the things that we made sure to do on all the rides was that nobody got left behind. Somebody, one of the group members, always made sure to ride back."

"We made T-shirts," says Pamela. "And we made these spoke cards that would say all the Florida bike laws on them."

Carolyn and other Skirts raced and placed in King of Evil II, the St. Pete Alleycat, and Key to Cortez. They played bike polo on the shuffleboard courts with the other hipsters and ended up with skinned knees and elbows. They rode all the way from Saint Pete to Ybor City for art-gallery closings and Mema's Alaskan Tacos. They carpooled to Orlando Alley Cat and the Orlando Rat Race, and even Faster Mustache in Atlanta.

"Carolyn was still in high school, still trying to figure out what she was doing in the world," says Erin. "Carolyn liked that The Skirts was a place where she was not looked at as 'just a kid' and where her opinion was valued. We took her seriously."

• • •

In fall 2008, Carolyn was a senior enrolled in Creative Writing, American Lit 1865–Present, Twentieth-Century Philosophy Trends, and American Government. She was tutoring at a Sylvan Learning center. She had also won the school's creative writing contest, against 115 other SPC students.

She wrote on her LiveJournal of once talking to a boy and hearing him use the word "cashmered" to describe a music video by Devendra Banhart. Carolyn remembered thinking, *That's not a real word*, and being kind of offended, and had even stopped speaking to him.

Then recently, she had rediscovered the camera Jim Bush had bought off the TV and then promptly lost. It had "the picture quality of scrambled 80's porn." And the name for the look of those pictures, from that camera? Cashmered. She calls the aesthetic "lovely . . . soft and ugly and romantic and tired." She can't wait to document her life with this camera. Tomorrow she was road-tripping to Orlando and Gainesville.

"She came to visit me a few times in college in Orlando," says Adrienne. "And she would ask, 'What do you think about Ian?'" who by this time had up and moved suddenly with his family to Mobile, Alabama.

"Well, he's been my best friend all this time," Adrienne would answer, whenever Carolyn asked. "If you like him, whatever."

"I think he's a good-enough guy to take my virginity," Carolyn told her.

"I remember quote for quote, her discussing it," says Adrienne.

"He's a fine-enough candidate," Carolyn said. "His legs are nice. He has bad teeth, but I can look past it."

Adrienne remembers thinking this was not how it happened for her.

On one of those trips to visit Adrienne, Carolyn's debit card froze, and Adrienne loaned her forty dollars for McDonald's and gas to get home. Later, Carolyn sent her a card. "Hey, remember that time you lent me forty bucks and I promised to pay you back within a week, but instead I waited six months?" she wrote. "That was funny. Not, I-am-such-a-flake."

"With hyphens in between," says Adrienne.

"But you my dear are one of my favorite people ever," wrote Carolyn, "not just because you are generous and patient, but because you are . . ."

"And then there's a scribbling arrow up to the top of the note card," says Adrienne. "The note card is a picture of elderly ladies and says, 'Thanks for being one of my best, best ladies.'"

Carolyn lists all the reasons why she loves Adrienne. "I hope to see you super, super soon and stay friends for a super, super long time. xoxo Carrie."

• • •

Pamela says, "At some point that year, I remember she went alone, took the PT Cruiser," and drove up to Mobile to visit Ian. Ian thinks his apartment in Mobile was a stop on Carolyn's way elsewhere, but he can't remember where. "I had an apartment with my cousin, and she came and stayed for a couple of days with us and hung out," he says. "We were hanging out at the apartment, and then we left and we went to this creek behind my grandmother's neighborhood. And we walked down along in the creek bed. And then sat in a drainage tunnel, and just talked, and caught up, and drank whiskey."

"I remember it being very awkward for sure," he recalls about that night. "She was nervous, and we had both been drinking. It was something she needed to take care of. I remember her telling me that. She seemed relieved afterward and calm. It also cemented that we were friends and not lovers, which I believe both of us knew from the beginning. Seems better for it to be a friend than a fling."

• • •

In December 2008, Carolyn was applying to Emerson (her number one), Boston University, NYU, Skidmore, Bard College, Brown, and New College. She specifically was applying for their literature or writing programs. She wrote in an email to Alexis Novak that in her essay answers, she wanted to get across how she approached reading and writing as an opportunity to experiment with craft and perfect it, which she says is true; she does that a lot. Even now!

She'd filled out a questionnaire given to her by her school counselor. She shared it with Alexis. It asked what she was looking for in a college. Carolyn wanted a hip, urban environment that would inspire her and offer interesting internships, an established English department, and a place where she could pursue a career with an interdisciplinary and broad curriculum.

Alexis provided her with a recommendation. "In my eight years plus of classroom experience, I have rarely encountered such a talent of a writer like Carolyn Bush," she wrote. "Her writing has a strong narrative voice, rarely found in the 10th grade set. This voice reflects how well she knows herself and shows she has the moxie to share her unique perspective with her peers and teachers regardless of their criticism. There is an authentic, self-sacrificing element to her writing that is refreshing and relatable. This made her an unofficial leader of her class; a distinction that I am sure she would shy away from but that she earned nonetheless."

"I remember being in Café Bohemia when Carrie showed me her college essays," says Pamela. They were "so well-written, that me at age twenty-three or whatever, she's seventeen, I was just like, *What?* I couldn't write that well. It wasn't just the thoughtfulness, it was the grammar, the syntax. It was all the more shocking because she was a kid. She wrote a lot of college essays about the Skirts."

Jim remembers Alexis encouraging Carolyn to go to Bard because of its writing program. Carolyn's school counselor also encouraged her. "I found out at that time it was sort of known for their accelerated education programs," Jim says. "That they took a lot of folks that had graduated early into their programming. St. Pete Collegiate being that you're getting all this advanced placement, that's kind of how I think the connection with Bard got started."

Jim took her on a college-discovery trip. "I actually didn't want her to go to New York," he says. "I drove her to almost every Florida college there was. I took her to Florida State, to New College and South Texas. There's a South . . ."

"South Florida," says Cindy.

"That's one of my schools," he says.

"But she wanted New York," says Cindy.

"And she wanted New York. She did."

"Originally, she wanted to go to Emerson, but then she went there, and I think she didn't like the urban campus," says Pamela. "She visited the Bard campus and she fell in love with it. She wanted to be in this pastoral setting. I was going to NYU and she wanted to go to Bard." Bard was one hundred miles north of New York City, among villages and farmland, across the river from the Storm King Art Center. The school's motto was "A place to think."

• • •

Carolyn was enrolled in ballet and Intro to Motion Pictures in the spring of 2009, her last semester of high school. Pamela, Carolyn, and Erin made a day trip to Cassadaga Spiritualist Camp, the self-proclaimed "Oldest Continuously Active Religious Community in the Southeastern United States." It's called the "psychic capital of the world."

"We would play the Ouija board," says Pamela. Pamela would also invite over a professional tarot reader and psychic to host reading parties at her house for her friends. This trip to Cassadaga was a culminating one. There, Pamela had booked three readings with a psychic who came highly recommended.

The Cassadaga Hotel was rumored to be haunted, and it had a restaurant with a piano in it, so Erin and Pamela walked in that direction while Carolyn was taking her turn. They passed through lush trees and nineteenth-century boardinghouses and wooden cottages that served as homes and offices for certified mediums, with statues and flowering citrus hedges in the yards. They explored the hotel gift shop and walked back down the quaint streets. "I have this very vivid memory of Pam and me waiting for Carolyn to come out of the room where the psychic was taking us to talk," says Erin. "One of her specialties was communicating with the dead. When Carolyn came out, she was absolutely in tears. Her face was wet, and she didn't want to talk about what she had talked about with the psychic."

A week after the trip, Carolyn wrote in the comments of an online obituary for her friend Frankie, who had died the previous fall. The medium who did her reading told her Frankie had come into the room with them and kept repeating, "It's so much fun when it's someone you know!" Carolyn took great comfort in imagining him having fun in the afterlife, hanging with old friends and doing things he couldn't do while alive. She had been fond of his sincerity, innocence, and humor. He'd once said to her, of his current job, "I just love the pizza industry."

• • •

Pamela sold everything she owned in preparation for her move to New York. "I had this garage sale," she says. "Carrie and I hauled everything from my house onto the front lawn. Brought my couch out on the lawn. Carrie was trying all these clothes on. We were sitting on my couch in the yard drinking Sparks and smoking cigarettes. We had orange-tongue. People would come up and ask us, 'How much for this?' And we'd be like, 'Make me an offer.' At the end of the day, we would just leave everything out, go in, go to sleep, come back the next day. If anybody took anything, who cares? Like three days."

Carolyn graduated in May. Her aunts Carol and Ann flew in for the ceremony. Everyone went to Jim's house afterward to open presents and cards, then to dinner at a restaurant on the waterfront. "Carrie was a little on the shy side in those instances," says Ann. "She grinned a big, big grin, and then kind of looked away. Trying to think of something intelligent to say to the older folks, and I definitely was an older folk."

"Jenny had asked me, or maybe it was Carolyn, to make sure that I told the family that it was a good idea for her to go to college at Bard, because they weren't necessarily wanting to pay for it," says Pamela. "It was a lot of money. At that dinner, I said something about Carrie being the kind of person that wouldn't mess up the opportunity, that she was incredibly smart and she had so much potential, and she wouldn't take this for granted. She would make something with her life. I felt it with conviction."

. . .

It was Carolyn's last summer in Florida before moving. She drove back to Orlando to visit Adrienne and to see Ian's new band, The Sunshine Factory. They had just put out their first album, *Vintage Revolution*, and were on tour, passing through. "We developed a live show with projections to supplement the fact that there was no band other than me," says Ian. His dad did the A/V. "I would dress to the nines and have plywood cutouts with art all over them. We'd bring like four old TVs and have those all hooked up to a VCR and play projections or videos."

Carolyn was taking a summer literature class and had to write an essay. Her topic was the Romantic form of Mary Shelley's *Frankenstein*. She emailed her work in progress to Pamela at the end of July, ten days before Pamela flew back to the US from two months in Paris to start her life in New York City. Carolyn had already written four hundred fairly organized words on the sublime, terror, the human psyche, and the book's context within the Romantic period, and she'd written another eight hundred words consisting of notes, ideas, and quotes from a reference text, which could be ordered into an impressive critical essay—which only had to be between six hundred and one thousand words to begin with. She pleaded for help.

. . .

In July, Carolyn flew to Houston, Texas. "When Hurricane Ike hit in September 2008, Ann and I, and our husbands, had to go down and get everything out of my mother's house quickly," says Carol. "Everything that we could salvage, fast before it molds. We threw so much away. Find boxes, stick things in boxes. Then it was taken to storage. We didn't know where was what, what was which." They moved their mother into an assisted-living facility and rented a condo to stay in while they dealt with her house. Ann remembers Carolyn coming to be there. Edith's second husband, Bill, died in October 2008, just a month later.

By the following July, after Carolyn graduated, all of Edith's belongings were still in storage. "Ann had this great idea that we should figure out what the heck we had in there and organize it," says Carol. "Carrie went to be Susan's eyes.

"I was there for a full week; Carrie was there for about four days," she says. "We would open things up, take pictures, and then decide where things were ultimately going to go. We were inventorying everything with the intention of later dividing things up. Of course, along the way, incidentally, Carrie would say, 'This is a cool shirt.'"

"Great, Carrie, take it," the aunts would tell her.

"She loved it," says Carol. "I'm positive she did. While her grandmother, my mother, was still alive, she would sometimes give things to Carrie or Jenny out of her jewelry box. Some of which, I was like, 'I can't believe you gave that. That's going to get stolen in a dorm room.'"

"One of the things I knew she wanted was that Victorian sofa," says Ann. "When we worked her too hard, it was the only place around that she could stretch out and stare up at the ceiling, relax. She said she would like to have that. It was originally Grandma Ruth's."

"My grandmother graduated from Vassar, in Poughkeepsie," says Ann. "She did very much enjoy antiques and poetry, lots of literature. She collected glassware, furniture, some gorgeous lamps. Carrie saw a lot of Grandma's furniture physically sitting in Mother's house, and so heard about Grandma Ruth, but never met her."

• • •

Ruth matriculated at Vassar in the fall of 1916, when Edna St. Vincent Millay was a senior there. A year later, Millay graduated and moved to New York City, where she made her name as a poet. Ruth was "kind of a New York elite," says Carol. "My father's people were from the Newburgh and Poughkeepsie area, the Hudson River Valley. Ruth was very intelligent, a writer. A teeny, tiny woman who wore hats all the time."

"Ruth graduated in 1920, the same year Grandjohngee asked her to marry him," says Ann of her grandfather, John Hilton Balfe. They married in August 1922. Their honeymoon was a road trip to California in a brand-new car. "Somewhere there are pictures of them tent camping and cooking freshly caught fish over a campfire."

John's uncle, Harry Balfe, had made millions producing mineral water and had gone on to become CEO of the world's largest wholesale grocer, which had made him the richest grocer in the world. In 1919, he bought 760 acres north of Fresno and founded the Balfe Ranch. It boasted a seven-room main house, five guest houses, its own racetrack, an airfield, terraced fishponds, an aviary with pheasants, and a garden that included four hundred rose bushes, a eucalyptus grove, a vineyard, and several orchards.

Harry made John principal and ranch manager. Meanwhile, Harry's interest was his thoroughbred horses, thought to be the best in the world. After them, his priority was Hollywood. With a private landing strip, movie stars visited regularly. Harry "put in a racing stable, a racing arena, an outdoor swimming pool, an airfield, a hangar for small airplanes," says Ann. All of those expenses ran the ranch into the ground.

John and Ruth moved back to the Hudson Valley in 1928, "with metaphorical tails between their legs," says Ann. Their son, Ann's father, was three years old. John McKinstry Balfe, or "Mac," Carolyn's grandfather, would be their only child.

The family moved into a drafty three-story Victorian in Newburgh, Ruth's childhood home. John went to work at a bank, as his father had. Ruth's father too—he was president of the bank where John worked, and of which he would move up to become president. John always missed the ranch. After the Depression, uncle Harry sold it for "next to nothing," says Ann.

By 1944, Mac was a regular midshipman and two-thirds of his way through the Naval Academy in Annapolis. "My husband and I feel very strongly that the United States must take an active constructive part in world affairs from now on," Ruth wrote to the *Vassar Alumni Magazine* that year. Further, "We feel that the concentration of wealth and industry in the hands of big business will lead again to the wrong kind of international entanglements. In an ultra-conservative, traditionally isolationist community, we are considered almost radical!"

She reflects on how her alma mater shaped her life. "I do know that I am now a more serene, a more tolerant, and still a more enthusiastic person than I was when younger, and for that growth I hold Vassar largely responsible."

. . .

At night, Carolyn, Carol, and Ann stayed at Grandma Edith's apartment at the assisted-living facility. Carol and her niece shared a pullout couch. "You can imagine," says Carol. "My mother has dementia. She's sweet as she could be, but she would go to bed about eight o'clock and Carrie and I would pull out the pullout bed and drink beer and watch TV. That's when she would read my palm and read my cards and do astrology."

Carol would ask her questions. "Do you really believe this?" she'd say. "Is this really going to happen?"

"Carol, just enjoy this," Carolyn would tell her. "Don't be too serious."

"She put me in my place a little bit, which I got a kick out of," says Carol. "Of course, it's flattering when somebody wants to read your astrology. It's like, 'Just shut up and enjoy this gift.' I think we got more of a kick out of each other because we were kind of on this island. It could have been really shitty, but it wasn't."

. . .

"This coincided with our neighborhood—Timber Cove, which is the area where we grew up, had planned a fifty-year reunion, sort of a retrospective, where everybody would get together and have a big dinner," says Carol. There would be a cocktail hour by the pool before a big barbecue. Susan and her sisters had grown up in a military family. "We are an exaggerating people," Susan told me. "My dad went to MIT, which my mom joked was a trade school. My father was groomed to be a doctor, and he decided that he didn't have the desire to be a doctor, so he'd be a fighter pilot, which was very cool at the time."

After retiring from the navy as a commander in 1964 due to complications from lupus, Mac went to work for NASA and then Boeing as an engineer. Timber Cove was a brand-new suburb of Houston back then, built as a home to astronauts and others working at the Johnson Space Center, which would soon send the first men to the moon.

By then, Ruth and Grandjohngee had moved from the Hudson Valley to South Carolina then to Kerrville, Texas, to be near Mac's family. Mac worked on the lunar module and then the backup flight-control system for the space shuttle. "His department was Reliability," says Carol. "I remember him answering the phone and saying, 'Reliability, Balfe.' He was in charge of the engineering of redundant programs. Everybody in the neighborhood worked for NASA. That was an interesting part of this reunion.

"Friday night was going to be a barbecue happy hour at the Timber Cove pool," she says. "We've been working and sweating in the storage shed. This pool was the center of our neighborhood. It was built in the shape of the Gemini capsule."

"My sister Ann is tired, and she and her husband decided not to go," says Carol. "I've always been the kind of person that was like, 'Oh, well. I don't care. I'll just go by myself.' But Carrie was like, 'Hey, I'll go with you,' and she wasn't twenty-one yet. Which surprised me, because most eighteen-year-olds would have no interest in going. Meeting people she would have no interest in, that she's never met before. But that was so Carrie.

"There were some people that I knew there, so I started talking to them," says Carol. "Carolyn would get a little bit bored and walk away and get a drink. I kind of felt bad that I abandoned her. You know how it is when you go to a party with someone. I was mingling and I'm like, *I wonder what happened to Carrie.* I walked over and she was standing at the shallow end of the pool. We kicked off our flip-flops and we're standing on the steps of the pool, and the sun was setting. I was sharing Timber Cove with her. She'd heard Susan and me talk about it. 'Our dad was a navy pilot and went to the Naval Academy and worked at NASA. Our dad worked on the lunar module.' Astronomy and astrology. It came from the blood."

20.

Day Five (Part One)

The trial reconvenes in the new year. On Monday, January 9, there are three witnesses for the defense. Finn testifies that Render moved out of their parents' house "relatively shortly after I did," in "2015, I believe." He says Render had been living with Carolyn between six months and a year at the time of the murder and that Render had been in a relationship with Sofia since his junior year of college, or for about four years. "To the best of your understanding was your brother's relationship with Sofia an exclusive one?" asks Smallman.

"Not through their entire relationship."

"All relationships have ups and downs; is that fair to say?" says Smallman. Finn agrees.

Smallman asks, and Finn affirms, that Render was not romantically involved with Carolyn in any way.

"Was there ever a time that there was a discussion between yourself and your brother about the woman who lived on Stanhope Street?" asks Smallman. Finn says he learned a little bit about Carolyn through Render. "Was there ever a time that any problems were indicated to you?"

"No," says Finn. "No serious problems at all."

Hughes asks on cross-examination. "You knew Carolyn Bush because you met her?"

"Yes, I had met her," says Finn.

Hughes has him confirm that all three had gone furniture shopping at IKEA together. He asks what Finn's "take" on Render and Carolyn's relationship is.

"My take on their relationship was that they were relatively normal roommates," says Finn. "Not a very close personal relationship between the two of them. Not—maybe a couple mutual friends, but not really a strong circle of mutual friends. No animosity between them."

"That's not actually true, is it?" says Hughes.

"There were no problems between them," says Finn.

"You were aware of an issue they had with Airbnb, right?"

"I am aware of that, yes." Finn confirms he had spoken to Render about his living situation with Carolyn on multiple occasions, and that more than once, Render had expressed an issue with Carolyn's Airbnb. "It was an ongoing thing," says Finn. "So, he talked to me about it more than once."

Render had shared that it prevented him from being able to use the apartment's common areas. It caused Render, "in my opinion, an understandable amount of annoyance," says Finn. He says he doesn't remember how soon before the murder Render had last mentioned it to him, but it was a while before the murder. The issue "largely" revolved around access to the bathroom.

Hughes asks how many times Finn has met Sofia Bonami. "More than I can keep track of," says Finn. "Dozens of times."

Finn agrees that it's fair to say Render's relationship with Sofia had changed over the years. While they were in college, they were exclusive. Afterward, they broke up for a time, and there was even a period when they were not in contact at all. Between seven and fourteen days before the murder, says Finn, they got back in touch.

"And you testified on direct examination that you believed that they were in a relationship at that point, right?" Finn says yes. "You believed that they were in an exclusive relationship at that point?" Yes. "You believed that because your brother told you that?" Yes.

At Finn's apartment on the night of the murder, Render was expressing positive feelings about Sofia. He hoped they would reconcile on a more permanent basis.

Then Render left, and Sofia texted Finn soon afterward, concerned about Render. Finn called Render to find out why. "It is fair to say that when you reach out to Render, he discusses Sofia again, right?" says Hughes. Finn says yes.

21.

A Children's Story

of an Enchanted Forest

In August 2009, Carolyn moved into her room in Tewksbury, the crumbling concrete brick freshmen dorm at Bard, a.k.a. the party dorm ("Pukesbury"), complete with a patio for smokers. She emailed her dad, mom, sister, aunts, and Pamela upon arriving. "I'm here!" she wrote. On the "backwoodsy campus" where she couldn't get a signal on her phone until she crossed the Hudson. While she had wanted to call and tell them all "how beautiful it is here and how many fleas there are on my ceiling," she couldn't. She didn't have a phone in her room, and wouldn't for several weeks.

Iggy Isaacson was her roommate: sheltered and blonde, from a Milwaukee suburb, she wrote. Iggy's favorite color was pink. She dotted her i's with hearts. She drank Diet Coke with Lime. She spoke "with an upward inflection," wrote Carolyn. But Iggy was also sweet and attracted boys their way. Her musical taste was "remarkably un-hatable."

"I'd never met someone like her," says Iggy. "We were so opposite." Bard had made them each fill out a questionnaire so they could "hand-match" roommates. Iggy and Carolyn speculated as to why they were paired. "I think it was that we both cared about aesthetics, even though our aesthetics were different," says Iggy. They both also loved poetry.

They divided their room down the middle. Iggy's side was all pink. On Carolyn's side, she channeled Grandma Ruth. She hung jewelry and decorative belts beside her vanity, piled with various cosmetic potions. She cut up and placed in four frames a piece of beige paisley fabric and hung the frames alongside smaller needlepoint works and film photographs. She'd brought a blue floral ceramic lamp. A bookshelf at the foot of her bed overflowed. The roommates' desks were set up back to back, between the beds. "We would talk at night, but you couldn't see the person on the other side," says Iggy.

Last night as she left her building, she encountered, "A BABY DEER," Carolyn wrote to her family. The campus reminded her of "a children's story of an enchanted forest."

"You're super isolated," says Iggy. "It's just college students around." Students couldn't leave the campus to go to the nearest supermarket without a vehicle, and the campus itself covered several acres of rural landscape bordering a wooded nature preserve.

"They do a great job of curating the whole class, so everyone has something a little interesting about them," says Iggy. "It's a 'smart misfit' vibe. The weird kids at school, all thrown together, with whatever would ensue. Francophiles, nature kids who live in trees, artists and photographers and sculptors, random athletes on scholarship."

For the first three weeks of Carolyn's time in Annandale, she spent all day, six days a week, in intimate, seminar-style classes alongside other incoming freshmen, learning how to read, think, and write on a college level. This is known as the Language & Thinking Program, and it is required prior to matriculation.

Her first semester, Carolyn was taking Race and Ethnicity in Brazil; History of the Decorative Arts with Professor Tom Wolf (whom she and Pamela joked must personally know the similarly named author); First-Year Seminar I, a required class for all freshmen, which teaches the Great Books, one section of which was taught by Leon; Written Arts: Poetry Workshop, with Max Agrio as her classmate; and The Harlem Renaissance.

In October, she posted on Facebook, throwing expletives at Bard's financial aid office, and asking her friends for help finding a job. Her need for one placed her in a different economic class than a large contingent of her Bard cohort, who hailed from Manhattan or were the children of celebrities.

Pamela came up to visit for Carolyn's nineteenth birthday. "I remember Carolyn telling me where to sit on the train so that I could see the Hudson," she says. "I remember there was a big yellow school bus that picked me up. I remember going through the dorms was very surreal." Pamela hadn't lived in a dorm as an undergrad because she owned a house already. She couldn't believe they put a bunch of eighteen-year-olds in a coed housing situation. "I was very confused that it was just twenty-four-hour party potential."

"I remember we went to a Bard party," she says. It was off campus. "There were so many couches in this house that it was like you couldn't move around them. They were all plaid and looked like you found them on the side of the road. Everyone is wearing nine flannels because the heat isn't going, even though it's November. It's this big Victorian house and everybody is waxing on about some writer that they could not fucking possibly understand. It was Joyce or Proust or something, and philosophy that is so complicated." She was just listening to them, thinking, *I don't even get that and you're, like, eighteen.* There was a bottle of Maker's Mark sitting on the table, "like a hundred-dollar bottle," she says. *Who are these people?* she was thinking. "They're living like squatters, not putting the heat on, talking about literature like they understand it when they don't, and then they have this super-fancy bottle of whiskey? This is rich-kid shit."

"It was very split into groups and very cliquey," says Danielle, about Bard. Danielle met Carolyn living in Tewksbury and formed a tight-knit group of friends with her that included Iggy, Casey Romaine, and Ally Davis. "Carolyn transcended the clique line. She hung out with the people that were constantly in the library and constantly studying and smoking and reading poetry. Then she also hung out with us. We were chugging forties and chasing boys." Carolyn didn't party, but the friends pregamed in her and Iggy's room.

The other group Carolyn hung around with was "The Literati." "The Literati was cool," wrote Danielle later, for the *Huffington Post*. "They liked poetry. They discussed philosophy. They were angry and brooding and took Ancient Greek." Kevin, Cameron, Max, Tommi, and Moira might have fallen into this group.

"There was a very academic crowd who hung out at the library and probably lived on campus or they lived in Red Hook," says Danielle. "That was its own part of Bard. Then there were the party kids that lived in Tivoli, and usually they had a lot of money and could afford to rent these big houses, and live there with all their friends and just throw these ragers. They were mostly from LA, New York, and San Francisco, and had famous parents or really rich parents."

. . .

In November 2009, Bard's dean of students, Erin Cannan, was copied on an email from another administrator. The administrator detailed conversations with two Bard students who relayed allegations that one of the school's administrators had been inappropriate with two other students. According to one of these reports, he had lured a student to his trailer in the woods and offered him drugs, and then pulled out his penis. When the student refused sex, he had then been stranded in the man's trailer overnight, without a car or cell phone service. In the morning, supposedly, the student awoke to find $300 on the table, took the money, and ran to the nearest highway.

Cannan consulted with the school's HR department, and then emailed a Bard email list called "Keepsafe." It consisted, as the name suggests, of administrators charged with students' safekeeping. "A bit of a shock," she wrote. She told them that the administrator had "been laid off for budgetary reasons." She did not mention the allegation of misconduct with students.

In January 2010, a Bard creative writing major, a senior, hung himself on campus. He had asked that his ashes be scattered at the school. He was buried in the Bard College Cemetery. "Another jumped in front of the fucking train," says Danielle. "That goes past on the Hudson River. I don't know how a lot of us made it out okay. A lot of people seemed to have mental breaks at Bard."

"It just was not a good place for my mental health," says Lizzy Crawford, who became close friends with Carolyn. "Mental illness was cool in a way."

"It had a lot to do with the kind of students they accepted, and that there was no support," says another alum.

"A lot of people that I knew who were highly creative and highly inquisitive and engaged in the work that we do there as students were also very troubled," says Lucas Baumgart, a friend of Carolyn's and Tommi's.

"I don't think there was really anyone trained to deal with these things," says Ally.

"We have a lot of students who come to campus with preexisting issues," says Ken Cooper, who was director of security at Bard for roughly twenty years. "Then you add to that the pressures. The stress of the college, it can be profound."

"My school does not do enough to support the mental health of its student body," student Allie Shyer wrote in the *Bard Free Press*.

"Angst, depression, and alienation are not phases for many Bard students—they are states of being," wrote another student, Lenny Simon, in the *Free Press*. "To ignore Bard's culture and ethos in exacerbating these problems, however, is naïve."

"She was very frank about having mental health struggles and not always feeling safe at Bard or at home at Bard," says Moira of Carolyn. "Mental health, which was a large and pervasive problem up there, had very little opportunities for treatment. You're in the middle of nowhere, which drives a lot of people crazy and also means there's no real resources."

• • •

It was Carolyn's second semester of college. She was enrolled in Survey of Latin American Art; Accelerated First-Year Spanish; and Poetry: Texts, Forms, and Experiments. "THE CURE FOR SEASONAL AFFECTIVE DISORDER IS NOT 0 DEGREE 20MPH WIND," Carolyn posted on her Facebook in February. The Sunshine Factory was coming to Bard in February and bringing a Brooklyn shoegaze band called The Qualia with them. Ian, his dad, and The Qualia all crashed in Carolyn's single dorm room. "It seems like one of those places where you have people like Carolyn, who are overjoyed and very serious about being there," says Ian of Bard. "Then you have a lot of rich kids who are like, 'I'm going to liberal arts college,' and their parents just pay for everything. They go there and get fucked-up the whole time." While they were there, some jack-ass went stomping down the Tewks hallway smashing lightbulbs. Ian swears the kid looked exactly like Render. Most of them did, though.

The Sunshine Factory played two shows at Bard. "I'm sure you've heard about the very distinctive Carolyn dance move?" says Iggy. "It's like one leg is stamping, and her hands are straight, and she's looking up at the sky."

"She stomped her front leg down," says Pamela. "And it was like she was putting out a cigarette. Then she'd waddle her hips like a duck. Lots of swagger."

"I have this one memory of me and her," says Ally. "We were drinking whiskey and we didn't have anything to chase it with, so we would just slap each other in the face." Carolyn called the game "Slap Shots."

"She was the first person who I ever did a shot with and chased it with a slap in the face," says Iggy. "You lock eyes."

"Then you take a shot and slap the other person as hard as you can," says Cameron. "It's a drinking game. Apparently, it came from Saint Petersburg."

"We just did shots," says Pamela, of growing up in Saint Petersburg. "No one I knew needed a slap in the face to take a shot. Maybe she just wanted to slap them in the face and made up a game for that."

. . .

Carolyn spent the summer after her freshman year in Brooklyn. "She would stay with me," says Pamela, who was living with another friend from home, "or rent an apartment from somebody nearby and we would see each other all the time," says Pamela. "Probably working weird jobs, like waitressing at some place you would never go."

Max wanted to visit. "We go to this grimy Williamsburg loft, classic dream-of-the-2000s-style loft building," he says. "There's this crazy rooftop party happening. Her friend came up to me and Carolyn. They're like, 'Oh, my god, hey! What's up?' Then they just open this grocery bag, and it's filled with mushrooms. Me and Carolyn are like, 'Might as well.' We ate a bunch of mushrooms together. It was beautiful. We were just talking, and tripping, staring out at Manhattan and loving life. We stayed there until we saw the sun rise, then we went back to this tiny, tiny apartment that she was staying in, this comically small apartment." At the time, Pamela and their other friend were living in a sixth-floor walk-up. "I was really depressed, and she would always bring me out of it and make me feel like more of a person, more fulfilled. I'm thankful for her because my first year at school was not great."

In July, another Bard student killed herself at her parents' apartment in the city. She was two years ahead of Carolyn. A mass email went out to the whole school, from Leon. "It is my sad duty to inform you of the death," he wrote. "Those needing further information should contact the Dean of Students Office."

. . .

At the end of September 2010, a Bard student named Katherine "Kate" Blake was hit by a pickup truck on Route 9, in Tivoli. She had been leaving a meal with her boyfriend, Henry Pfeffer, who grew up in Rhinebeck around the corner from Render, just a five-minute walk. It's not clear if they knew each other since they went to different high schools. Henry graduated from Poughkeepsie Day School, where he'd met Kate.

As Henry would tell in a later psychiatric evaluation, after suffering his first psychotic episode at the University of Vermont in January 2009, he had returned home to Rhinebeck to recuperate and seek ~~treatment. He and~~ Kate had reunited over the summer, and she'd ~~decided to~~ enroll at Bard, where she was studying to be a ~~writer~~ in September, eventually declaring a studio-art ~~major. They~~ began an intense sexual relationship, Henry's ~~first. It was~~ overwhelming to him.

~~That night in~~ Tivoli, Henry would explain, Kate had told him ~~she loved him~~ and didn't want to spend the night alone. He'd told her he needed space. She'd left the restaurant distraught. Moments later, she was hit by the truck. Doctors stabilized her in a traumatic brain injury unit, where she lay in a coma. Henry blamed himself and began struggling in his classes. He asked his psychiatrist for something to help him focus. The doctor prescribed him Ritalin, then Adderall.

. . .

That fall, in 2010, Carolyn was enrolled in Jerusalem: History, Theology, and Politics, and she volunteered for a project digitizing the first modern census of Palestinians in the West Bank and Gaza. She took Philosophy and the Arts; Reading Religious Texts; and Reading as Writing as Reading: Exploring the Contemporary, with Professor Ann Lauterbach. Lauterbach says, "The subject of Carolyn

Bush is not an easy one. She seemed at the time to be 'troubled,' and to want more reassurance than was possible, at least for me, to give."

"I never saw Carolyn as troubled," says Cameron, who was in the poetry class with her. "She could give the appearance of being abrupt. Carolyn did suffer; I don't want to make light of that. Carolyn sometimes needed to spend a lot of time alone. She would also say things like, 'It takes up a lot of my time being crazy.' But the relationship that Carolyn and I had was so fun that I took great refuge in Carolyn a lot of the time, and I hope or think that she did in me as well."

Though, "There was a time when I remember she slapped me in public," he says. "I said something she construed as rude."

"She believed she had ADD," says Jenny. "Which she might've. She certainly struggled with focus and she was struggling in school as a freshman. She kept getting bad grades and they were going to boot her, and she would go on academic probation, and then she would sit in front of a panel, and she would have to plead her case."

• • •

Carolyn posted on her Facebook in December that she had moderated. It is the Bard term for declaring a major and a process that requires approval from a faculty committee, which is not guaranteed.

"CONGRATULATIONS!!!!!!!!" Cindy responded. "Wahoo!!!!!!! Yippeeeee,,..what else can I say? Proud of you!!!!!!!"

"Yippy ki yeah!" said Jim. "Way to go . . . Proud papa here!"

"I'm late getting my congrats in, but they are nonetheless heartfelt!!" said Ann. "Love and hugs!"

"What does this mean?" said Carol. "I'm in the dark (in so many ways)."

One issue of the *Bardian* explained, "As it has for nearly 80 years, Moderation, in which all students assess their academic progress and anticipate their courses of study for the next two years, signals the transition from the Lower to the Upper College." It is typically done midway through a student's sophomore year, and preparation for it begins early.

The way Carolyn explained it was that she wrote a bunch of critical papers and poems, then "sat in a room for two hours with three of my most intimate professors where they told me all kinds of things about my life as an intellectual failure (kidding, kind of)." They also told her how she was "magnificent and complicated and brilliant (kidding, mostly)." She said it's required for Bard students, and that she had now officially declared herself a Written Arts major.

There are no classes on Carolyn's transcript for the following semester, spring 2011. But she had initially planned on taking at least one—she had asked Danielle if she could buy her old copy of the *Iliad* for it. They arranged to do a transfer.

The next day, Danielle wrote, "i have the books and am in kline. Please claim them because they are heavy."

Carolyn said the plans had changed.

"do you not need them anymore?" said Danielle.

She did not.

"Mom thinks you are suffering from, 'despair,'" Jenny wrote on Carolyn's Facebook that week. "Seriously, direct quote. I tried to tell her that you are without phone and really just inherently literal, but to no avail. Please send her a bat-signal shaped like this: ☺."

• • •

In February 2011, five months after Kate was hit by the truck, Henry penetrated the ward where she lay in a coma. In a lawsuit he filed later against his psychiatrist, he claimed that the Adderall he had been improperly prescribed weeks earlier had triggered a psychotic episode in which he believed he had to take Kate's breath away. He stabbed her twice, on either side of her ribcage. Then he walked out of the hospital, still holding the six-inch knife, made from an animal's jawbone. He was arrested, still holding it, in the parking lot and was charged with attempted murder. Kate survived the incident but died in April from complications related to the initial accident with the truck. Henry was found not responsible by reason of mental illness and was institutionalized, then released. According to his website, he lives in Kingston, across the river from Rhinebeck, and is an abstract fine art painter.

• • •

"When I first lived with Carolyn, I was worried about her," says Alexis Graman. It was spring 2011. "She was taking a semester off and planning on going to Bard the following semester. She seemed like she was just dealing with shit."

They lived in a flea-infested red house just over the bridge spanning a little creek, leading into Tivoli. "We would hang out on the long, narrow wooden porch. The house was sort of pushed back. The house across the street was a party house. I remember, she kept a big bottle of whiskey in the freezer. Every night we'd have whiskey and ginger ale, and we'd sit on the porch and talk and talk and talk and she'd always go really far with whatever she was thinking about. She wanted to be a writer. She wanted to take great classes.

"We would walk at night and smoke cigarettes," he says. "She would talk about Florida. We talked about romance. She was always crushing on people. Tommi for instance. She loved Tommi, and Tommi's a really interesting, strange guy, but she would only talk about how good-looking he was.

"Mysticism," he remembers. "The occult. Predictions to do with the future. People's personalities. We talked about poets. California poets. We were talking about Jack Spicer, John Wieners.

"We probably spent the most time together of the people in the house," he says. There were five total. "She'd never really get along with anybody else. Carolyn would take up all the space she needed."

Even when she wasn't enrolled in classes, Carolyn liked to smoke cigarettes outside the Stevenson Library; lots of Bard students were heavy smokers, so many that there were articles about it in the *Bard Free Press*. She loved to read on the benches of a meditation garden enclosed in Canadian hemlocks, next to the chapel. The garden is dedicated to Anna Jones, the Bard student whose throat was slashed by her boyfriend, a recent graduate, in the parking lot of a nearby church in 1998.

Carolyn worked at a coffee shop on a busy corner in Red Hook. It had a charming facade with hand-painted windows, a striped awning, a white balcony, and trees shading the sidewalk. Lizzy Crawford was a senior when Carolyn worked there. The two had met through Cameron. Lizzy's boyfriend came up with the name Coco.

"He had forgotten her first name, but he knew that it started with a *C*, so he just started calling her Coco," says Cameron of Lizzy's boyfriend. "I imagined her as this eccentric flapper: 'Carolyn could be a Coco.' It started to catch on a little bit after that but none of her close friends called her Coco. All of us called her Carolyn."

"Something about her essence," says Lizzy. "He thought it was funny and she really liked it. They came up with this idea that her pen name should be Coco B. Either she kept going with it or it came back again later. She reclaimed it." In New York, her Wendy's Subway family would call her Coco.

. . .

After living in the red house, Carolyn lived in a shady large yellow two-story house with Cameron. "Carolyn and I wanted to host a cocktail party," he remembers. "We wanted to get cocktail glasses and a mixer, so we went to Kingston," which is where places like Bed Bath & Beyond and Linens 'n Things are. "We're looking for cocktail glasses, and we run into this woman, and this woman said . . ."

"Oh, are you also looking for champagne flutes?"

Rather surprised, they said, "No, we're looking for cocktail glasses."

And she was like, "Well, I don't think you'll find them here, it is so uncivilized. This whole area."

The friends decided to play it up. "Oh, we know," they said.

"We were sort of amazed that this woman saw us as her equals, and we went with it—that we were struggling in this wilderness."

They ended up going to HomeGoods next. "And this woman was there again," he says.

She told them, "I called in advance."

Cameron made meatballs for the party. The whole night, he and Carolyn took on this woman's persona, "Really pronouncing *wh*'s."

"*Wh*ere did I put my cocktail? *Wh*at shall we put on the stereo?"

Carolyn moved out at the end of summer and lived in an apartment now, five minutes west of the café on foot, in a red building on a corner, above a lawyer with a wooden hanging sign. "It was beautiful," says Cameron. It was a studio, so the main room held her bed, a table in the corner for writing, and all her books, all in one place. "I guess this is the last place she lived at Bard."

"Carolyn stayed up very late a lot of the time, as all of us did," he says. "You could always see that light on when you were walking home.

"She had a sort of business scheme in which she would order books from Amazon and then keep the ones that she liked but resold the other ones," he remembers. "She was basically just always collecting books and selling them for a cent. I think, not to make money, but so that she would have credit. I remember one time we had fifteen copies of *Antigone*."

She continued to write voraciously. Cameron remembers her poem "A Magnificat," calling it "a breakthrough poem" she had written that year. Gabe would later quote it in "Regression," the poem he dedicated to her, writing:

like the day that's over
but clings to your nerves a while, "Still wading
sentimentally in a year
That ended sentimentally in the middle of a season,"
is how you put it,

She was also reading a lot of György Lukács that year, the Hungarian Marxist philosopher and politician. "He was kind of popular at Bard," says Cameron. "A lot of poetry, and Julian of Norwich." They shared a fascination with the medieval Christian mystic. "There was a period where we'd sit in bed together and she'd read *Dubliners* to me."

"She loved Mina Loy," says Max. *Stories and Essays of Mina Loy* had been published by Dalkey Archive that August. "I feel like she was kind of this reincarnation of Mina Loy. She definitely wanted to be. The kind of 'swathed in fur, holding court in a smoky parlor talking about the firmament and the fixture of the stars.' That's the world that she wanted to inhabit."

22.

Day Five (Part Two)

Margulis-Ohnuma calls to the stand Dr. David Cherkas, the emergency doctor who treated Render at Elmhurst Hospital. Cherkas says he reviewed Render's medical records briefly before testifying, a portion of which Margulis-Ohnuma offers into evidence and attempts to project on the document camera, if only anyone can get it working.

Render had arrived at Elmhurst about a quarter after midnight, covered in blood, cuffed to a stretcher. Upon examination around 5:00 a.m., his neurological state was grossly nonfocal, meaning he showed no apparent paralysis or severely altered mental state; however, he did show a constricted affect. "He was not very interactive with me," says Cherkas. "I see a fair number of patients who are both victims and perpetrators in crimes and they are usually emotional or agitated, and I felt like he was neither of those." A "constricted" or "blunted" affect could be symptomatic of several illnesses, including traumatic brain injury, depression, PTSD, a personality disorder, or schizophrenia. It could also be a side effect of marijuana or other drug use.

In his book *The Brain Defense: Murder in Manhattan and the Dawn of Neuroscience in America's Courtrooms*, Kevin Davis details the story of Herbert Weinstein, who, in January 1991, confessed to killing his wife and then throwing her out of their twelfth-story window on the Upper East Side, to make it look as though she had committed suicide, immediately after committing the crime. "It was completely out of character—he had to have been out of his mind. That's how Weinstein's friends and neighbors reacted to news of his arrest," Davis writes.

Noting Weinstein's inappropriately calm demeanor afterward, his lawyer ordered a psychiatric evaluation. The psychiatrist who examined him "found nothing wrong with Weinstein," writes Davis. "He noted, however, that Weinstein didn't show any feelings about his wife's death, 'no manifestation of guilt, depression, or anxiety,' as he wrote in his report."

One of the examining doctors, noting some slight irregularities in Weinstein's motor skills, ordered an MRI. It revealed an orange-sized cyst sitting on his frontal lobe, the part of the brain that governs impulse control. Decreased blood flow to the frontal lobe is responsible for the impulsive behavior of people under the influence of marijuana and alcohol. In Weinstein's case, it wasn't an intoxicating substance inhibiting its function but an enormous fluid-filled sac.

Weinstein's defense team sent these findings to the prosecutor, who feared a jury seeing them would be forced to conclude that Weinstein's brain was defective when he murdered his wife. He decided not to press the murder charge, and Weinstein instead accepted a lesser charge of manslaughter. The judge handed down the minimum sentence of seven years. Davis writes, "Weinstein wasn't insane in the classical sense—his mental health evaluations confirmed that. But Weinstein, he could argue, had been temporarily insane—at the time of the crime, Weinstein had not been Weinstein."

At Render's first exam, the resident psychiatrist, under the supervision of the attending psychiatrist, gave Render a working diagnosis of substance-induced psychotic disorder. Elmhurst was prepared to send him to Bellevue Hospital for evaluation by a forensic psychiatrist; however, this never happened because at his second evaluation that afternoon, Render was found not to be suicidal or homicidal. "Patient has no overt psychosis," the doctor wrote. "Mental status has improved . . . Patient recalls what happened yesterday leading up to his injury, but refuses to communicate, stating his lawyer told him not to mention anything . . . Patient currently denies auditory hallucinations, visual hallucinations, suicidal and homicidal ideations."

On cross-exam, Hughes asks Cherkas, "You'd agree with me the defendant indicated he's never experienced any significant mental health episode before, right?" Cherkas confirmed. "Says he never had taken any sort of antipsychotic medications?" Cherkas confirmed that too. "Never indicated taking any sort of antidepressant?" Correct. "Never indicated he was under the care of a psychiatrist?" Correct. "Never under the care of a psychologist?" Correct. "Never under the care of a therapist?" Correct.

Render's blood had been drawn and a toxicology done the night of the murder, showing a blood alcohol level equivalent to about one beer—but the results of his marijuana test, for organic and synthetic marijuana, are dated January 2017. They show no marijuana in his system.

Margulis-Ohnuma thinks that the 2017 results are dated correctly, and the blood was likely drawn while Render was at Riker's. He says that the original test results, from 2016, have been lost. Hughes believes the 2017 results are dated incorrectly and that they are from blood drawn on the night of the murder.

"We've been asking for this for three years," Margulis-Ohnuma argues with him on sidebar, in the back hallway. "We have never seen a toxicology exam that says, 'Yeah,' or that he had marijuana in his system, that is from this time period. It doesn't exist."

"There was tox testing done on the defendant's blood both for the presence of cannabis and synthetics," Hughes says to the judge and Margulis-Ohnuma. "One done by the Office of Chief Medical Examiner's toxicology lab and one done by an independent laboratory. The results that come back say, 'None.' Mr. Margulis says that blood didn't come from the blood that was taken in Elmhurst Hospital. My belief is it did."

"I think there's a very serious discovery violation here," Margulis-Ohnuma argues. "We tried our entire case on the assumption that Jack Warsawsky gave us all the discovery he said he was giving us. We looked high and low for those test results that are associated with that night, with a sample that was taken that night. What we were given was something from January 2017. This must have been from something at Rikers or something later. There's nothing associating it with this night. That tox screen has been lost. Not only is it a discovery violation; our office has investigated and has engaged for three years now with Elmhurst Hospital to do that. We would have tried our case very differently." The trial proceeds without anyone obtaining the original toxicology tests.

23.

Sparkies
___

David Shein's character witness statement for Render says he was his dean until he graduated, and at times served as his academic advisor. David arrived at Bard in 1999, the year Janet joined the admissions department. He currently serves as associate vice president for academic affairs and dean of studies. "Render was always calm and kind and peaceful and serious about his work," he writes. "I can't say for sure, of course, but I can say from a lifetime of working with 18 – 22 year olds (who are, as we know, prone to psychiatric illness) that what I was reading about sounded like someone who had experienced a break with reality."

According to a former Bard employee, David oversees a secret group of students called the "Sparkies." The students themselves aren't told they're in this group. "Sparkies is for people who get admitted, not for merit, but for how much money the school thinks their families can donate," says the administrator. "It's like the equivalent of those special programs they have for athletes where they give them 'a different experience.' Make them feel happy so that they'll want to donate money. That's the entire reason behind the program." David is assigned as their advisor. David neither confirmed nor denied the existence of the "Sparkies" or his role overseeing them.

Danielle Sinay recalls Leon calling her into his office during her sophomore year at Bard because, "I wanted to transfer out," she says.

"I don't know how he hears things. I don't know who tells him, because I never would tell Leon I was applying."

"I hear you're looking to transfer," Leon said in his office. He sat her in a little chair, so he was looking down on her. "You know, you're a very pretty young woman." She thanked him because she didn't know what else to say. "That means that it doesn't matter from where you get your degree. You just have to depend on that."

"I was nineteen, I was very anorexic, I was very addicted to Klonopin, and had an abusive boyfriend, so I would listen to anything anyone powerful said to me," says Danielle. Asked about saying this, Leon denies it, saying, "I would not make such a comment."

"Leon literally summoned David to the office," says Danielle.

"Hi, Danielle wants to leave," Leon said to David Shein. "Can you please work with her to make sure she likes Bard?"

David was made her co-advisor. Asked whether this occurred, Leon said, "I don't recall, though a large part of all of our job here is to ensure all students are supported." Leon denied the existence of the Sparkies.

"He was equally nice to my little sister, and everyone I know who is wealthy," says Danielle, of David.

• • •

"I loved Bard as much as I did because the administration wanted it that way," Danielle wrote in an open letter, which she published online soon after Render's sentencing. "While my last name is Sinay, I am known to the administration as granddaughter of Lynda and Stewart Resnick," billionaire owners of The Wonderful Company. She lists some buildings that her grandparents have endowed on campus: "Resnick as in the Resnick Commons, Lynda and Stewart Resnick Theater, and The Lynda and Stewart Resnick Science Laboratories (among others)." She says Leon is her grandfather's "very close friend." "I've known Leon since I was young, and still don't know if I would've been admitted to Bard if it were not for this connection."

• • •

After learning, at Render's sentencing, that Leon had written a letter of support for him, Danielle resigned from the Bard Alumni Board of Governors, which helps with the school's fundraising. When Leon found out about her resignation, he emailed Danielle and her grandparents together. Danielle's grandfather, Stewart Resnick, sits on Bard's Board of Trustees. "I hate operating by rumor," Leon wrote, "but word has reached me that Danielle has resigned."

He didn't ask why. Instead, he explained that the letter he wrote for Render is "self-explanatory." He attached it to the email. "My voice was that of a parent who survived the senseless killing of his own daughter. And, as President of Bard, I try to do my best to help our graduates, when they are in trouble and need aid, even when they have done something grievously wrong. I stand by what I did. I stand by what I wrote. I wrote in the spirit of my daughter's death, her memory, and her loss."

His letter in 2020 was nearly three times as long as the one he sent in 2017, the latter of which I wouldn't learn about for another year, through an open record request. In his second letter to Justice Buchter, he cited the Bard Prison Initiative (BPI), the largest prison education program in the country, which brings liberal arts higher education and the chance to earn a degree to incarcerated people throughout New York State. He directed Buchter to the Ken Burns documentary about BPI released earlier that year but did not mention that his daughter Sarah had coproduced it, nor that the BPI director is his son-in-law, Sarah's husband.

He described himself as "a college teacher and administrator with many years of experience observing and dealing with young people between the ages of 15 and 35." In his first letter, he had written: "The reader of this statement should be aware that I make this claim in the context of having spent over four decades running an institution of higher education and living on a campus surrounded by young men and women between the ages of 17 and 22, and an equal number of years teaching undergraduates and counseling students and their parents, as well as being responsible for disciplinary actions for students who violate the law and codes of conduct enforced on the College campus for which I am responsible."

In 2020, he told Buchter, "There is in my opinion no danger of anything remotely similar happening as a result of any behavior on Render's part in the future," and, "Whenever he is released from prison, he will live out his life as a model citizen," and, "In short, I believe Render is a danger to no one but perhaps himself."

. . .

"Part of me thinks that he would do it for any Bard student," says Danielle. "Maybe he really would, and I think that's what he wants people to think. But also, Janet worked at Bard and went to Bard, and knew Leon for a very, very long time, and they had a close relationship. To the Bard administration community, she was a very important person."

Danielle says, "Jane Brien, the head of [alumni] at Bard, was at the trial, sitting on their side," meaning Render's side. "I made eye contact with her. She knows me because she had chased me around for donations. She knows my family. She hid under a blanket after she made eye contact with me."

Martha Tepepa was a recruiter for the Levy Economics Institute at Bard in 2017 and had shared an office wall with Janet in Blithewood Manor, after Janet was promoted, and her office moved there. Martha remembers how close the relationship between Janet and Leon was then. One day, Janet had emailed Martha. "She sent an email that I didn't reply to." It was just a busy day, she says. "I was running up and down and up and down."

"So, Janet barged into my office," she says. "Started screaming and yelling. And I'm like, 'What?' And giving me all of this lecture. 'Oh, you have to be a professional. You cannot do that.' This was so weird. She's like, 'When your president asks you to do something . . .' I'm like, 'What president?' She's like, 'The president of the college.'"

"She believed that she had, how should we say, the touch from the president," says Martha's husband, Jan Kregel, who also worked alongside Janet in Blithewood.

One former administrator tells me that soon after they started working at Bard, they were having dinner at a local restaurant with another professor and administrator, Thomas Bartscherer. "We're seated next to Leon and Janet Stetson," they say, who looked like they were having a very private conversation. "It was awkward, because Thomas was new in his position, and I was new there." They felt like they were seeing something they weren't supposed to see.

In response to a question mentioning rumors of an affair, Leon informed me, "I am not now nor have I ever been romantically involved with Janet Stetson."

"From my experience at Bard, I can tell that Botstein is a controlling freak," says Gennady Shkliarevsky, who had worked at Bard since 1985, and was Render's history professor and academic advisor. He lives in Rhinebeck and is friendly with Janet, having been her neighbor and colleague since she started working at the school. "He knows how to manipulate people and enjoys enormous power at Bard. It is not difficult to imagine that this enormous power creates its own seductions.

"The fact may have been known to Render too," he says.

24.

Day Six

After Dr. Cherkas, the defense calls Dr. Alexander Bardey, a forensic psychiatrist and frequent expert witness. He is a consultant for *Law & Order* and is known for coproducing and consulting on the movie *Side Effects*, directed by Steven Soderbergh. In it, a mentally ill woman is prescribed an experimental drug by her psychiatrist, resulting in side effects that drive her to kill her husband. "Across all of mental health, mentally ill people are no more dangerous than anyone else," Bardey said in an interview about the film. "That being said, there are certain subgroups of people, because of their symptoms, that do represent a greater threat of danger to themselves or others."

Bardey later wrote for CBSNews.com that, to diagnose mental illness in criminal cases, "Inferences are drawn from later interviews, police reports, medical records, and sometimes, in this day and age, internet and social media postings . . . The psychiatrist's conclusion about sanity lies in his or her analysis of these data—in other words, an opinion. An opinion can be contradicted by another psychiatrist, leading to courtroom 'battles of the experts,' which then only confuses juries."

On the stand, Bardey says he had an opportunity to review Render's health records from Rikers Island and the Northern Dutchess Hospital, prior to writing his evaluation report. He interviewed Render four times for a total of about eight hours but did not record the interviews or provide transcripts. The prosecution's expert witness, Dr. Kostas Katsavdakis, did record his five interviews with Render over nearly ten hours.

Before writing his evaluation, Bardey also interviewed Render's parents, Finn, Sofia, and Arun. When he diagnosed Render with cannabis-induced psychotic disorder, he says, he had not yet seen his complete health records from Elmhurst. "The records that I had reviewed from Elmhurst Hospital did not include the evaluations, the consultations by the psychiatrist there," he says. He says he was unaware that Render had been diagnosed with substance-induced psychotic disorder already when he was writing his report.

After writing the report, he watched the thirty-one minutes of video excerpts from Render's taped interviews with Dr. Katsavdakis. Katsavdakis had reached the conclusion that Render wasn't suffering from psychosis but rather a catathymic reaction brought on by a panic attack. Asked what a catathymic reaction is on the stand, Bardey says, "The assailant may not even realize what button is being pushed or what trigger initiated it, but it's an act that the assailant responds to unconsciously, subconsciously, and then is filled with explosive murderous rage."

Bardey disagrees that this is what occurred in Render's case. "I did not see anything that would provoke it," he says. He does not think it is significant that Render's relationship with Sofia was uncertain. He does not think that Render and Carolyn's disagreements over Airbnb rose to the level of a provocation. He also does not think it's significant that Render told a reporter he had always "buried his anger at small annoyances."

"There was no antecedent behaviors by anyone that would have immediately caused him to react in such a way that he would stab himself and then go through the motions that he described," he says. Bardey says that Render stabbed himself before stabbing Carolyn, despite him telling police it was afterward—he'd changed his story by the time he was interviewed by Bardey and Katsavdakis.

Katsavdakis had used the words *depersonalization* and *derealization* in his report.

"Derealization is a sense of being in a kind of strange—you don't recognize the surrounding around you," Bardey explains. Time slows down in a moment of depersonalization or derealization, which may happen after a traumatic event like a car crash, or discovering your spouse in bed with a lover. "You could almost feel as though you're watching yourself in a video," he says. "There's a protective mechanism so as not to be overwhelmed. And it also lets you not be paralyzed by panic. You can act, in fact, without being troubled by your emotion in that moment in a way that may be life-saving." What Katsavdakis fails to appreciate in his evaluation of Render, says Bardey, is the severity of his symptoms. "So, in his opinion," he says, "it stayed below the psychotic line."

Margulis-Ohnuma asks Bardey what conclusion he reached about Render's mental state at the time of the murder. "As a result of the cannabis that he had ingested," says Bardey, "he had an unusual psychotic reaction that caused him to have a break with reality. He at that point no longer could distinguish what was a thought in his head from what was going on around him.

"He thought that he had died," says Bardey, "and he was caught in this almost cinematographic loop where the same events would keep occurring over and over again until infinity with slight variations each time. He had lost the ability to recognize that the actions he was taking were actually impacting the well-being of other people. As a result—because he was in a psychotic state, was divorced from reality—he could not appreciate the nature, and the consequences, and wrongfulness of his actions." Bardey says that substance-induced psychosis is different from cannabis intoxication. The core difference, he says, is that when someone is high, they can reflect on their experience from a manageable remove. Whereas when someone is experiencing psychosis, they lose the ability to understand what's real or not.

Margulis-Ohnuma plays the video excerpts of Render from Katsavdakis's interviews with him. Katsavdakis interviewed Render in a conference room in the district attorney's office. Margulis-Ohnuma pauses intermittently to ask Bardey how he interprets Render's various statements.

"It was the only time I really wrote anything down," says Alexis Graman, who was present in the courtroom. "I wrote a bunch of quotes," from the screening of Render's interviews with Katsavdakis. "I wrote down, 'Some people say when you die you have a final thought and that is the afterlife.' This is before he killed her. 'By stabbing Carolyn it was part of my mind I was destroying. It had a reality.' 'This is going to be the present future for eternity.' His own death, I think, is largely what he was talking about, because he's saying he's dead," says Alexis. "He had a premonition that this is the afterlife in the Uber before he killed Carolyn, and now this is the rest of his life. 'I died in the Uber and it existed as a final thought in my own head. I was asking for some amount of control. I want people to understand the truth of what happened. That is very important to me.' I think the truth of what happened to him is it didn't happen. For him, it still never happened. For everybody on that side, it's like this couldn't have happened."

"What he is saying there is," says Bardey of one clip, "in his opinion, he was not appreciating the fact that he was actually harming anything real or any real person." Pressed on this by Margulis-Ohnuma, he explains, "He was killing someone in his mind, not in reality. So, no, he did not know he was actually killing somebody."

"You're saying he's out of contact with reality?" Buchter asks. Bardey says yes. "Could you explain to me what caused the violence?"

"Because the reality that he was in was filled with these violent thoughts that somehow he was in purgatory," says Bardey. "He had to suffer and had to experience pain himself and watch people suffer and experience the horror of watching that. That's what populated his psychosis. In other words, psychosis represents a type of thinking."

"Now," Hughes asks Bardey on cross-exam, "you'd agree with me that nowhere in those medical records says anything about his feeling like he was experiencing an infinite time loop, right?" Bardey agrees with this.

"Doesn't say anything about believing he was already deceased, does it?" says Hughes. No, says Bardey.

"All of those statements come based upon his interview with you, right?"

"Over time," says Bardey. "He did not remember a lot of that initially."

Bardey is not neutral in his responses to Hughes. He gives lengthy answers that meander from the point. Emotion and insistence seep in. "This is an anomaly," he says, when Hughes has him confirm that marijuana-induced psychosis is very rare, and that Render does not meet the criteria for being at risk: early onset usage, heavy usage, and smoking high-THC cannabis or cannabis products. A handful of times, Bardey utters some version of the phrase "I think I just explained what I meant by that." He twists his own words, contradicts himself, and is sarcastic.

"He does say he had feelings of impending doom, right?" Hughes asks.

"Yeah," says Bardey. "And I explained to you where that comes from. It doesn't come from 'I'm having a heart attack because of the intensity of my panic attack and I'm going to die.' It comes from 'I'm in this purgatory where I'm going to be suffering for eternity, there's impending doom.' That's where it comes from."

Bardey says that he sees no evidence that Render was experiencing acute anxiety, though Sofia testified that he seemed "jittery" on the phone. Render also told Katsavdakis in his interviews that he felt intense panic just before the murder.

Bardey speculates that the marijuana Render smoked may have been laced with something, though there's no evidence for it, and Finn smoked the same weed with no adverse reaction. Bardey testifies that he thinks Render may have a genetic predisposition for substance-induced psychosis, though Katsavdakis will later testify that he's not aware of any literature supporting the idea that substance-induced psychotic disorder is genetic.

Janet had provided Bardey with a mental health history of her family. There are anxiety disorders throughout her side. There is substance abuse on Danny's side but no psychotic disorders.

"You also cited, too," says Hughes, of Danny's interview with Bardey, "the adverse reaction that he says he had to marijuana, right?" Bardey says yes—Danny had also reported, during his interview, he'd once had an adverse reaction to marijuana.

"Are you aware that he never mentioned having an adverse reaction to marijuana during his testimony?" says Hughes.

"He did during my evaluation of him," says Bardey.

"Are you aware that he never mentioned having an adverse reaction to marijuana when he spoke to Dr. Katsavdakis?"

"Sure," says Bardey. "He didn't mention that in his report."

"Only you he mentioned it to?" says Hughes.

"Yes."

Hughes points out that Render smoked weed voluntarily even though he knew he had had a prior negative experience with it.

"Yes," says Bardey. But it "was mitigated by the fact he smoked it on specific occasions since then and had no such reaction." In Render's interviews, he had told Bardey that he'd smoked weed between ten and twelve times since the 2007 incident.

"But in your report, you also detail an experience from December of 2015, right?" says Hughes. Render felt buzzed from smoking marijuana on that occasion. "He told you, also, though, that his body was pulsating?" says Hughes. Bardey says yes. "He also indicated he experienced visual distortions?" says Hughes.

"Minor visual distortions, yes," says Bardey.

"But he denied paranoia?"

"Exactly."

"And from that point on up until this event, based on your interviews with him, he never smoked marijuana again?" says Hughes.

"That's true, that's what I reported."

"I think Judge Buchter already on questioning pointed out that the defendant actually told you that he urged someone to call the police, right?"

"He did."

"The police come when crimes are committed?"

"Or when someone is injured or when there is a crisis," says Bardey. "There are a lot of reasons to call the police."

"Defendant told you he wasn't experiencing any pain, right?" Bardey agrees with this. "He said that the dagger stab really didn't bother him very much at all?" says Hughes.

Bardey does not answer the question but instead explains what hasn't been asked: he says that Render told him that stabbing himself in the leg would put "bookmarks" on the infinity loop, starting from the time he was in the Uber to the police arriving at the apartment. "Is it possible," says Bardey, "just like when he is leaving the apartment for the second time calling his brother, that he has some, at that point after the event, some shred of appreciation that something really bad happened? I think so. He may not understand what happened. When he gets to the hospital he is not clear in terms of, he said someone might have gotten hurt, but it is very unclear that he even appreciates that he is the cause of that."

"You were here when Finnegan testified?" says Hughes. Bardey says yes. "Finnegan was asked by me about a statement his brother made to him during the course of a phone conversation after this incident, right?"

"Right," says Bardey. "About the lease being terminated."

"Right," says Hughes.

"I think that is consistent with what I'm saying right now."

"Just to clarify for the record," says Hughes, "did you hear what he said, his brother told him that he needed to get a new lease, right?" Yes. "You are also aware that Carolyn Bush was the defendant's roommate, right?" Of course. "And that Carolyn Bush, are you aware her name was the one on the lease?" Yes. "Not the defendant's?" Correct. "So, if Carolyn Bush wasn't in the apartment anymore, he wouldn't have a lease, would he?"

"He wouldn't be able to live there anymore," says Bardey. "Sure."

"So, you'd agree with me in that moment he is in recognition of his potential continuing living status, right?"

"Yes," says Bardey. "I think that's consistent with what I just said. Which is consistent with wanting to call the police. That he has, at that point, some understanding that something bad has happened. But I don't think he understands much more than that."

Hughes asks Bardey about his income. He has few private clients, he says. Seventy percent of his income comes from private individuals or the defense bar. He has been paid about $20,000 thus far in connection with this case. That does not include his fee for testifying, which has been "incremental over time."

"So, for each additional annoying question that I ask," says Hughes, "your fee could rise, is that fair?"

"That's one way of looking at it," says Bardey.

. . .

Render would say later in a parole interview that he and Carolyn had not attended Bard at the same time. Danny testified that Render may have told him he was renting his room from someone who wasn't a Bard student. But Render was a year ahead of Carolyn at Bard.

On the stand, Dr. Katsavdakis testifies that Janet told him she'd encouraged Render to see a therapist or psychiatrist while he was in college because he was falling behind in his classes, but he didn't follow her advice. The first time he would do so would be after the murder. Depression was "something he had been struggling and dealing with most of his years," says Katsavdakis. Render "was underperforming based upon what I was told by the family, as well as Ms. Bonami had indicated in the records that he wasn't doing as well as he could have been doing."

Katsavdakis says Render told him his depression and panic episodes first manifested in high school and persisted after college graduation. His salary at Atelier 4 was about $30,000 annually, the doctor recalls. "It was a problem in a sense that he was looking for other opportunities." Render had even been planning a trip out west on his motorcycle to contemplate his future. He had not told Sofia of this plan. By his own account, "He was hoping to do something different, especially with the art packing," says Katsavdakis. "Especially with his skill and artistic ability."

"He had the love of his family?" says Smallman.

"I didn't ask him if he had the love of his family."

"Did you have any reason to think otherwise?"

"Well, I do . . ."

"Go ahead," says Smallman.

"Mr. Stetson-Shanahan was, as I said, and from the family, was suffering from some depressive symptoms," says Katsavdakis. He highlights that Bardey had indicated as much in his own report. Katsavdakis had also interviewed Render's family and Sofia. "It is unclear to me why the greater effort was not made to try to get him some psychiatric care either in high school," he says, which would have been easier, because he was still a juvenile, "or that it wasn't attended to, even on the one instance of smoking marijuana—which juveniles do, especially nowadays—at least to seek some care to follow up with that."

"Did he have the love of his family, in your opinion?" says Smallman.

"I don't know."

• • •

"It is pretty shocking," says Carol afterward. We're in a Thai restaurant down the street from the pizza place, down the block from the courthouse. "I don't think we're supposed to know this." She says that when "Dr. K" was leaving with Carolyn's family at the end of the day, he told Hughes's paralegal, "I don't want to go out there. I was approached by the family in an unpleasant way," meaning Render's family. Carol asked him what they'd said. He wasn't sure if he should say it, but Hughes's paralegal told him to. Supposedly, some of Render's family had told him, after his testimony, that they hoped he could sleep well after what he said.

"I didn't hear that," says Ann.

"Can you believe that?" says Carol. "After our restraint in not going off on those freaking people? You can't even walk down the damn hall, as you know." At one point, Carol had compared the congregation of Render's family and their well-dressed friends in the courthouse hallway to a cocktail party. "We never said anything like, 'Oh, I hope you can sleep at night with a murderer as a son.' We never said shit to any of them."

"The attorneys talk about the remorse Render feels," says Ann. "But he has not expressed it and we haven't seen it on video. Not one member of the family has mentioned it. Smallman is the only one of all of them." He had finally, at the end of the prosecution's case, approached the aunts alongside Margulis-Ohnuma and given his condolences.

"Yeah, I mean that's real nice, Smallman," says Carol. About Katsavdakis, she says, "That's a kick in the butt, isn't it? He said he's been doing this for thirty years and he has never had anything like that happen to him before."

25.

In Loco Parentis

"Myths die hard, especially those that appear to
symbolize the purposes and identity of a college."
-Leon Botstein, *New York Times*

Leon Botstein became president of Bard in 1975. He'd begun his
career at twenty-three, five years earlier, at a soon-to-be-defunct
college in New Hampshire with a student body of about 250. There,
he'd been the youngest-ever college president in the United States,
through a family connection: his brother-in-law was a student, and his
father-in-law was on the board. Showing up to Bard at the age of
twenty-eight, he was still the nation's youngest college president.

He was now at the helm of a private liberal arts school with a student body of 660, an endowment of roughly $300,000, and $1.8 million of debt. In 1975, it hadn't raised a new building in about fifty years
and it had recently been made famous by the Steely Dan song "My
Old School," featuring a refrain about never returning.

Bard's rolling hills and lush gardens with Romanesque statuary
and columns overlook the Hudson River, whose golden diffuse light
and wide waters served as inspiration for the nineteenth-century
Hudson River School of painters. The quaint surrounding farmlands
and villages were second homes to many elites, at one time including
Bard faculty Saul Bellow, Ralph Ellison, and Mary McCarthy. The

pastoral setting, proximal to New York City yet peacefully isolated, gave a feeling of privileged insularity.

Leon started his own undergraduate studies at sixteen and completed his bachelor's in history and philosophy at the University of Chicago in 1967. He then went to Harvard, where he earned a master's in history. He began his PhD the year he was hired at Bard. He would complete it over ten years later, with a 1,500-page dissertation.

"The trustees understood my being a very young person that I had to have time," he said in an interview later. He wanted to develop his own interests, not be an administrator stuck in endless meetings, limited to making boring decisions for which he would have to be liable, like most college presidents. He did not want to act "in loco parentis" and be responsible for the safeguarding of his students, or their parenting; he believes, as he has repeatedly stated, that students should be regarded as adults and in charge of themselves. "So the presidency that I developed," he said, "the way of working, I'm not a professional administrator." He is, instead, a figurehead, fundraiser, and guardian for his institution.

• • •

When looking at Leon's approach toward shaping Bard's culture, it is hard to overstate the significance of the University of Chicago's influence. The importance of Leon's affiliation with the University of Chicago is due in part to Robert Hutchins. Hutchins had retired as president and then chancellor there in 1951, over a decade before Leon enrolled, but in some ways, he is the proto-Leon. Before Leon, Hutchins had been the youngest college president in US history; he was thirty when he was hired at Chicago in 1929. The pedagogical reforms he instituted became blueprints for Bard's curriculum in Leon's hands. And perhaps, to some degree, for Leon's greater worldview.

Shortly after arriving at Chicago, Hutchins convinced the university to hire a friend of his. Mortimer Adler was an instructor at Columbia University, where he'd studied under John Erskine, credited with launching the "Great Books" movement, which holds that the quality of a liberal education, classically defined, is based on a core curriculum of the great books of the Western tradition, curated by white scholars and philosophers like themselves, and replicating their elitist values in a liberal democracy. This curriculum is based on the Greeks and Enlightenment philosophers, Plato and Aristotle, Hobbes and Rousseau, and their protégés and devotees.

Adler and Hutchins instituted a program like Erskine's at Chicago, choosing what they considered canonical works of literature and employing Socratic dialogue in roundtable classes rather than lecturing in halls. Leon would later bring these same values to Bard. Adler and Hutchins believed scholarship in the Great Books reconnected the privileged man with the divine and instilled a morality that prepared him for life as an elite citizen, an aristocrat. To them, this was a role that entailed participating in government or perhaps philosophy, leading the "ignorant" masses, and gifting them with "real" culture.

In the classical sense, liberal education carries a specific definition, one that has lent influence to the modern sense of the term. "Liberal education is the ladder by which we try to ascend from mass democracy to democracy as originally meant," writes University of Chicago political philosopher Leo Strauss in "What Is Liberal Education?," a commencement address he delivered in 1959.

This classical liberal education has its roots in the veneration of the ancient Greek philosophers. "Liberal education is the necessary endeavor to found an aristocracy within democratic society," says Strauss. In the classical definition, a liberal democracy separates the elite, or aristocracy, from what Strauss calls the "vulgar classes." Then of course there are those below the vulgar classes: the slaves. Under this system, not everyone can afford to have a liberal education and therefore is not qualified to participate in this so-called democracy; under this model, the poor and uneducated must be ruled for the good of the whole.

In his essay "Liberal Education and Responsibility," published in 1962—the year before Leon enrolled at the University of Chicago—Strauss says, "Originally a liberal man was a man who behaved in a manner becoming a free man, as distinguished from a slave." Yet he says, even free men often live like slaves because they must work and have no time for leisure; a true aristocrat does not work to manage his own wealth, he has others do it for him, a trusted inner circle (say, of vice presidents—in 2022, Bard had seventeen of them). The rulers of today's city are the aristocrats, the politicians, and philosopher-kings; those who have received a liberal arts education. The ruler of Bard would be Leon.

Strauss's interpretations of the Greeks have been called dangerous by some; the American neoconservative movement would co-opt, among other aspects of Strauss's philosophy, his interpretations of liberal democracy as dependent on the separation of the aristocracy from the masses. Leon would later call him "unfairly notorious."

Leon has said that his ideal syllabus, a personal version of the Great Books, would include *The Republic* by Plato. Book III is one that Strauss lectured on extensively, especially a concept called the noble lie. In Book III, Socrates says, "It's appropriate for the rulers, if for anyone at all, to lie for the benefit of the city in cases involving enemies or citizens, while all the rest must not put their hands to anything of the sort." A few pages later, he continues, "Could we . . . somehow contrive one of those lies that come into being in case of need, of which we were just now speaking, some one noble lie to persuade, in the best case, even the rulers, but if not them, the rest of the city?"

Strauss argued that it is nobler under certain circumstances for a ruler to lie for the greater good of the city. This is another core concept loved by neoconservatives. I would argue it was often employed by Leon in the years to come, for the benefit of the institution of Bard.

. . .

In August 1991, while she was still a student at Bard, Sara Davis sued another student, with Bard and Leon as codefendants. Sara's complaint stated that the student had raped her during their Language & Thinking period and accused Leon of being "unsympathetic and callously indifferent to her concerns for her safety and that of other women" on campus.

According to the lawsuit, Leon "went so far as to publicly state that no rape had taken place" and "privately sought to bring pressure" on Sara to withdraw her complaint after she reported her rape to the school. Sara further believed that Leon had gone easy on the fellow student because his father, an influential Manhattan gallery owner, was a donor to the school and had helped with fundraising. Accusations Leon denied, calling the last of them "childish."

Sara lost her lawsuit in March 1992 and appealed for four years, then gave up. "I needed to be free of him," she says now, meaning Leon. "Bard and all that shit." She moved west, putting as much distance between herself and Bard as possible. "It's not a safe place physically," she says. "Plus, they'll mentally fuck with you."

By August 2009, nearly twenty years since Sara filed her lawsuit, and the month Carolyn arrived as an incoming freshman, the culture at Bard of men versus women had remained largely the same. That month, Sara's alleged rapist was invited back to Bard's campus to perform with his band for Bard SummerScape, during the L&T period.

In 2013, Sara's alleged rapist's father died. The school's report of gifts listed a donation in his name by Jane Brien, director of Alumni/ae Affairs. Brien is the close friend of Janet's whom Danielle saw attending Render's trial with her.

On December 14, 1992, a shooting rampage at Bard College at Simon's Rock, the school's Massachusetts early college, left two people dead and another four injured. The shooter was eighteen-year-old sophomore Wayne Lo. Within hours of purchasing an SKS rifle, Wayne had loaded it with bullets he'd ordered in the mail and opened fire in the school library.

The ammunition Wayne used had arrived at Simon's Rock addressed to him that morning. The box was marked "Classic Arms." Administrators, including the vice president and dean of students, Bernie Rodgers, had sat around a conference table with the package between them, discussing its potential contents and whether it should be delivered to Wayne. They'd concluded that since opening another person's mail was a federal crime, they would ask Wayne what was inside. The package was sent back to the mail room, where Wayne picked it up. Later in a meeting, Bernie asked him about its contents. Wayne showed him an empty cartridge box and said it was a Christmas present for his father. Bernie would seem to have believed him.

More than three hours before the shooting, a friend of Wayne's called campus security to warn them that Wayne was about to use a gun. He got the answering machine. He then called a dorm advisor, who called Bernie, who in turn called the provost, Ba Win, and asked him to investigate the anonymous tip. Ba Win then called another residence director, so they could confront Wayne together. None of them called the police or alerted students. Before they reached Wayne, he had already opened fire. During the shooting, his gun repeatedly jammed. He eventually walked to a nearby dorm to call police.

Wayne's lawyers entered a plea of not guilty by reason of mental illness. Their psychiatrist argued Wayne suffered from paranoid schizophrenia. The prosecution's psychiatrist said he suffered from narcissistic personality disorder. He was found guilty on all counts and sentenced to life in prison without parole.

Gregory Gibson's son Galen was one of Wayne's victims. After the murders, Gregory visited Leon in his home to interview him, and he recounts the conversation in his memoir *Gone Boy: A Father's Search for the Truth in His Son's Murder*. At the time of his visit, Gregory and his wife were locked in a lawsuit with Simon's Rock and its administrators that would drag on for another year, as were families of other victims; they were suing the college for failing to prevent the shootings. But that wasn't the only reason they were suing, and it wasn't the only reason Gregory was visiting Leon.

He was not at Leon's house to ask about the timeline of events before the shooting, but rather to discuss what had happened afterward, once his son was already dead. The Gibsons, and families of other victims, had been stonewalled by the institution after the tragedy, despite their efforts to find out why it had happened.

"Along with Bernie Rodgers's refusal to accept responsibility," he writes, "this failure of communication was, I realized, a big part of the reason for my anger. It was why we were suing these guys." Gregory suspected that, along with other administrators, "Bernie Rodgers failed to communicate because he was covering up."

When he spoke with one residence director, Irvinia Scott, she told him that a month after the shooting, a cleaning woman had given her bullets she found in the workout room that Wayne Lo used. She took them to Bernie and asked him what to do with them—and he told her to throw them away. Instead, she took them to the police. Bernie "now claimed that he had told Irvinia to take the bullets to the police in the first place," writes Gregory. "She became angry, almost obsessively so, about what she considered to be Bernie Rodgers's lie."

Gregory also suspected that Ba Win might also feel guilty and, "Perhaps he would have liked to say more" to the families of the victims, but was directed not to by the school, along with other administrators. Some of those administrators confirmed his theory. He writes of his conversation with another residence director that he'd been told, "There were people . . . who'd otherwise be acting differently, especially with regard to the Gibsons. I got the distinct impression he was referring to Ba Win."

Gregory states that his questions for Leon were, "Why did we have to learn about the Classic Arms package from the newspapers? Was this failure of communication the result of an executive decision made by Bard College, or was it Bernie Rodgers's personal decision?"

Leon's "answer was no. And yes. And, well, let me give you an example." He said his role as a college president was to "maintain a way of life that was becoming impossible in the world outside." The college, he seemed to say, should be a hyperbaric chamber preserving the kind of life that a liberal arts education was meant to cultivate: that of the gentleman. It necessitated that they, as college administrators, "ignore certain ugly realities that confront the rest of the world on a daily basis," as a matter of duty. Even if those realities exist inside the college's walls.

"Wonderfully, the explication of this doctrine flowed into a sympathetic analysis of Bernie's role in such an institution," writes Gregory. Leon questioned, "If the institution existed to make the world a better place, what were the standards by which Bernie's actions were to be judged?" In other words, if Bernie was, by denying basic answers to victims' families, protecting the institution, then shouldn't we view his actions as, well, noble? It serves to note that Bernie is also a graduate of the University of Chicago.

"I had my grief, certainly," Gregory continues, attempting to summarize Leon. "I was entitled to it. But what about the greater good? What about the true function of the institution? What if . . . Bernie and Ba Win acted the way they acted out of concern for the greater good, for the life of the institution?" If Bernie obfuscated to protect the institution, Leon argued, then he was doing so in the normal course of his responsibilities toward it.

"If I had to be responsible for the safety and well-being of my students," Leon told Gregory, "I'd quit my job."

"In a sense, it was always Us and Them," writes Gregory. "The people at Simon's Rock were engaged in a very special mission and they, better than anyone else, knew how best to execute it. . . . The politics of loyalty, and a common attention to the nurturing institution were sound principles for the efficient operation of a place like Simon's Rock. It had been going on since cave-times. A bunch of people would get together under the protective cover of a larger entity and do the bidding of that entity while the larger entity took care of them. They didn't question things and they didn't make waves."

Bernie Rodgers would continue on as vice president and dean of students of Simon's Rock until 2003, at which time he retired as VP and dean but remained a teacher. Ba Win retired in 2018 as vice president of Bard Early College Programs and Policies. His wife was Simon's Rock's director of psychological services until 2012, then was a therapist at the school until 2022. A room in the library bears their name.

• • •

Say you are arriving at Bard as a freshman in the fall of 1997. That first weekend, when you and your classmates are dropped off, you may hear Leon address the parents and students gathered in the auditorium. He may say something to the effect of, *We will not watch your students. If they do drugs, if they try risky behavior, that's up to them. We don't condone it. I don't think that students are more enlightened or more creative if they take drugs, but we won't be policing your students. We won't be watching your students.*

Hopefully, he will then inform you that, just a few months earlier, a Bard student and her seven-year-old daughter were bound with wire and raped in the Tivoli Bays nature preserve bordering campus. Further, that the rapist is still on the loose, possibly even among you now. Police sketches of his face paper the campus and the nearby towns.

You will soon learn that another student had been raped on the other side of campus in a similar manner two years earlier. At the time, security guards and students were discouraged by administration from talking to police on campus. The dean of students was quoted in a *Bard Observer* article warning that they couldn't be sure the rapist wasn't a Bard student, and that anyone appearing to be a police officer may be an undercover news reporter, so not to trust them.

Amanda Harris was a student in 1995, at the time of the first rape. She would give campus tours to prospective students and their parents. "I remember they had a pamphlet that listed the percentages of crimes," she says of the college's promotional materials. "And they had zero percent for sexual assaults. But I also volunteered at the women's center, so I carried a beeper one night a week. There was a serial rapist who everybody knew. I think his dad donated a lot of money. Women came forward and they didn't push them to go to the police. They wanted to keep it in the campus police, and they didn't discipline him. He got to graduate." Amanda did not know if he had anything to do with the rapes in the nature preserve.

The former mayor of Tivoli, Marcus Molinaro, would later tell the *Observer* that in 1997, "When the last rape occurred, we didn't have any communication going on and we should have. Bard was busy dealing with it in its own way just as we were. It is just as much my fault as it is theirs. But that's no excuse."

"Marc's body language says another story," the paper reported. "He fidgets constantly in his chair when discussing Bard."

As an incoming freshman, hearing all of this, you may feel terrified. On day one, you are told to walk in groups and not go in the woods. Ken Cooper, who would arrive at Bard three years later, and who served as the director of security for roughly twenty years, says, "They gave women whistles. Whistles. I would have given them machine guns.

"Leon is not thrilled with law enforcement in general," says Ken. "He has an attitude about it." When Ken arrived, he says, "I think there were problems with the way they thought people sometimes use their badges. Locally, we had some issues with the sheriff's office, long before I got there. It left a bad taste in everybody's mouth."

In his position, he would work on improving Bard's relationship with local authorities. "I was able to translate from cop to college and back and forth, so law enforcement learned to respect the college and vice versa," he says.

Once something appears in a police report, it becomes part of the public record, a historic artifact. It can also appear in the news, where the public may find out what patterns of misconduct are being cultivated, protected, defended, or hidden from view.

"The issue is," says Marc, "what's been on campus that we don't know about, I couldn't say."

• • •

Soon after beginning college in the fall of 1997, you catch on to a trend among your classmates.

You are all brooding loners. You were the kids who didn't fit in at your high schools. You are psychologically on the edge. "Bard attracted a very creative type," says Eric Holzman, a painting and drawing professor during this time. "It seemed many were struggling. The air of nonconformity and freedom offered and encouraged gave no grounding."

Arriving at Bard, you are unsupervised, many for the first time, and isolated from the world outside, and from your previous support systems, making you vulnerable. Drugs and alcohol are rampant. The American Psychological Association says fifty percent of mental illnesses begin by age fourteen, and three-quarters by age twenty-four. Your brain won't finish developing until around that time, or later. Away at college, you need protection from yourselves and from each other, even if you don't think so. Yet, you notice that risky behavior and dangerous masculinity are not being discouraged by your college's administration. You witness, hear about, and personally experience several instances of overdose, suicide, stalking, physical violence, even false imprisonment, among fellow students.

"It was such a weird environment," says Amanda. "There were so many people on hardcore drugs. I'm very liberal sexually, but there was such a sexual undertone to everything, like sex parties and food, sex parties and ménage à trois." One of the annual parties is called The Ménage; another is called Drag Race. There is a phone-sex line set up in the basement of Tewksbury, leading up to one Ménage. Leon is known to make an appearance at most of the Drag Races. "There were only eleven-hundred students there," says Amanda. "So, everybody knew everybody."

The campus-wide parties that are school-sanctioned and on-campus are organized by student clubs, funded by official student activities dollars, and attended by faculty and administrators. You are at school for about a month when you go to your first one. There are drag acts, but it isn't anything like the drag shows you've seen before. It is way beyond what you are looking for as an eighteen-year-old. The raunchiest. Everyone is nearly naked, wearing bondage attire including dildos, and lingerie, or simply, a thick layer of pudding. Administrators and faculty are there, dancing with students. There is a sex tent.

In 1997, your freshman year, the *Observer* reports that, "According to Bob Brock, Bard Security Director," before Ken Cooper, "approximately 450 partygoers showed up to partake in the cross-dressing, overtly sexual atmosphere of the night . . . The catwalk was crowded with dancers, in all stages of undress, grinding to the music and each other."

Leon would say, on the talk show *Firing Line* with William F. Buckley, Jr. the following year, "When you step away from the legal issue, [it] has to do with the human realities of the way we interact with one another in the workplace, where sexuality has always been part of it from the very beginning." The 1998 episode, called

"The Sexual Harassment Mess," was filmed at Bard. "It's a fact, whatever one's sexual preference is, that the reality is between employers and employees, between colleagues, between professors and students, sexuality is a factor and it's a factor of human life.

"It's also a factor of individual judgment," Leon says. "And the difficult question of course is applying general rules to specific issues where emotions and individual circumstances are very important and guiding the dividing line between public and private behavior. The workplace is a public place, and at the same time, there're private relations between individuals. And there's a tremendously awkward and difficult fact as we try to regulate the variety, unbelievable, unimaginable variety of human behavior."

• • •

In 1998, painting and drawing professor Eric Holzman met every Wednesday night with a group of students for a life drawing class. A few would go out to dinner afterward. Sometimes a student named Anna Jones would be among them. Eric calls Anna "a thoroughbred." Her parents were professors at Oberlin College. She'd been schooled in Italy and had a strong background in the arts: violin, dance, theater, painting. "We got to be incredibly close," Eric says. "We were similar in temperament. I gave her emotional, philosophical, and spiritual grounding in her art studies."

Anna's boyfriend, Tor Loney, was a Bard student when they met, set to graduate—after which he would follow Phish on tour and continue his experimentation with LSD. Anna had moved to Annandale to be with him, enrolling in the school as a senior studio art major in 1998. When fall came that year, the town of Red Hook hosted its annual Hardscrabble Day, a street fair. Tor and Anna wandered around, enjoying the cool sunshine before catching a ride in a friend's truck to a dinner party at another friend's apartment, a mile from Bard. That night, as their friends were upstairs cooking, Anna and

Tor stayed in the parking lot to finish a conversation. From inside, people could hear them arguing.

Their friend had left his hunting knife in the cab of his truck. Anna's friends would later describe hearing her scream, "No, Tor, no." Tor apologized as he pulled the knife across Anna's throat.

"We decorated the chapel for Anna because the school did nothing," says Eric. "They didn't bring together the school to talk. They didn't bring together the school to light a candle. The chaplain wasn't in the chapel. I was in the chapel one afternoon between classes and somebody comes down."

"The dean and the president want to talk to you," they said to Eric.

"As we walk up to their office, I'm thinking to myself, *Be careful what you say because they're not your friends*," he says. "So there I was, and they're telling me, 'Don't talk to the students about it.'" Students came to him because they knew he and Anna were close. "I asked Leon why he hadn't brought the school together even to light a candle," says Eric. "I suggested the school do a little more."

He was fired. "There was no reason necessary for firing me," he says. Which is legally true: an employer can fire an at-will worker at any time for any reason that's not discriminatory. Eric didn't yet have tenure.

Asked about Eric's firing, Leon responded through Bard's associate vice president of communications, Mark Primoff: "It's against our privacy policies to discuss personnel matters."

"Either right before or right after, people needed counseling, really bad," says Eric. "A lot of people. Being an art student myself, and being around art students, it's a hard time in people's lives. They're not people who usually fit in everywhere."

The school hosted a small memorial in the Chapel of the Holy Innocents, three weeks after the murder. "Bard officials decided to delay the memorial service in the hopes that her family will be able to attend," the *Observer* reported. The paper noted this information "is included to help dispel some of the rumors."

"They dedicated a little park outside the art school for her," says Eric, of the garden that Carolyn liked reading in.

Tor was charged with second-degree murder, which came with a sentence of twenty-five years to life. Like Wayne Lo, Henry Pfeffer, and Render, he pleaded insanity. Psychiatrists for the prosecution and the defense agreed that symptoms of Tor's schizophrenia had begun several years earlier. Both sides recommended that he be found not guilty by reason of mental illness. There was no trial.

Anna's father addressed Tor in the courtroom. The *Poughkeepsie Journal* ran an excerpt of his statements. Among other things, he said, "I wish no vengeance. But I hope that through this court and any other court, you will be kept secure for many, many years. I cannot trust that whatever led you to kill Anna would not also lead you to some other terrible act."

Marjorie Smith was the prosecutor assigned to the case and told the *Journal* she believed accepting the insanity plea was right, "But she also said she had some 'serious reservations' about the laws governing what happens to a defendant following an insanity plea . . . Smith noted that the current law does not provide for any minimum time that Loney will be confined. As soon as mental health experts determine he has recovered sufficiently, he is eligible to seek release."

Tor was sent to a psychiatric center in Albany. He took classes at SUNY Albany and graduated with a master's in Library Science. He has worked for Albany Public Library since October 2009. He's currently a library development specialist at the New York State Library. His folk band, Tor & the Fjords, has performed all over the Hudson Valley since the late 2000s. He is married with a son.

Leon invoked Anna Jones's murder in his second letter of support for Render. In doing so, he places the two murders side by side, encouraging a comparison. Indeed, both crimes were committed by former Bard students, against Bard students; both perpetrators were white men; both victims white women; both perpetrators were artists, and so were their victims; both men used knives in the murders; both men used the insanity defense.

. . .

In 1999, Leon published an opinion essay in the *New York Times* with the title "Let Teen-Agers Try Adulthood." It recycles ideas in his only book, *Jefferson's Children: Education and the Promise of American Culture*, a loose collection of cultural essays published by Doubleday two years earlier and largely forgotten. In the acknowledgments, he thanks Ba Win and Bernard Rodgers.

Jefferson's Children makes much of a "1992 study of nearly 5,000 adolescent Flemish girls [which] indicated that menstruation now takes place almost a year and a half earlier than was the case during the late 1930s." Leon does not credit the authors of the study nor cite the journal in which it appeared nor say anything more about it that might help someone locate it today, though it's broadly established that girls menstruate earlier. Still, the study's supposed findings form a large part of his basis for the proclamation that "the American high school is obsolete and should be abolished."

High schools were invented a long time ago for children, writes Leon, but because of this dropping menstruation schedule, teenagers today should in fact be considered adults, on all levels—only they're still being treated as children. They're horny and distracted, he says, trapped at their desks, so no wonder they have behavior issues. They require more stimulation—of all kinds. "Our high schools," he says, "more frequently than we care to think, [are] breeding grounds for violence, drug and alcohol abuse, vulgarity, and a totally thoughtless, rampant expression of sexuality."

Whereas in the book, Leon bases his call to action on a study of Flemish girls that allegedly showed they menstruated "almost a year and a half earlier" than they used to, in his op-ed in the *Times*, which cites no studies at all, Leon writes that the age at which girls were menstruating was earlier by "at least two" years. He adds, "and not surprisingly, the onset of sexual activity has dropped in proportion." He does not address the discrepancy between the number of years in his book and in the article; he does not provide any sources for his conclusion that the onset of sexual activity has fallen "in proportion."

Leon appeared on NPR, interviewed by Diane Rehm, soon after the op-ed dropped. Again, he cited no studies, and his examples differed even further from his sources in the book; he claimed the onset of menstruation and sexual maturity was even earlier. Yet his argument was "simple," he told Rehm: "Sixteen is now what eighteen was several years ago." He seems to be saying that we cannot afford to hold kids back—we must treat them like adults. Even if they are not, I want to venture, technically, or legally, adults; and even if, I surmise, the ramifications of treating them like adults when they are not ready to make adult decisions or deal with adult consequences are severe and lifelong.

A caller asked to what extent he was indebted to Robert Hutchins, "who admitted seventeen-year-olds, sixteen-year-olds, really, to the University of Chicago back in the '30s and '40s?" Leon admitted that he owed a great debt to Hutchins. But then he said, "He didn't really pay attention to the developmental side of people. He thought it was all a matter of reason, sort of a brain without heart. I think he's wrong."

The New York City school system later helped Bard found the Bard High School Early College system, which admitted students to Bard Early College campuses as young as fourteen.

• • •

In 2011 and 2012, Bard accepted, according to differing reports, either one or several unsolicited donations of $75,000 from convicted sex offender Jeffrey Epstein, for the Bard Early Colleges. Leon visited Epstein's Manhattan townhouse to personally thank him, he would later claim; he would continue visiting Epstein, nearly two dozen times, over the ensuing four years.

Two years after Epstein's 2011 donation, in 2013, a helicopter landed on the Blithewood lawn, and "a man wearing a polo shirt and jeans" stepped out of it "with three women," wrote the *Bard Free Press*. A then-student tells me that this person was widely known, even then, to be Jeffrey Epstein. Leon picked up the man and girls. He told the *Press* that the male passenger was "an unaffiliated financier." In 2015, Bard accepted another donation of sixty-six laptop computers from Epstein.

"According to Epstein, the age of consent, if dictated by anything other than biology, was arbitrary," writes Bradley J. Edwards, Esq., in his book *Relentless Pursuit: Our Fight with Jeffrey Epstein*. "How could a female whose body was able to bear children not be given the choice to perform the acts necessary to give birth? Society, through the years, had created these concepts of marriage and monogamy that not only contradicted human nature, they unbearably constrained and killed people's freedom. Sexual freedom."

Ten years later, in April 2023, the *Wall Street Journal* reported on Leon's meetings with Jeffrey Epstein. Leon told the paper that after thanking Epstein in person for his initial donation, he continued meeting with him over four years to try to solicit more donations. He claimed he'd stopped contact with Epstein at a certain point because he realized the sex offender was "stringing us along" and wasn't going to make any more donations to Bard.

Soon after, the *Journal* reported that in 2016, Epstein in fact hired Leon as a "consultant" for his charity, Gratitude America. Epstein paid Leon, personally, $150,000, over several increments. Leon claimed he gave that money directly to Bard, as part of a $1 million donation he made that year. He said he didn't know why, but Epstein didn't want to donate under his own name. Asked why he did not reveal this $150,000 donation from Epstein in those earlier interviews with the *Journal*, Leon claimed he forgot about it.

• • •

Thomas Bartscherer has been at Bard College since 2008, the year Render matriculated, and in 2010, he was made director of L&T. He taught philosophy and classics during the school year and had Render as a student. "I recall being very impressed with his drawings, which he had shared with me on several occasions," he writes in his letter of support. In 2012, Bard investigated reports of Thomas having a romantic affair with an undergraduate student. Though the investigation was not made public, a rumor about Thomas's behavior circulated around this time.

A former administrator who worked with him recalls being summoned into an investigation and interviewed by a lawyer about their experiences with him. "No one told me anything about what was happening," they say. "They just asked me about his general character. I told them that he just has this whole romantic affect." He would leave flowers on a female colleague's desk all the time, but the administrator didn't think he meant to be harassing.

The investigation found that allegations about Thomas with an undergraduate were not substantiated. Later, the administrator confronted Thomas about a rumor they were hearing, but he denied it and they believed him.

In the summer of 2012, Allannah Capwell was personally summoned by Leon to return from Bishkek, Kyrgyzstan, where she had been for two years, running the Institute for Writing & Thinking (IWT) at one of Bard's partner institutions. "There were aspects of the [L&T] program that he felt were not being addressed as deeply as he felt they needed to be," Allannah says of Leon. She was made director of the newly restructured Institute for Writing & Thinking, in Annandale, which now housed L&T. Thomas worked underneath her and was "highly monitored," she says. "Yes, I had heard of a rumor." She claims she didn't hear of it until she got back to Annandale.

"Young academics," she says. "Whether male or female, though it tends to be more male, especially when there is a cultivation of the intellect, and on wonder, that that Bard supports, especially in the Language & Thinking Program, lines can—boundaries get crossed very easily."

In 2013, Bard issued a "Consensual Relations" policy governing faculty-student relationships, its first. The policy said that failure to report a faculty-student relationship could result in a verbal warning or dismissal.

At the time, Thomas was writing the libretto for what would become *Stranger Love*, Dylan Mattingly's opera. In Thomas's artist statement, he writes, "Rousseau's Julie and St. Preux are nothing like Héloïse and Abelard, and yet Julie is also the new Héloïse," referring to two famous stories of teachers having romantic affairs with their students.

"He was supportive while he was Dylan's thesis advisor, and he was very excited, and very much going on about how brilliant Dylan was," says the administrator of Thomas. He was also uniquely supportive of another of his students, a young woman who has asked me to refer to her as Penelope and who had come to work for L&T, underneath him. "So, it wasn't totally implausible that he was just a very enthusiastic instructor who just really wanted to support," she says.

Penelope was set to graduate in 2015, as a classics major. "I had him for freshman seminar, and I have to say, I flirted with him," she says, agreeing to talk to me on the condition of anonymity. "The first meeting that we had to talk about a paper of mine was scheduled for fifteen minutes and went on for an hour." At the time, she was vaguely aware of a rumor about Thomas, but avoided finding out more.

"Nothing physical happened between us until after I graduated," Penelope says. However, things had begun to heat up between them during her junior year. Thomas became her thesis advisor, and they sent numerous emails, and spent hours alone in his office, talking over "pretty rarified subject matter." The thesis Penelope wrote under his direction was on the erotic in Plato's *Phaedrus*, a spin on the subject of Thomas's own 2011 PhD dissertation from the University of Chicago, where he had hosted a conference, "Erotikon," and afterward, coedited an anthology by the same title.

Thomas gave Penelope's thesis its title. She dedicated the work to him, and also thanked him in the acknowledgments, following his name with, "but where to begin?"

Of their relationship, though, she says she would honestly be surprised, "unless he heavily fictionalized it and sublimated it, if that was what the opera was about." Meaning his libretto for *Stranger Love*. "To be honest, I just don't think I meant enough to him."

Penelope and Thomas spent, at the most, she says, five nights together, just after her graduation, always far from public view, and usually only after dark. They sometimes met at the empty lake house of one of Thomas's friends.

In the libretto for the 2018 unstaged performance of *Stranger Love*'s first act, which Thomas sent me upon my request, his male lead, Andre, sings, "Magnolia blossoms scatter near the house by the lake."

The libretto tells a story about the ephemerality of love. "Nature's first green is gold," sings Andre, a line from Robert Frost. "The hardest hue to hold."

How fleeting love can be, how time bound. "Time is their enemy," says another character, Uriel, of the lovers. "A thief in the night."

"We are not heroes," sings Tasha, the female lead, Andre's lover. "You and I. I am not Héloïse. I am not Ilsa."

"I was certainly hoping it would unfold differently than it did," says Penelope. "He was very explicit with me before I slept with him that we were not going to have a 'let's go out to dinner' kind of relationship. There was a need for tightly managed expectations, and if that wasn't okay with me, then I should go."

It broke her heart. "The pain of the affair didn't come at the end," she says. "It came at the very beginning when I saw he was capable of such insipid carnality and cynical rationalism. He must have known that I just adored him. But he thought that was okay to do as long as I more or less verbally signed a waiver.

"I've fallen in love again," she says. "But the loss of respect for a beloved teacher, for me, it involved a kind of grief and mourning as though someone had died."

Thomas declined to discuss his alleged relationships with students or the letters of support he wrote for Render.

• • •

In June 2015, a month after Penelope filed her thesis, Allannah approached Thomas about making his position a full-time administrative one, without the "undue burden" of tenure. That the position's tenure expectation, alongside administrative duties, was a burden, was not only her perspective "but that of the academic vice president of the college as well."

Thomas rejected her offer and quit his position as director of L&T before the session began. Allannah says now that she felt she was doing Thomas a favor, as he wouldn't have gotten tenure; he had not published enough. Her offer was not related to the fact of the investigation of Thomas. "My job was to realign L&T with the Institute," and Thomas was "well-known as an excellent teacher who had been under incredible expectation as a young faculty member and administrator."

With the previously planned date of Thomas's tenure review still approaching, Leon called him into a meeting, which he recounted afterward for his administrative colleague. "I like you," the colleague says Leon supposedly told Thomas. "Maybe this tenure meeting is not going to go very well, but I've arranged something else."

In this scenario, Leon might have considered that Thomas would not easily find work at another college. "His file was going to follow him no matter where he went," Allannah explains. The mere fact of an investigation in his background would work against him in a job search. Leon approved a five-year renewable contract for Thomas as the Peter Sourian Lecturer in Humanities. Today, Thomas works closely with the Hannah Arendt Center for Politics and Humanities at Bard College.

I reached out to Leon over email to ask about this story. "I am sure that you understand that even if, hypothetically, an employee of the college was under investigation, or had been, for violating laws and regulations governing the conduct of employees, I am constrained by law and ethics from discussing or commenting on such a case," he responded. "So let me respond by clarifying the processes that govern appointment and re-appointment. I approve or reject all appointments to the faculty, but after reviews and recommendations by faculty committees. I do not act alone or in a vacuum. I also do not grasp the connection between what you are now asking about Carolyn Bush and Render Stetson-Shanahan. But to answer your question, after the process of faculty evaluation, it is not uncommon that the duties of a faculty member are adjusted to improve their effectiveness and value by making the duties line up better with the strengths of the faculty member."

I informed Leon that Thomas, like many employees of Bard, on Bard letterhead, had written letters of support to the court for Render. He claimed he did not know. I told him that, separately, Thomas's name and various stories about him had come up in interviews with Bard students, alumni, professors, and administrators.

"It is perfectly possible that students and faculty are engaging in conduct which is explicitly forbidden but if so, they are doing so without seeking redress from the institution," Leon tells me. "It is also the case that in the past, allegations against faculty members have been made, have been investigated by third parties and action taken by the college. However, absent a formal complaint or allegation, we remain stuck in the shadow world of informal and unverified allegations and speculation."

"Sadly enough, we have to have these regulations," says Allannah, referring to Title IX regulations. Working at Bard, she recalls having conversations with Leon about similar matters. "I don't think, in heart, that the president of Bard is against them. I think at heart, what he's against is that we don't have some moral amplitude to navigate that. He looks at another human being and says, 'In truth, you are a sovereign being. You're responsible for you.' And yet, we grow up in these social and complex systems and don't manage them. I think at heart, it's a disappointment. He's also highly conscious of creative lives, people who have tremendous creative lives, and the things that have occurred in their lives. Infidelities, tragedies, all of this."

In March 2023, Bard released a revised "Consensual Relations" policy, prohibiting such faculty-student relationships altogether. Leon tells me that he is unaware of any current investigations. He allows that given certain "prohibitive policies," he would certainly be the last to know about them.

• • •

"Bard did not actually have a set-in-stone sexual assault policy until 2015, which is the year I graduated," says novelist Nicola Maye Goldberg, who matriculated in 2011, and had been raped on campus her freshman year. She delayed reporting it because she didn't know who to report it to. Even once there ostensibly was a policy, it gave Leon the final say in all Title IX outcomes. He had sent Goldberg a letter in March 2015 stating that the college's investigator "did not find that a preponderance of the evidence supported an allegation of rape."

Later that same month, another senior, who had been raped in February by a fellow student, attempted suicide by overdosing on pills. Paramedics arrived in time to save her, and a police officer discovered a letter in her room like the one sent to Goldberg. The officer asked her if she wanted him to investigate. She agreed upon the urging of her family and friends.

Her rapist was arrested in April. Local papers and news stations reported on the arrest. The victim claimed she'd been discouraged by the school from reporting her attack to police. A later report would allege that both the victim and her companion, who had accompanied her to report her attack to Bard's Title IX coordinator, had both been pressured by the coordinator to sign nondisclosure agreements.

Leon held a town hall at his home. Someone asked about the college's handling of sexual assault, and secretly recorded him. "Are we in a position to regulate your private life in a way that gives us assurance that nothing is going on?" he asked those gathered. "It would essentially put a secret police, a surveillance system in place." No one interrupted him for nearly ten minutes.

"But you can't equate sexual violence to intimacy," a student finally said.

"Clearly not," he fired back. "But the interpretation of what is violent is subjective, is not objective. That's the problem."

"It's about power."

"She's ready for law," said Leon. "Now I may be an idiot, but I have actually never been involved in a . . . I can say this: in an intimate circumstance where I actually thought it was about power."

"I'm talking about sexual violence. I'm not talking about intimacy."

"But sexual violence is not only about power," says Leon. "It only doesn't come—" The recording cuts off. Soon after, the *Huffington Post* reported that he'd also said, "You have to use common sense. A girl drinking a bottle of vodka and then going to a party is as wise as me walking into a Nuremberg rally while wearing the yellow badge." He has never denied saying it.

Less than a week later, Bard's director of security, Ken Cooper, sent a campus-wide email. "On May 5, 2015, a report of possible sexual assault, to an incapacitated student, was made," he wrote. "The matter is currently under institutional investigation." He noted that he was sending the email in compliance with the Jeanne Clery Law, which required him to report such occurrences.

By January 2016, the *Huffington Post* reported that Bard was facing three federal Title IX complaints with the U.S. Department of Education, writing, "Activist group End Rape On Campus helped recent alumnae file two of the three complaints."

The student-run Bard Anti-Sexual Assault Initiative (BASAI) filed a third Title IX complaint in response to Leon's comments at the town hall. "BASAI is currently petitioning for the removal of President Botstein from the Title IX process and for his replacement with a more 'suitable alternative,'" the *Bardvark* reported.

BASAI wrote on Facebook that Bard's Title IX response to Goldberg had listed, as one of her rapist's charges, "erotic asphyxiation without consent," which trivialized the severity of the attack. "This is not an actual legal or medical term," it said, "and it indicates Bard's disregard for the experiences and safety of victims of sexual assault." What happened to Goldberg was actually *strangulation*.

In March 2016, Bard College of Simon's Rock students filed two more, unrelated, Title IX complaints with the DOE.

• • •

In December 2020, Danny Shanahan was arrested and charged with possessing child pornography, and in July 2021, he died of multiple system organ failure before going to trial. Leon hosted a private memorial for him at the Chapel of the Holy Innocents at Bard, with a reception afterward at his home. "A *New Yorker* cartoonist drew the map and the invitation to this funeral," says Martha Tepepa. "I took a picture because this lady," meaning Janet, "moved into our offices at Levy," meaning the Levy Economics Institute, in Blithewood. "She used to leave stuff all over. I was like, 'Do kids know about this? Do students? Do they even know that he's hosting the funeral for a child molester?'" meaning Leon hosting the funeral for Danny.

"Bard College," Leon tells me over email, "regularly, and often more than ten times each year, hosts memorial services, funerals, burial ceremonies for members of its community, alumni, colleagues, neighbors and their families in the Chapel of the Holy Innocents. The memorial service for Daniel Shanahan was one of these events. The President's House, my home, is right across from the Bard College Cemetery and therefore I routinely make it available for receptions connected to memorial, funeral and burial events held in the college Chapel."

Shanahan's memorial was not listed on the Chapel's schedule. A review of the schedule since 2020 shows only two memorials: one was for a former L&T faculty person, and the second one was in December 2021. The latter was for a graduate student from Russia who killed herself in her dorm room, and whose body was not discovered for four days, until it began to smell. She is buried in the Bard College Cemetery.

· · ·

In the course of my investigation into Bard, I reached out to Leon a handful of times to verify information. In one of his replies, he states: "If my memory serves me correctly Carolyn's murder happened years after her quite brief tenure as a student here, and therefore Render's crime happened years after he graduated. You should know that I believe individuals, not educational institutions, bear the responsibility for their actions, even when they are enrolled as students, and certainly after they graduate or leave."

However, the values that pervade Bard as an institution—a privileging and protecting of wealthy white men; the elitism of an institution that protects its own at all costs under a perverted rationale of the "noble lie"; and the abdication of responsibility for the health and well-being of its students—did impact Carolyn in significant ways.

There is evidence that Carolyn struggled with mental health issues during her time at Bard. In Render's trial, the prosecution's expert witness testified that Janet had also encouraged Render to seek help for his mental health while he was a student at Bard but he did not.

A great many other Bard students have shared with me that the school didn't provide adequate mental health services while they were there, and that the culture of Bard directly contributed to their unwellness. Professors have shared that mental instability is so much the norm that it can be hard to tell which students they should actually worry about. Surely an institution tasked with educating students who attend classes there for four years on average, and often live on campus, must also be tasked, to a degree, with their mental well-being.

Despite Leon's claims about the increasingly early onset of adolescent maturation, neuroscience holds that the human brain does not stop maturing until the mid- to late-twenties, including the area responsible for sound decision-making. Additionally, most mental illnesses present before the age of twenty-four, and the most common age of onset for psychotic disorders is between eighteen and twenty-five.

Given the slew of rapes, murders, and suicides that have happened in connection to Bard, it seems unconscionable that the school has not taken more deliberate and robust measures to support the mental health of its student body, before or after such tragedies occur.

During their time at Bard, both Carolyn and Render struggled to complete their degrees. Carolyn struggled to keep up with her coursework until she was forced to leave. Render struggled completing his thesis, required for graduation. While likely both could have benefited from support, Bard's handling of each situation reveals the inequity of its troubling moral ethos, beyond its failure to care for the mental well-being of its student body.

For her academic challenges, Carolyn—a young woman from an unknown family out of state who received financial aid for her tuition—was put on probation and forced to plead her case before a faculty board until eventually she left Bard.

For his part, Render—the son of parents endowed with generational wealth and minor celebrity, one of whom worked at Bard, and both of whom donated to the institution, including in Render's name after his incarceration—was, at the behest of the dean of students, given the mentorship of not one but two faculty members to help him complete his thesis to a sufficient degree that would allow him to graduate. After their sons graduated, Janet and Danny began donating money to Bard each year. So did Finnegan. Render, in turn, donated money to Bard once he was incarcerated.

The principle that there is an elite who deserve consideration beyond the laws that govern the general populace was applied in a more disturbing way in the aftermath of Carolyn's murder. Letters of support attesting to Render's character included (not counting his own mother's) eight writers who were Bard faculty and administrators, and all but one of the letters were sent on the college's letterhead.

In our judicial system, a defendant is presumed innocent until proven guilty beyond a reasonable doubt. In a murder trial such as Render's, all that the defense must do is cast reasonable doubt on a defendant's intent to kill. The letters from Bard personnel helped cast that doubt. In these same letters, Carolyn is mentioned in passing, barely at all. The school was careful, in its comment to *DNAinfo*, to clarify that she hadn't graduated.

26.

Coco and Sunshine

One former Bard student asks, "Have you ever seen the *Town &
Country* Bard College write-up? It's hilarious." It came out in
the September 2011 issue, just a few months before Carolyn's final
departure from the school, and it was written by a Bard alum, journalist Matt Taibbi. Its logline reads, "For a certain sort of high-schooler
(too cool for Yale, too socially savvy for Harvard), Brown was once
the university of choice. But now that sort of student is turning to a
little patch of emerald green on the Hudson River."

The article was structured as a photo essay with the story conveyed
through its captions. "It has all these photos of students," says the student. "It was photos of the rugby team and it's like, 'The athletes.'"
(The caption for this photo, in fact, said, "The brotherhood.") "And
then it was photos of 'The It Girls.' It's these three girls who are really
rich and skinny and wearing cute outfits. Then there's a photo of Lola
Kirke. Her sister is Jemima Kirke who was on *Girls*. It's her and then
this other girl with their ukuleles, sitting at Blithewood." The caption
says, "The Musicians."

"We have a conservatory full of international, classically trained
musicians," says the student, "and this is who you're saying the musicians are?"

Two photos showed "The Graduates." "LA is a mecca for Bard
alumni, such as filmmakers and writers Ben Greenblatt, Sam Freilich,
Gia Coppola (who's following in her family's footsteps), and Nick

Shore," read the first caption. The second one read, "Bardies also love New York. Jane Moseley (left) is a sculptor in Brooklyn, and mini-mogul Hannah Bronfman runs a clothing line and record label with her brother Ben. (Their father is Warner Music CEO Edgar Bronfman Jr.)"

• • •

Carolyn returned to Bard for one class in the fall of 2011 but did not come back for the following semester. Instead, she moved to New York City in the summer of 2012. "She did say something to me about how it was hard for her to finish," says Lizzy. "I knew that she had taken a break from Bard, a leave, because she wanted to be in New York City. When she tried to say, 'Okay, can I finish my classes now?' I remember her saying Bard said, 'No, you can't finish your classes.' It wasn't medical. It could have been financial. She just wanted to delay finishing her coursework."

"You have an institution that doesn't want to become de facto parents," says Allannah Capwell, who shares the school's view. She says, of Bard professors and administrators, "They want to be creatives, intellectuals. They want to live in that realm where people," meaning the students, "are accountable to themselves. They try to inspire that in students. It's a big load if you haven't come from families where you've had that instilled in you."

Allannah remembers Leon saying, "I'm not interested in being a de facto parent. I've got my own kids." Being encouraged to take a leave of absence seems to happen not infrequently for certain students at Bard. "It's not uncommon, if you're not ready to be there and commit to the work," says Allannah. "It's just a normal part of the process to reflect on your learning."

"I think it happened three times," Jenny says of Carolyn's academic probations. "The head of the poetry department would come to bat for her." This would be Robert Kelly, who was actually head of Bard's

Written Arts department until 2022 and had been at the school since 1961, longer than anyone else. His wife was a Bard student when they met. Generally, students worship him; Tommi is one of his protégés.

Carolyn took a poetry workshop with Robert, and he was her academic advisor, according to her résumé. "She stopped into my office once in a while, and our talk was always about academic matters of the moment," he says. They would chat over books she was reading and her classes, especially his workshop. "She seemed quite intelligent and witty."

"He would talk about how she was a singular talent," says Jenny, referring to Robert in Carolyn's academic-probation panels. "So special, she deserved another chance. It happened twice, that he did that, and what a cool and special thing, but she kept taking this gift and throwing it away."

"Nothing so formal," says Robert of the so-called faculty panels. "I did stress to her other teachers that her work was cogent and well-written."

"On the third try, he wasn't going to show up for her again," says Jenny. "She finally was kicked out, and she moved to Brooklyn."

"My perception," says Carol, "was that she had taken incompletes because she's such a perfectionist and always had difficulty completing and turning in final projects. She took too many incompletes and was asked to leave. It's not that she flunked out. It's just that she wouldn't finish courses."

"I know that toward the end of my last year there, Carolyn was not feeling well health-wise," says Masha Mitkov, Carolyn's friend from Bard. "She was super, super tired. She was sleeping a lot and couldn't get out of bed. I remember she was always trying these different supplements and herbal teas, trying to figure out why her energy was so low. Maybe she was depressed. Then later when I saw her in New York, she was really lively and a lot better."

"A lot of kids drop out," says Christopher Qualiano, an alum, who also struggled with his mental health while he was a student.

"A lot of people don't finish at Bard," says Moira. "It's really expensive. It's really high pressure."

. . .

On December 30, 2012, Michael Assiff visited his hometown of Saint Petersburg. He was at a new downtown bar called The Bends, one shockingly reminiscent of the ones he frequented in Brooklyn. He was waiting to order and feeling impatient when his friend swiveled his barstool to face the two girls sitting next to him, "prompting me to greet them," he says. One of the girls was Carolyn. "I attempted small talk, trying to find the right kind of charm to normalize the situation. Skeptical yet amused, they entertained my presence, but it was clear Carolyn was much more entertained by me." Michael joked that it would be easier for him to order "in actual Brooklyn" where he lived, he says. "It was then, with much excitement, that we learned we lived stops away from each other, off the JMZ in Bushwick."

"Carolyn and I had a very immediate magnetic pull toward romance," he says. "She was borrowing her mom's big boat of a car. We made out in the back seat. I grabbed her nude foot. She said 'Oh, you're a foot guy!' and I sheepishly said that I am not but that she did have a nice one. She drove me to my mom's and stayed the night." Michael's mom, seeing Carolyn in the morning, greeted her with "girlish giggles," as Carolyn would call them.

"The next day she suggested we meet at exactly 11:59, New Year's Eve, and make out," says Michael. "We did."

A little over a week later, one morning, Michael and Carolyn went to Crescent Lake Park, where she and Callie used to sneak out to in middle school. It was just a few blocks from the Flamingo Bar and Jim's old house. They sat "with the low sun shining in our eyes, watching the ducks in the golden light," says Michael. "Even though there was a chill in the air, I had my shirt off. I had the idea that I wanted to sun-damage and effectively pre-weather a tattoo that I had just received from my friend, of the numbers *2013*. I remember thinking about what a complete and perfect moment it was sitting next to her in the grass."

. . .

They continued their romance back in New York, where Carolyn was enrolled at The New School and trying to make money on the side. "She was applying to jobs," says Michael. "She was working as a waitress in Bed-Stuy. She told me amusedly about how the restaurant, for some extra amount of dollars, would make the customers omelets with organic eggs by request, but, in reality, they were the same eggs. I got her a gig installing vinyl lettering with my former studio-mate. One of the jobs she was applying to was a sales job at Hugo Boss." Carolyn and Michael texted about her upcoming interview for it. She was deciding whether to wear a black mini skirt. Michael told her, "The real question is what purse will u have draped over your shoulder." She responded, "The monstrosity of course."

It was during this time that Kevin helped her get a job in the McNally Jackson Books café. I was then cohosting the Essays Book Club there. We would meet in the travel section. Often each session drew no more than six people, my cohost and me included. Carolyn attended the Anne Carson *Decreation* meeting in March. It was my first time talking to her, though I had noticed she was new to the store. During the discussion she left us all speechless with her deep knowledge and affinity for Simone Weil, the French mystic about whom Carson writes in the book. I remember sensing that she expected more from the conversation, and I remember wanting to meet her at her level. She also came to the meeting for Chris Kraus's essay collection *Where Art Belongs*, the following month.

Other than those meetings at the bookstore, which were held while we were on the clock, we did not have much chance to interact. The bookstore's owner catered a company picnic in Prospect

Park in the spring, where we all played whiffle ball and ate sitting on the grass, and stayed in the park until the sun went down. Afterward, Carolyn and I went to a nearby bar with my then-husband and another friend. We talked about Agnès Varda and playing Scrabble together sometime, and lots of other things that I wish I could remember now, so it's wild to me that I didn't learn she was then dating Michael, my friend since high school. We didn't ask each other where we were from.

"She lived in three different places in Bushwick, that I visited," says Michael. She was trying to find a stable living situation, live "less precariously," he says, and also "have time and space to write." One of these apartments was next to Woodhull Hospital, off Ellery Street. "The apartment was a loft that had a second floor built into it," he says. "She was on the first floor in a hastily constructed room without windows. There was a hole cut into the drywall to move furniture into it." Then the drywall "was just sort of placed back." She described the replaced drywall as "like a loose tooth." "There was absolutely no privacy. She referred to this zone as the 'survival trench.'"

"Later, on Facebook, I asked her about her new place off Kosciuszko," he says.

"the worst part is over," she responded. "my back is killing me, but last night after doing laundry till 4am i got to sleep on my brand new super mushy ikea foam mattress that i got from a real nice rich girl from tennessee in the east village." Carolyn's new room came with a bed too. "an iron one with BARS!"

Her new landlord was "the oldest man in the world," she said, "and a christian spaceman, which sounds cute but it's not. we've already decided to hate each other." He lived in the building and would watch her coming and going. He was trying to "exorcise me with song," she said. "again not as cute as it could hypothetically be."

"She introduced me to the concept of rewilding extinct ecosystems," says Michael, "and tardigrade water bears. She had TMJ, she used dry shampoo, her breath smelled like sweet milk." One of his nicknames for her was Milky Breath. He also called her Carob and Sweet Potatah. She called him Sharky and Sunshine.

Much of their time together was spent on a bed, which they called "mattress mountain," reading to each other, watching movies, and ordering in. One night they watched a movie together called *Trees Lounge*, on Michael's laptop, and ordered Egyptian food from a now-closed restaurant called Amun, in to his apartment. "Then in the morning ordered Dominican mangú and ate it in bed," he says. "Time was endless once we were together."

Sometime in February, they went to see the movie *Side Effects*, at Williamsburg Cinemas—the movie Bardey coproduced. "Afterward we were livid at how bad the movie sucked," says Michael. "I don't know how or why we sat through the entire thing. It was so cold and self-serious and corny and implausible, stretching credulity to the breaking point."

• • •

One thing Michael and Carolyn bonded over was a love of art. Carolyn was writing, as always, and Michael is a painter. He and Carolyn would go to art openings and museums together, and he would go with her to lectures and readings. She loaned him CAConrad's *The Book of Frank* and Robert Kelly's *The Scorpions*. "I remember one night we went to Tandem, a bar that was on Troutman Street in Bushwick," he says, "and we read about ten of her in-progress poems. She was interested in my perspective as someone outside of her literary circle. I dialed up the criticism at a few moments, which would get her really excited. She wrote notes and drew diagrams on the pages as we went line by line. A lot of my criticisms, I believe, were due to my own lack of fluency in the craft, but I thought it was very generous and open-minded how she wanted to grapple with me as a reader."

As they grew closer, she began to open up about her family. "Her relationship with her parents seemed complicated," he says. "She was convinced they would work it out over time. She opened up slowly about her mother, talking about the things she would do to care for her mom and the possibility of moving back or at least spending more time in Florida to care for her. Her friendship with Pam seemed very important to her.

"The relationship feels long in my mind," he says. In reality, it only lasted about seven months, until July 2013. "A source of guilt is how blunt and tactless I was in some of our breakup drama. Not that we had a lot of drama. Most of it was an outgrowth of the precarity of our lives back then. While we were having serious discussions, she was so incisive without being harsh, could be teasing without eviscerating. She could strongly advocate for herself while giving the other person grace to maneuver and reconnect. I attempted to try an impression of that back at her and it came out terrible. I also was carrying so much baggage in my twenty-something-year-old boy brain that we really didn't stand a chance. Somewhere in my deep fantasy imagination I envisioned a future in which we reconnected when we were older."

● ● ●

By November 2013, Carolyn's living situation in New York was still constantly in flux, and for a time she lived with Lizzy in Queens. "She and Kevin were supposed to live together and then he pulled out and moved in with Gabe," says Lizzy. Living with Carolyn, "It's one of the only times I've lived with someone who really, really knew me," she says. "She and I smoked cigarettes on our stoop in Astoria/Long Island City and drank copious, copious amounts of red wine. We imagined what we would do with the money from the circle," a new group they had joined for empowering women financially. "We talked about astrology. She was often wearing her astrology pajamas. We tried to share parts of our creative selves, like where our writing was coming from, which was tied to the movement of our lives and our erotic yearnings.

"Michael Assiff, he was someone we talked about," she says. "Also, friends at Bard. We had this cradle of care for each other. She cooked dinner for me. Mali would come over and we'd have dinner and drink wine and just listen to music all night." Amalia "Mali" Scott would later be Carolyn's roommate on Stanhope Street. "That was one of the times I felt closest to her."

Their birthdays were both at the end of November, so they held a joint celebration. They invited friends out to Soda Bar, in Prospect Heights, Brooklyn, across the street from Unnameable Books, where I was giving a reading that night in the basement. "I remember she felt really connected to you," says Lizzy. "I'd met you through Kevin, and we went to that reading because we were like, 'Oh, Sarah!' We both invited friends to the reading and then to go across the street to get drinks for our birthday.

"I remember she was calling herself Coco," she says. "Then she was like, 'Well, what's your name going to be?' Then she called me Sunshine," the same name she had used for Michael. "She thought I was so positive all the time," says Lizzy. They made a Facebook event: "Sunshine and Coco really know how to age," they wrote in the description. "we'll be bringing our rose rocks and green glass to the bar on friday to celebrate. Come into woemanhood with us—buy us drinks!! Get sarah gerard one too, cause you'll have just heard her stop time at unnameable. locay subject to change maybe."

Wendy's Subway was in its most nascent form, cells multiplying in the primordial ooze of ambition. Kevin had just found the nonprofit's first location, and on the day of Coco and Sunshine's celebration, he would be viewing it for the first time and meeting the building's owner. "I remember her telling me, 'Wendy's is my golden ticket,'" says

Pamela of Carolyn. "She felt like the people that were involved with Wendy's had a vision. I feel like her relationship to Wendy's Subway wasn't purely philanthropic. It was a part of her success."

"She found that very intellectually fulfilling," says Jenny, "and found so much joy there."

27.
Airsoft

"It is that whiteness which invests him, a thing
expressed by the name he bears."
—Herman Melville, *Moby-Dick*

R ender Elvis Stetson-Shanahan was born on February 19, 1990, on
the Aquarius-Pisces cusp, making him an artist, and very sensitive. Janet's sister Diana was present at his birth. "Thus technically
I've known him longer than anyone else except his own parents," she
writes in her support letter. His birth came one month after his cousin
Chandler's. They were the first two grandsons. "The cousins spent a
lot of time together," writes Render's aunt, Bonnie, Chandler's
mother, in her letter. "The two boys hiked, explored, played, and went
to preschool together."

Render was "quieter and more contemplative" than her own son,
according to Bonnie. "He loved being read to, he loved dramatic play.
From an early age he was incredibly funny and a talented artist. He
was never aggressive, did not fight with other children or (as some of
the boys in our neighborhood did) hurt the lizards or other desert
creatures in our backyard."

When Render was born, the family was living outside Albuquerque,
New Mexico. Danny writes in his letter, "From a very young age
Render loved being outdoors, at my side, as I landscaped and

maintained our home." They "hiked the irrigation roads, visited national parks, and never missed the annual hot-air balloon festival."

During this time, Danny published his first *New Yorker* cover. Janet had been dancing professionally but stopped when her sons were born, and she continued teaching dance to children. When Render was two, she appeared in a *Los Angeles Times* article about why men don't dance. "I always had boyfriends who wouldn't dance," she's quoted saying. "I've heard women over and over say how their male friends don't dance and how much they'd like to go out dancing."

Janet's own husband "is willing to dance—but only in the privacy of their home," writes the *Times*. "Her experience with teaching dance to boys has convinced her that most men become inhibited early in life."

• • •

Finnegan was born three years after Render. The boys' "births were planned," Janet writes in her letter of support. She put her career on hold to raise them. "Money would come and go, but there is only a single window of time to raise a child." Render was five when they moved east, to the Hudson Valley. Finn was two. Danny was six years into his contract with the *New Yorker*. They had been in New Mexico for seven years, and they missed the seasons, "the beaches, the green of the valleys and woods," Danny writes in an anthology he later edited, called *Some Delights of the Hudson Valley*, to which Leon contributed an essay.

They bought an 1860 Federal Colonial, in the heart of Rhinebeck Village, a historic district. It had a big, shady porch, where they hung baskets of flowers. "Surrounded by fruit trees, the house is decorated with Shaker furniture that Shanahan bought at auctions (or received as gifts) and refinished in his garage," the *Hudson Valley News* reported. "Here and there are other auction purchases, including Bakelite items, eighteenth-century tools, and early baseball gloves," plus framed drawings throughout the home, by *New Yorker* cartoonists.

Render enrolled in kindergarten at Chancellor Livingston Elementary. He met Seth Oclatis on the first day. "I called him by his nickname, Renny," Seth writes in his first letter of support. Render was the first person he ever dubbed a "best friend." They both liked art and stories and making blanket forts. When old enough, their parents let them ride their bikes the half mile between their homes. "In those elementary school years Renny was a showman," he writes. "He never picked on anyone, and he could crack jokes without victimizing others." In Seth's second letter of support, he would write that Render always included Finn. "For comparison, my big brother never wanted to hang out with me when we were growing up."

Render met Arun Saxena in kindergarten too, and would attend school with him through senior year, staying close afterward; Arun would testify at his trial. Arun writes in his letter to the court that Render "always engaged in classes and played an active role in classroom activities. All of our teachers adored his kind demeanor," and he was a "popular favorite among them." Arun and Render played at recess every day and "he had no rivalries with any of our classmates," he writes. "There was absolutely no reason that you could dislike Render."

Lisa Ilene Cahn moved in next door to the Stetson-Shanahans in the late 1990s. She saw Render and Finnegan playing together in front of their home. She wanted to have children someday and was looking for "parenting role models," so she knocked on the door and introduced herself to the boys' parents. "I was always intrigued that such a normal, well-adjusted, seemingly mainstream kid had also managed to find time to develop refined artistic and intellectual esoteric interests," she writes of Render in her letter of support. When he was still young, he demonstrated for her the technique of Japanese calligraphy. "How sure and smooth his brushstrokes were and how calmly and confidently he explained the characters for me."

In a photograph of Render's family from that time, the four stand before the white picket fence encircling their new home. It's fall. Center frame, Finnegan crouches devilishly among a pile of dead leaves, nerdy glasses on his tiny nose, cold hands in jacket pockets, mugging for the camera. Render kneels before him to the left, in a yellow polo shirt tucked into light-wash belted jeans. He wears an enormous navy blue backpack, which looks weighed down. He gazes sideways into the camera with dark eyes and doesn't smile. Instead, he seems to slightly frown at the viewer. His parents laugh together on the other side of the frame.

. . .

"That's their house," the Stetson-Shanahans' neighbor Mark Lytle tells me, gazing from his open back door at a second-floor terrace and rolling green backyard. I am in the Hudson Valley to learn about the place and its people, which helped create Render. I'd emailed Janet prior to coming and she'd responded through Render's lawyers. Margulis-Ohnuma invited me to direct any questions to him. I later called his office to test this invitation, and he laughed at me. "I'm not going to help you with your book," he said.

Mark's enormous cat scratches at the screen, and he opens it for her. Mark wrote in his letter of support for Render, "His family and mine shared a backyard fence; I watched him and his brother Finn grow up." His daughter was one of their babysitters. He would be Render's professor and thesis advisor at Bard. A history major, Render's thesis subject was whaling in Nantucket.

"We knew them socially," says Mark of Janet and Danny. He and his wife would see the couple at parties or book signings. They all lived down the block from Oblong Books, an independent bookstore that hosted local writers and artists, including Danny. Mark and Danny were both golfers and would talk about the sport or see each other on the green. He'd see Janet on his strolls through the village, and they would chat about Bard. In 1997, she'd returned to her alma mater to teach dance at the new Abigail Lundquist Botstein Nursery School, before joining the admissions department.

Over the years, as the boys aged, Mark would often hear Finn practicing his violin on the home's veranda. "They didn't play in the yard, these kids, they played music on the porch," he says. "I don't believe that either of them was much into sports. Interesting, because Janet is a dancer and Danny is a good athlete, so probably they had the physical capability. I think they were aesthetically driven."

Render "loved to climb trees and was always on the move," writes Janet. "He was cautious though. When I taught him to ski, he chose to follow me as I crisscrossed from one side of the trail to the other in control of my speed." In contrast, Finn "preferred to take aim for the bottom and go with abandon." When Janet pushed Render on a swing set, he would plead with her, "Not too high!"

Danny's cartooning studio was off the family's kitchen. He could often be seen taking breaks to meander around the village. Rhinebeck is small enough to navigate on foot and the kind of place where you can gather all the major gossip in an afternoon. Its biggest claims to fame are the Beekman Arms (which is the longest-operating hotel in the United States, a place where Revolutionary War heroes took shelter) and the fact that Chelsea Clinton got married there in 2010. Danny passed time in the local cafés and bars, which often featured in his cartoons. "He and I began meeting on a fairly regular basis in a Rhinebeck coffee shop, usually on a Thursday or Friday morning," writes Michael Maslin, a fellow *New Yorker* cartoonist and friend of Danny's. "We came to know Danny as someone with an uncanny ability to fire off hilarious, often dark jibes, machine-gun style."

Danny was publishing cartoons regularly in the *New Yorker*. The magazine celebrated its seventy-fifth anniversary with a show of its artists in a Manhattan gallery, where his works hung alongside those by contemporaries Roz Chast and Lee Lorenz—as well as masters like Ludwig Bemelmans and Jules Feiffer. *New Yorker* illustrators at that time were paid $1,200 per cartoon, $4,000 for a first cover of the year, plus $500 for each successive cover that same year.

Each week, ten or twenty cartoonists commuted into the city with portfolios for the "Tuesday Looks." Danny would sit in a small room of the magazine's office with a dozen black-and-white drawings he'd prepared, chatting with others while waiting for their names to be called by Bob Mankoff, the editor. Bob would look over Danny's cartoons. Then on Thursday around dinnertime, the phone would ring, and Danny would find out if he'd sold anything. He aimed to sell one or two per week. Still, "Ninety percent of my work is rejected; I never know why," he'd say in an interview.

By this point, Danny couldn't walk from one end of Market Street to the other without running into several friends and fans. He was a regular at Le Petit Bistro, Terrapin, Gigi Trattoria, and the village's bars. One of his cartoons from this time shows a man in a bar saying to another, seated beside him, "What I don't, like, get is how, she, like, figured out I was, like, having an affair with, like, the babysitter."

The parents at his sons' school were impressive too. When Render was in fifth grade, the parents devised a fundraiser for his class trip to Cape Cod. "The students go there every year to study whales and their environment," the *Poughkeepsie Journal* reported. Danny was among "more than 50 Rhinebeck artists who decorated a birdhouse to help raise money."

"I have a very small collection of Big Bird feathers, which are very hard to get," *Sesame Street* writer Nancy Sans told the paper, and she used some to create a birdhouse for the fundraiser. James Gurney, *Dinotopia* creator, had a son in the same class as Render, and he contributed a *Dinotopia*-themed birdhouse. Liza Donnelly made one, as did "renowned artist Richard Artschwager." Then also, "Marvel Comics' Howard Mackie created a storyboard on his birdhouse," featuring "Spider-Man, disguised as a naturalist."

"From everything I have seen, Render comes from a loving, supportive, highly 'functional' family," writes Rachel Cavell, a close friend of Janet's. Cavell and her husband, Norton Batkin, were colleagues of Janet's at Bard and lived a few doors down. Their children went to school together. Batkin would announce Janet's promotion to the position of director of graduate admissions at Bard in January 2017.

. . .

In a book about Hudson Valley writers, the author says of Danny, "Now he works in the Rhinebeck home he shares with his wife, Janet Stetson (of cowboy hat royalty), and their two sons." It's a common misconception that Janet is a direct descendant of the Stetson hat lineage. Her family is proud of its very distant connection to John Batterson Stetson, the iconic milliner and namesake of Stetson University, in DeLand, Florida, about two hours from Gainesville (and with a law school campus in Gulfport, ten minutes from Carolyn's childhood home near Flamingo Bar).

Like John B. Stetson, Janet's father, Chandler Alton Stetson Jr., is descended from Cornet Robert Stetson, who emigrated to Plymouth Colony from England in the 1640s. Cornet Robert served in a military unit, and according to the Stetson Kindred of America (SKOA), "met with Natives both in warfare and as a commissioner, negotiating in the settlement of their differences with the colonists."

I reached out to SKOA to confirm John B.'s relationship to Janet's father. "Chandler Alton Stetson Jr. is indeed a descendant of Cornet Robert Stetson as follows (tracing backwards thru the generations)," the secretary replied. "Chandler Alton Stetson, Jr., Chandler Alton, Sr., Furber Alva, Daniel C., Josiah, Benjamin, Amos, Robert, Joseph, Cornet Robert."

She continued, "This is not the same line of descent as John Batterson Stetson . . . John B. descends from Cornet's son Robert, and Chandler descends from Cornet's son Joseph."

Chandler Alton Stetson Jr. earned his BS at age twenty and his MD from Harvard three years later, then served as an associate in medical research in the army. He became an associate professor of pediatrics at NYU in 1957, two years before Janet was born. Chandler enjoyed building furniture and boats and restoring or reproducing antique cabinets, using period tools he gathered from around the country. He was a sculptor of wood and stone, making flint arrowheads and polishing semiprecious rocks and gold he found, turning them into jewelry. He played piano, violin, saxophone, and recorder. He scouted for uranium in Wyoming and was an amateur archaeologist. He served as a South Nyack village trustee, a deputy mayor, and the town's PTA president. He and Betty Jean Stetson raised four daughters on the west bank of the Hudson River, twenty-five miles north of Manhattan and an hour south of Poughkeepsie.

"Not certain about the photo on the right, but the one on the left was taken at his cabin in upstate New York," writes Render, posting two photos of his grandfather, Chandler Stetson, on Reddit. In the cabin photo, Chandler looks more than a little like Bryan Cranston, as one user points out. He wears a denim jacket and smiles ruggedly at the photographer. In the second photo, he looks like a young Hank Williams, perhaps on holiday in France. He wears a white shirt with black stripes and smokes a pipe. "He was an avid sailor and outdoorsman," Render says of his grandfather. "Very much a man's man, I'm told. Died of a heart attack 13 years before I was born. Wish I could have known him."

South Nyack was 82 percent white when Janet was born on December 5, 1959. It had a population of just over 3,100 people. In 1964, Janet's mother, Betty Jean Stetson, completed a land-use map of the village based on her own survey of residents. It was "preliminary to a study of how the village can be most advantageously re-zoned to preserve its present character and enhance its attractiveness," she told the paper. She wanted to safeguard against apartment developers and, it follows, the people who would live in those apartments.

Then a Black man applied for a job in the fire department, via the village board rather than through the department itself, accusing the fire department of racial discrimination. "Dr. Stetson told me if he were a Negro he would not apply to the fire company," the applicant told the board, about Janet's father. "I took that as pretty sound advice." The fire department denied that the firemen of South Nyack were racists, but the *Record* reported, "It has been noted that no Negro applications for membership have been received in the company's history."

In 1968, Johnson was in his last year as commander in chief of the Vietnam War, Martin Luther King Jr. was assassinated, and marijuana had finally reached the white middle class, which was enjoying it after all. Consequently, social and political views on the drug were shifting. Chandler published a letter to the editor responding to an editorial claiming marijuana was "so probably dangerous that it should be even more strenuously outlawed." Chandler, as a doctor himself, charged that to call marijuana dangerous was "neither logical nor in agreement with informed opinion such as that of the Surgeon General of the United States Public Health Service . . . It is not the use of marijuana but its abuse that is dangerous."

Soon after, Betty wrote her own letter to the editor of the *Journal-News* defending the village's recent purchase of riot-control equipment. The South Nyack Democrats penned a response to Janet's mother in which they questioned "whether such riot control equipment as an electric shock prod and automatic repeating riot shot guns are truly necessary." They also questioned Betty's assertion that the purchase of such equipment in their small village was intended to meet the "minimum potential needs of the community in these times."

That year the village was forced to consider abolishing its police force for financial reasons. In response, Betty raised concerns about the policemen's salaries being too high. Then the village board voted to pay its trustees a modest salary. She argued against it, saying their work was a community service. The treasurer responded, saying, "Salaries for board members would make village elections more democratic, rather than merely having 'the moneyed elite' run for office." The moneyed elite, he implies, are the Stetsons.

In 1972, Janet's sisters had already gone away to college, and she and her parents moved to Gainesville, where she attended high school. Render would later write on Reddit about her being a "total surfer girl" and "blasting" around town in her dad's T-Bird, until he took it away, like in the Beach Boys song. Chandler was now dean of the medical school at the University of Florida (UF).

Within a few years of arriving in Florida, Chandler co-owned a small island off the coast with the president of UF. With other administrators and faculty of the medical school, he was also taken to task by the *Tampa Bay Times* and *Miami Herald* for "siphoning off nearly $9 million from fees paid by patients," at the university's teaching hospital, to "spend much of it on themselves."

Janet's father suffered a heart attack after serving the school for just five years. He died in May of Janet's senior year. His eyes were removed and given to a blind person. His name was given to a medical school building on UF's campus. Janet moved back to the Hudson Valley that fall to go to Bard.

· · ·

Daniel Shanahan was born in 1956, in Brooklyn. He was raised on Long Island, and in Bethlehem, Connecticut, in what his nephew describes as "a gaggle of Irish-Catholic Brooklynites." He was the fourth in line of eleven children whose father managed an electronics company. Their mother was a homemaker. "He was always drawing," Janet would tell the *New York Times* about Danny. "His parents had a large family with a modest income, but they always had lots of books and lots of paper on the table."

When he was twenty-five, Danny moved back to Brooklyn and found work as a bartender at a nightclub in Greenwich Village called The Bitter End. Bob Dylan, Joni Mitchell, Duke Ellington, and just about everyone else you can think of had played there. He kept drawing. One day, he was playing tennis with a friend who edited *World Tennis* magazine. The friend asked Danny to submit a cartoon strip. He got fifty dollars for it and went on to do one a month. He cut back on the bartending and devoted more time to cartooning. "Hoping to break into the *New Yorker*," he began "bombarding them" with stacks of cartoons.

Then he met Janet. "She thought I was a stalker," he'd later say in an interview. "She'd noticed me eyeing her on Christopher Street." Imagine Janet early in her dancing career. She's leaving a performance at night in Greenwich Village, flushed, sweating, and tired, while Danny is leaving his shift at The Bitter End, soaked in ten kinds of liquor and who knows what else. They see each other on the platform. "When she took the subway home to Brooklyn, there I was in the same car," he says. Imagine Janet watching this dark-haired stranger out of the corner of her eye as the subway lights flicker. "I got off at the same stop," says Danny. He follows Janet down the dark abandoned streets of Cobble Hill, toward her apartment. She steps into the warm light of her vestibule, thankful the creep doesn't follow.

"It turned out we were neighbors, living two blocks from each other," says Danny. "Some stalker!"

Janet had graduated Bard the year prior, 1981, moving to the city around the same time as Danny did and enrolling at Columbia University Teachers College the following year to work toward her master's in dance education.

Janet had thrived at Bard. She shared the story of her senior thesis with BardCorps, an oral history. "The story is about how closely students back then, and I think still today," she says, "very much so, how intimate the relationship between your faculty and students can be."

"I choreographed seven pieces over the course of a year to perform in a concert," she says. "One of the pieces was inspired by a photograph of three men," depicting a performance by the dance company Pilobolus. The dancers in it "were naked and one sitting on top of each other's shoulders with their back to the camera on these rocks. It was just a beautiful photo."

She wanted to make something like it. "I took the three dancers, made them all women, of course, and put them on their side. So, they weren't vertical, they were horizontal and had one's head between the other's legs . . . So, really what you saw were torsos. It was very sculptural and beautiful." Originally, Janet had planned for her dancers to wear flesh-colored unitards with spaghetti straps. The evening before the performance, at the lighting rehearsal, she was sitting next to Aileen Passloff, her advisor, watching the light hit the dancers. The fabric of their unitards was flat while the dancers' skin was "luminescent."

Passloff turned to her. "I don't need to see any more. Do you?" she said.

"No, I don't," said Janet.

"Well, it's your senior project and it's your lighting tech. You can stop it."

"That's exactly, verbatim, what happened between us," says Janet. "That's how close we were."

"Can everyone stop for a minute?" Janet said to the rehearsal.

The lights went up.

"Could you girls take your unitards off and do this piece in the nude?"

The lighting guys tittered. The dancers initially hesitated, then followed orders.

"They took off their clothes, stripped right in front of everybody, and laid down and began the whole piece," says Janet. "There were some awkward moments that we had to re-choreograph, but it was a great example of how that relationship between both the faculty and the student was almost . . . symbiotic."

In 2004, Render started at Rhinebeck High School. He worked at Samuel's Sweet Shop, a candy store and coffee shop on Market Street, in the center of town. It was a short walk from their home and next door to Handcrafted Builders, where he later worked as a carpenter for his father's friend. Across the street is Bread Alone, where Danny could often be seen having coffee with friends. It is diagonal from the Rhinebeck Artist's Shop, where Danny and Render would buy their supplies.

"Throughout high school, we often talked about different martial arts and which ones we find most unique, including cultural aspects," writes Arun in his character statement. He says he was the assistant instructor in some of Render's martial arts training sessions, and he saw Render avoid aggression even when it was the goal of the exercise. He calls Render "gentle" and says he "avoids conflict whenever possible as I have seen in multiple situations."

A record request to the Rhinebeck Police Department revealed that in October 2006, at 8:15 at night, when Render and Arun were in eleventh grade, a local man reported a white Mercury Sable "being operated on Livingston Street with youths discharging some type of air gun at pedestrians." When officers approached the vehicle, they found Arun and Render inside and could plainly see an airsoft rifle at the passenger's feet.

Airsoft guns are often designed as imitations of real guns, including military weaponry, which makes them difficult for the untrained eye to distinguish from, say, an AR-15, an M16, or a Kalashnikov; they are so much like real guns that the military uses them for training. They operate the same way as firearms, but they use compressed air, battery power, or springs to shoot projectiles, instead of internal combustion. They shoot pellets up to 340 miles per hour, or 500 feet per second, and can cause serious injuries or even death, if the person being shot at—say, a pedestrian—is not wearing protective equipment. The most common injuries associated with airsoft guns are to the eyes, causing blindness; people have also died from the pellets going through the eye socket into the brain or through the abdomen, piercing the lungs or heart.

Rhinebeck police confiscated the airsoft rifle and gave it to Arun's mother at five minutes to nine thirty. No charges were filed.

28.

Verdict and Sentencing

I n February 2020, Justice Buchter hands down a ten-page decision letter containing his verdict. It outlines the charges against Render: murder in the second degree, attempted assault in the first degree, menacing in the second degree, criminal mischief in the third degree, and criminal possession of a weapon in the fourth degree.

"At the request of the People and the defendant, the court is considering the lesser included offenses of manslaughter in the first degree and manslaughter in the second degree," writes Buchter. There is no disputing that Render is the one who took Carolyn's life and committed the other offenses in question. "What is very much at issue in this case is whether the defendant, on the night in question, by reason of his ingestion of cannabis and alcohol, possessed the mental state required to be found guilty of the crimes charged in the indictment or the lesser included offenses, and, if so, whether the defendant lacked the substantial capacity to understand the nature and consequences of his acts, or that they were wrong.

"Although the defendant did not ingest a large quantity of beer or marijuana," he writes, "the two experts who testified at trial agreed that the ingestion of marijuana impacted the defendant's ability to function." Therefore, Render is convicted of manslaughter in the second degree. "A person is guilty of this crime when he recklessly causes the death of another person."

"Credible evidence was introduced at trial that the defendant had a history of experiencing severe psychological effects from the ingestion of marijuana," he writes, "including depersonalization or an outer body sensation and panic attacks." He also brings up the doctor who treated Render as a teenager and warned him not to use weed anymore. "Knowing the likelihood that he might experience an adverse psychological reaction by ingesting marijuana," Buchter writes, "the defendant disregarded that risk.

"Furthermore," he writes, "to the extent that the defendant was unaware of the risk that Ms. Bush's death would occur when he stabbed her with a knife, any such inability to perceive and appreciate this risk is directly attributable to his ingestion of marijuana. Thus, the defendant's ingestion of marijuana, and the impact that the ingestion of marijuana had on his ability to function, does not negate the mental state of recklessness."

• • •

In May 2020, three months after the verdict, a former Bard student sues the school, naming Leon as a codefendant. She says she was forcibly groped and kissed by her music teacher in a soundproof practice room under the Fisher Center for the Performing Arts, during a private lesson. Afterward, according to the lawsuit, the teacher warned her that it would be pointless to file a Title IX complaint against him because, as he said, he "always wins." The student later found out that the instructor had already been fired previously after two Title IX complaints—and then given his job back, after appealing to a senior administrator and Leon. "They obviously protected somebody who didn't deserve protection, when in fact their whole commitment is to protect students," the student tells the *New York Times* in an interview.

• • •

"Carolyn was an uncommonly kind and gentle young woman," Render says at his sentencing over Zoom, the following month. He has just listened to Jenny's victim-impact statement, read by Mike, because Jenny could not bear to attend the hearing; he has heard Jim's, in which he cried and struggled to gather himself; and he's heard Susan's, read by Carol, as she sat weeping beside Jim and Cindy.

"A rare artistic sensitivity," says Render, "and her death constitutes an absolutely senseless tragedy that has no place in a just world. Every day I think of Carolyn, and every day I consider my role in her death. At these times I can only hold to certain convictions. I know that I was raised by good people to be compassionate and that I would never put an innocent person in danger. I have no doubt of any of this and yet Carolyn Bush is dead because of me. Because of me, she was most unfairly denied her future, her aspirations as a poet, and all the unfathomable dreams and passions to which none of us are strangers. All of that is gone. The fact that I am finally responsible for so great a loss is impossible to reconcile with what I know to be my true character and so I am left with a most acute sense of defilement and profound sorrow, and I am sorry, so deeply sorry that those who loved Carolyn must endure even worse than I do, that their unspeakable suffering and grief continues, and that the world has been denied such a remarkable person. I owe everything to my family and close friends who offered their unerring support and love since my arrest. Today I recognize fully the serious responsibility I have to safeguard my mental health. I will never use illegal drugs or ever again take marijuana in any form regardless of its legal status. I promise before this court to remain vigilant of my mental state and prioritize ongoing professional therapy. I appreciate as I did not before the vital importance of such commitment, which now represents a permanent facet of my life. Thank you, Your Honor."

"I just was like, that's a fucking weird way to put it if you're editing stuff," says Pamela, in response to Render's statement that Carolyn's family "must endure even worse than I do." "When I'm editing things for communication with people," says Pamela, "I don't talk about myself when it's not appropriate. The right way to structure that sentence is, 'It's so painful to confront the pain of the family.' Just be humble about it, rather than bringing yourself into the equation."

"I ask you to be especially mindful of the letters written to you on his behalf, in particular the letter that was written by the president of Bard College," Margulis-Ohnuma says to Buchter, before the judge reads Render's sentence.

"The Court believes, in light of all the circumstances, to sentence the defendant to only time served, as requested by the defense, would be a miscarriage of justice," says Buchter. "I read the presentence report, the People's memorandum and over twenty letters submitted by the defense, which extolled the defendant." His sympathy goes out to Render's family. "There is another young person who was also the light of her mother's life, and she is no longer here because of this defendant." Render is sentenced to serve five to fifteen years. He has already served nearly four.

"Is there any justice in this case?" says Jim. "I think that young man purchased himself a—that it's evidence of privilege. If a Black man had killed Carolyn, he'd get murder two. If the situation were that he was Black or brown, he would have not been able to get that kind of conviction or sentence."

In a 2023 article published by *The Conversation* about racial disparity in incarceration rates, the nonprofit media outlet wrote that, from 2000 to 2019, "States incarcerated Black adults for violent offenses at a rate over six times that of white adults."

"People use white supremacy," says a former Bard administrator. "This is it, concretely. You can kill someone and get away with it. And then you scratch the surface, and you find that there are literally several white male Bard students who get away with raping, they get away with assaulting, they get away with harassing, and stalking." And murder.

29.

The Circle

In January 2014, Wendy's Subway was a fledgling group of poets sitting in a circle on the splintering wood floor of 722 Metropolitan Avenue, Brooklyn. "I was definitely aware of the generation of writers that preceded my generation," says Francesca Capone, a visual artist and early supporter. "What I loved about what Wendy's was doing was that it felt like the next generation of artists and writers. I attribute that energy to, obviously, all the founders, but also to Carolyn, and the warmth and acceptance that was part of her personality.

"I remember really vividly," she says, noticing Carolyn, out of the corner of her eye during one reading, "seeing her legs crossed and her little slide hanging off the back of her foot. Something really fashion-based, but also just tender and sweet about her presence, and how she presented herself. It was both casual and elegant."

. . .

In February, for the first time after nearly two years of living for short periods with various Bard friends in the city, Carolyn had found her real home: 1861 Stanhope. At the time of her lease signing, she was living in the room with no windows.

"It was really nice," says Kevin of 1861. Carolyn's unit occupied the whole second floor. "It had a nice living room, kitchen. It was a standard New York apartment, small. It had little amenities like a little bit of a nook, nice nook, where it was clear she did her writing."

"That was her home that she was never going to leave," says Pamela. "Yet she couldn't afford it on her own."

"She was doing a ton," says Rachel. "She was always looking for a job. When I first met her, she was working at a café, I never knew which one. She did odd jobs. I hooked her up with a gallery once, to gallery-sit."

· · ·

In the spring of 2014, Carolyn asked me to hang out. We'd always planned to do so after we both left McNally Jackson the previous fall. We met at Café Loup in the West Village, a haunt of many famous New York artists. We sat near the door. I ordered french fries and we drank red wine and talked about writing and books and people we both knew. She might have mentioned having recently moved into a new apartment in Queens. We talked about Wendy's, for which I had recently helped organize a small fundraiser.

Then she told me about "the circle." She described it as a "women's circle," a sort of weekly support group, and a way to raise money for fellow women, who would in turn raise money for me. The process involved bringing other women into the circle, who then brought in others. Each woman's buy-in was $5,000, but someone had found her a sponsor, and she could probably find me one. It would be a loan, and I could pay the money back as I brought more women in.

As Carolyn described it, as more women came in underneath me, I would ascend a hierarchy, the levels of which were labeled like dinner party courses, "appetizer," "dessert," and so on. Alongside this commitment, which really was a gift to myself, I would have weekly phone calls with my circle. Lizzy had brought her in, and it had really transformed her perspective, to trust the love and support of other women. When a woman had earned back some amount of money for herself

and her circle, then her circle would graduate her out and gift her
$15,000, or maybe it was $50,000.

"Oh my gosh," says Lizzy now. "It was one of the dumbest things
I've ever done but it all worked out. None of us paid money." Her
boyfriend's mom had convinced her to join. "It is a pyramid scheme. I
didn't even know what that was. You have these weekly supportive
calls, and it was mostly really nice, hippie, middle-aged ladies. Carolyn
and I were both really struggling with money. I was like, 'This is going
to work. This is going to be awesome.' I was so into it. Carolyn was
skeptical."

The structure of the calls was to share on a theme in your life, like
love or gratitude. "Carolyn talked a lot about Spiritualism, and psy-
chics, being able to speak to the dead, when we were doing the circle,"
says Lizzy. "She said her grandfather spoke to her and told her to
focus more on math. I had a similar experience. I had a dream that my
own grandpa, who was a mathematician, told me to pay better attention to 'math.' I think we were both getting messages that the mathe-
matical model of the circle made no sense."

Later, Carolyn emailed me about the circle. She invited me to call
her if I wanted to talk more, and invited me to listen in on one of the
weekly calls with her circle. "no pressure to commit," she said. She
still treated the circle "like a strange experiment, a really real, good
conceit."

Home from work, I responded: "Hey Carolyn! So good to hear
from you, and I'm so sorry I didn't get back to you about this sooner.
Unfortunately, I don't think I can commit to it, as awesome as it
sounds. I'm afraid I wouldn't be able to bring in other women, or
commit time to the circle, itself. But I wish you all the best with it! And
please let me know if/when you'd like to hang out again. I'd really
love to see you." I never saw her again.

. . .

In May, Lizzy did a poetry reading at Queens Tavern, with Tommi as her coreader. A mutual friend had set it up. Carolyn attended. After the reading at Queens Tavern, Carolyn and Tommi walked to the train together. "I think we felt open around each other," says Tommi. "I've felt similarly with other Scorpio friends. I had little interest in astrology at the time I knew her, though her enthusiasm for that science proved to be provocative for me."

On their way to the train, "Carolyn and I stopped at a bodega where she got a cheese sandwich," he remembers. "Maybe there was lettuce and tomato on there too—however that may be, she insisted that such sandwiches were part of the secret to successful living in the city. Carolyn beneath the streetlights, pale as always, wearing red lipstick, eating a miserable cheese sandwich at midnight—the very image of a poet." Within months, Tommi would facilitate Render moving into Carolyn's vacant room.

• • •

"Obviously, Carolyn enjoys the occult and is drawn toward alternate energies," says Max Agrio. "I never heard anything about the circle, but I do remember one time she made a very weird request." They had gone to a reading at Peninsula Art Space, curated by Rachel for an opening of visual poetry by Francesca Capone, and were hanging out in their friend's apartment afterward. "I mentioned that I was doing software engineering," he says.

"Oh my god," said Carolyn. "I forgot that you were good with computers. You need to help me. My computer is haunted."

"Haunted?" he said.

"I keep getting weird messages, and my mouse moves around," she said. "It feels like someone else is controlling me, and occasionally it'll talk to me."

"The computer will . . . talk . . . to you?"

"Yeah, it'll say weird phrases."

"Um, okay," he said. "I can take a crack at it."

"She was completely convinced her computer was not hacked but haunted," he says. "You never knew how real it was. I believe that she believed her computer was haunted. I one hundred percent believe that. She truly believed in the energies and the different spirits that she would write and talk about, but she had such a developed sense of irony."

· · ·

"She was having a stalker at the time," Mali says. Mali was Carolyn's roommate prior to Render. "Someone was hacking into her computer."

Carolyn did have a stalker. He was named Isaac. He grew up one block over from Render, on Chestnut Street, in Rhinebeck. Born in 1988, he was a senior at Rhinebeck High School in 2004, when Render was a freshman there. I can find no sign that he went to Bard, except perhaps that in addition to using Carolyn's Gmail address, he also used her Bard email. The only way to know how he found her email addresses, whether he was the one hacking her computer, or how he met Carolyn in the first place, would be to ask him. None of Carolyn's friends or family know him, though a few people at Wendy's would eventually meet him.

Isaac emailed Carolyn incessantly and threateningly between 2014 and 2015. On June 18, 2014, he forwarded Carolyn an email thread between him and his public defender. In it, he reports that "the PROS therapist continues to have a positive outlook on my progress and my compliance with the treatment regimen." The Personalized Recovery Oriented Services (PROS) comprises programs run by the state of New York for individuals with mental health needs who are involved in the criminal justice system.

A records request to the Rhinebeck Police Department revealed that on November 14, 2013, Isaac had "walked in front of a fire truck on its way to an emergency with its lights and sirens activated," right outside of the Rhinebeck courthouse. He had been in court that day for "a criminal matter." The truck sounded its air horn to no avail. Finally, Isaac moved.

Later, in June 2014, Isaac emailed his public defender again out of the blue in another exchange he would forward to Carolyn. He was irate that he didn't have an attorney present for two former arraignments, one for a 2013 incident, the other for one in 2011 in which he had tried to break into a clothing store on Montgomery Street. His attorney responded sympathetically. Isaac forwarded the attorney's response to Carolyn with a message that said "coming soon."

A week later, he forwarded her an email he'd sent to two people: one a writer, and the other the publisher of HarperCollins. The email to them said, "FUCK THIS asshole." Above it, Isaac wrote to Carolyn, "bundle the emails fucking quickly, you FUCKING BITCH." About a week later, he emailed her again and said it would be the last time she'd hear from him. It wasn't.

• • •

Pamela moved to Ridgewood in August 2014 and began Airbnb'ing the extra room in her apartment to make rent while living alone. She was only a few blocks away from Carolyn's new apartment, and they shared keys. Mali was planning to move out of 1861 Stanhope in January, and Pamela encouraged Carolyn to run her own Airbnb instead of finding a new roommate. However, Carolyn wanted the stability of a roommate and an assured source of monthly rent.

Carolyn had really liked Mali. "Almost girl crush liked her," says Pamela, "and was bummed when she was leaving."

Around this time, she had said to Pamela, apropos of nothing, "I think I want to have sex with a woman. Just to see what it's like."

"I remember Carolyn telling me about her vision for her life, that she would probably eventually be married to a woman and living in

Europe with a bunch of kids," says Lizzy. "That was what Carolyn was attracting. That was who she was."

Carolyn, Lizzy, and Mali had spent a lot of intimate time together over the year Mali lived with Carolyn. She'd occupied the room that would become Carolyn's, and Carolyn lived in the room that would be Render's. She was also the original owner of Ally the cat, whom she would leave behind when she moved to California. "We loved Josephine Foster," says Lizzy. "Sibylle Baier, Nina Simone, Karen Dalton. I was constantly in a dizzy fixation with dudes with super-alpha personalities, and Carolyn knew how to take up more space. But also, she felt, I think as I did, everything break open and just flood, flood out of us when a man rejected us."

• • •

In September 2014, Carolyn spent ten days in Portland, Oregon, helping Jenny plan for her wedding. "She arrived and unpacked all this green," says Jenny. "She was doing wheatgrass and unpacked oodles of bottles of health products. I was like, 'Are you kidding? What are you doing?' and she was like, 'Oh, I'm vegetarian.' I was like, 'How could you not tell me?' I had planned all these meals around what I thought her diet was."

Jenny and Mike drove with Carolyn to the Washington coast and they stayed at a glamping resort near Jenny's chosen bridal boutique. "For $150 a night, at least in the fall when it's pouring rain, you can stay in one of these refurbished Airstreams, and each one has a record player in it, and it's so twee and adorable," says Jenny.

One night, the three played one of Jenny and Mike's favorite games. "You pick a theme and then everybody has to play music that fits the theme," she says. "We were playing and she got very drunk, and she was elbowing us and laughing hysterically and then just punching me in the arm, very demonstrative and physical every time she would laugh. The rain is pouring down on this Airstream trailer and she and I went out for a cigarette and she's just punching me in the arm as hard as she could every time I told a good joke. She's so intense."

· · ·

In November, Carolyn emailed Lizzy. She had borrowed a book from her: *The Sword Went Out to Sea: Synthesis of a Dream* by Delia Alton, also known as the poet H. D., and Lizzy had asked for it back, not for the first time. Carolyn wrote back telling Lizzy she was right, and apologizing—she'd been avoiding her. Finally, she found herself "consciously hoarding the book thinking that in it I'd find the perfect language" to say so much to her.

Carolyn was leaving the circle.

She wanted Lizzy to know that she'd given it deep thought and come to the decision with peace. She was grateful for all the circle had given her. She was so proud of Lizzy and wanted her to know how ready Lizzy was, for what was to come. She added a postscript that if Lizzy's first reaction was resentment, it was okay. "Go with that," she wrote. She was eager to hear from Lizzy but also patient.

"p.p.s. Newsy things?" If Lizzy had the energy to read on, that is. Carolyn said she was writing poems, and asked about Lizzy's poems too. She said that as much as she had scoffed at it before, she was excited to finish her undergraduate degree in creative writing.

· · ·

On New Year's Eve, Carolyn and Lizzy sat alone in a room at a crowded party and shared their "thorns and roses." Isaac had emailed again at 9:13 that morning, saying only, "now I'm angry"; however, she didn't tell Lizzy. Lizzy's thorn was the circle. "I'm embarrassed Carolyn saw that it wasn't going to work before I did and I am embarrassed at how much meaning and beauty the experience brought to my life even though it was a New Age working-middle-class white-women pyramid scheme," she says. "Thank God she only lost time over it. The Carolyn I knew, we were seeking peace, we were seeking temperance."

Carolyn's rose might have been Wendy's Subway. On December 17, the organization hosted its one-year anniversary celebration, with a cash bar and a "Secret Santa" exchange. It had lived through its first trials, intrinsic and extrinsic, and grown into a fully operational art space, with a donated letterpress machine, several reading series, and a steady membership and volunteer base, with rotating duties. Bookstores, individuals, and independent presses had donated books to the ever-growing library, stored on rough-hewn, handmade bookshelves, alongside handmade plywood study carrels. Members brought in folding chairs and tables and kept the space clean, airy, light, and energized. The year ahead was full of promise.

30.

Burning the Fat
from Their Souls

"The mystery of what is space and time may be made
more understandable by this explanation, but now the
burden of sustaining the order of the universe rests
on 'facts.' What are facts?"
-Robert Pirsig, *Zen and the Art of
Motorcycle Maintenance*

"**A**bsolutely, a suffering soul," says Render's academic advisor and
history professor at Bard, Gennady Shkliarevsky. He's known
Render since he was a freshman. He also knows Janet well and calls
her a "gentle creature." Despite Render's suffering, when Gennady
heard what he had done, he couldn't understand it. "He had that kind
of gentle attitude," he says. He reflects on his own misspent youth. "I
had a rebellious stage in my life. When I encountered the world and
the world proved this competitive ruthless place, I rebelled. I wanted
to exceed the world in its cruelty. I didn't kill anyone, but I was pretty
nasty."

In 2008, the year Render matriculated, Danny published the humor
collection *Some Delights of the Hudson Valley*, featuring locally famous
artists and writers, and to which Leon contributed an essay about living in the area as one who dislikes nature. Render also contributed an

essay about drawing. *New Yorker* cartoonist and friend of Danny, Michael Maslin, designed the cover. "Michael's daughter, Ella, just finished her first year at Bard," Danny wrote in his introduction. "My son, Render, just started his first year there this August." Danny called himself a "raging Ordinary Joe Pro-Bardite, an OJPB."

. . .

"Though we shared mutual friends, it wasn't until 2010 that we became close friends and quickly fell in love," Sofia writes of Render in her letter of support. "He was one of the kindest people I had ever met, and he made me laugh every day. He was more than I could have ever dreamed of, and we loved each other deeply." It was during this year that she gave him the inscribed copy of *Zen and the Art of Motorcycle Maintenance*.

"*Wow, what a beautiful couple*, is always what I thought," says Danielle. "I know a lot of guys really loved Sofia and were jealous. Render literally didn't talk ever. Like, ever. I don't think he's ever said a word."

Sofia is also really quiet, says Danielle, but "She was always friendly and nice to me. And anytime he was around, it was like he was a statue. I remember seeing him around campus because he has a very striking face. He is objectively handsome, but he just didn't speak. Now I wonder what was going on in his mind."

"Render was in Hawthorne, Melville and Literary Friendship," says Moira, "this class that all the lit majors in my year took, not because it was required but because it was such a great class. If you ever get to read Melville's letters to Hawthorne, do it because they are beautiful. They were so in love. A lot of us became Melville nerds after that, so it makes sense that he did his thesis on whaling."

. . .

By the spring of 2012, Render was struggling against his senior-thesis deadline. "I had a friend, we'd jog through the village two or three times a week, and we used to run into Janet occasionally," says Mark Lytle, his neighbor and thesis advisor. "We'd talk about his progress, or lack thereof. She was, obviously, as a mother, concerned, and worried that he might not finish in time. I reassured her."

As a father himself, Mark told Janet, "If you give him the chance to fail, he probably won't, but if you try to stop him, he might."

"He'd been in my class a couple times before that," says Mark, a history professor. "Although in class, he was very reserved. Bard is a very Socratic teaching environment, and we expect a fair level of active participation, and he was not particularly active. My sense of him was that he was very private, very self-contained.

"I think what happened was that he was having trouble getting underway," Mark says of Render's thesis. "I believe the dean of students," David Shein, "asked me if I would step in and if I could do something about this.

"I was totally dumfounded by the choice of topic, whaling in Nantucket," he says. "He never really quite explained it to me. I think maybe because he'd read *Moby-Dick*, he had some vision in his head." Mark owns a summer house with his wife on Nantucket. "I was very familiar with some of the literature about the island. I suggested to him that he go to a couple of the whaling museums. 'Get some visuals,' which he obviously did. He went to one in Bedford. I don't think he ever went to the one in Nantucket." To supplement his lack of text, Mark suggested Render include illustrations, maybe give himself another way into the material.

Since the thesis was slow-coming and substantively thin, Mark sent him to see Jane Smith, assistant director of the Bard Learning Commons and visiting instructor of writing. Render enrolled in a class usually meant for second-semester juniors who are beginning work on their projects. Jane and Render began meeting outside of class to discuss his thesis further, and he'd share his research, writing, and drawings with her. Jane recalls one drawing of a whale and her calf. "We talked about how his perfectionist tendencies were both a blessing and a curse: while they allowed him to produce splendid writing and illustrations, they also slowed him down," she writes in her letter of support.

"I believe Render came to the realization that his true vocation was in art late in his college career," writes Leon.

Render titled the thesis "Burning the Fat from Their Souls: An Illustrated History of the Early American Whaling Industry on Nantucket Island and in the Eastern Colonies, 1640–1775." He dedicated it to Sofia, for her "amaranthine affection." Ultimately, Mark says, "I think we gave him a B+."

• • •

After graduation, Render lived at home. He and Sofia broke up and she moved to New York City. That first Christmas came and went. "Every 26th Dec, some bloke off 4chan posts a picture of all the cum he's saved up over the past year," someone posted on /r/WTF. "Here's this year's haul." It was a picture of what appears to be two two-liter bottles full of murky yellow liquid, another one-liter full of the same stuff, and three-quarters of a second one-liter, with a thin layer of white froth at the top. "So now what," one user asked. Render responded, "Overpass."

That year, Render bought his 1973 Triumph T100R Daytona motorcycle and began restoring it. He bought a precision rifle, a Marlin XT-22TR, and custom-outfitted it. He played video games. He designed logos and signs for local Rhinebeck businesses and drew a wall-sized chalk mural inside one farm-to-table restaurant. His friend Gil came over for Thanksgiving dinner at his family's home. The family's dog died. Render worked as a carpenter for his father's friend, who owned Handcrafted Builders, next door to Samuel's Sweet Shop.

In 2014, the owner of Samuel's, Ira Gutner, also died suddenly. Janet writes in her letter of support, "Render promptly stepped up to cover shifts and oversee the well-being of the store while Ira's close friend and business partner struggled to find his footing after the loss." On the verge of closing, a group including actors Paul Rudd and Jeffrey Dean Morgan, who lived nearby, and whose children loved Samuel's, bought it. They made Render's colleague, John Travers, a partner.

Inside, Samuel's smells of sugar and coffee and unvarnished wood floors. The walls are lined with colorful gummies in glass jars and the front counter is a display case for gourmet chocolates. I introduce myself to John, behind the counter. His blond hair styled into a small Mohawk in front gives the impression of an old-timey soda jerk hat. He tells me that he and Render were close in high school, but he doesn't want Render's affiliation with Samuel's to hurt the business, and he hopes I understand that there's nothing he can say. I take his card. He says he might answer if I use the number on it, but he seems impatient with me, and I am shy, so I never call. When I approach him on my next visit to Rhinebeck, he declines to talk to me.

"He was a very larger-than-life figure," a local Rhinebeck resident tells me of Ira. Their child had gone to high school with Render and Finn, and they ask to speak anonymously due to the contagion of town gossip. "He would have a lot of kids, mostly boys, often with family issues, work in that coffee shop. It sort of was like a little society. He started them working extremely young. Render continued to do work there even after college, making artwork for him." Rhinebeck had loved Ira. It was devastated.

• • •

That year, 2014, Render illustrated the cover for Tommi's first book, *Blue Sun*, which had begun as his Bard senior thesis and was published by a small press run by Max Agrio. Max remembers meeting Render when he and Tommi were living together, while students, in Graves House. "Graves House is this old, creaky rundown student house, and it has a big wraparound porch. I'd be walking and I'd see Tommi on the porch. I'd be like, 'Hey, guy,' and chat, and Render would come out of nowhere and he would just sit on the porch in his corner and not say anything, just be there drawing, occasionally maybe laughing at something. He was like a shadow, and I was always off-put. No one had really seen him around campus. Everyone was like, 'Does he even go to Bard?'

"Someone told me that they're heirs to the Stetson-hat fortune," he says. They're but distantly related, I say. He'd found the rumor believable, he says. Render wore a Stetson hat. Further, "Bard is a weird, traumatic, violent place. There's this whole coterie where it was disaffected, rich children who were talented. They would stare right through you."

Soon after Tommi published *Blue Sun*, Render posted, "Cover art for 'Incense Games' by Tamas Panitz," on Reddit, with his illustration for the next book. Finn writes in his letter of support that in addition to pulling shifts at Samuel's, Render was also "building his reputation as an artist by doing graphic design work and art commissions for businesses," and, "seemed content with his life and the work he was making upstate." He and Sofia had been broken up for nearly two years, but, according to her letter of support, and her mother's, they still frequently talked, and they saw each other about once a month.

Finn was graduating from Bard that spring and already living in the city, commuting back and forth, playing regular gigs with major musical artists. Tommi had lived near Bard after graduation until he too moved to the city; Gil too before he moved away.

That spring, Render went to visit his mother's family in Albuquerque. While there, he rented a motorcycle to take on a pleasure ride through the landscape. "You should remember that it's peace of mind you're after and not just a fixed machine," writes Robert Pirsig in *Zen and the Art of Motorcycle Maintenance*.

Render moved to the city in the latter part of 2014. For the first six months, he lived with his parents' friends in upper Manhattan. He and Sofia got back together and would stay together until May 2016. He got a job at Atelier 4. He posted on the /r/guns Reddit board, commenting in response to the question "What are some of the best weapons, that are rarely represented in media such as movies or video games?"

Render answered, "H&K P7. You'd think it'd be in more spy films," referring to the Heckler & Koch P7 semiautomatic pistol.

In October, he posted about shooting his friend's rifles in upstate New York, to test the zeros.

The day after Christmas 2014, he commented on a video with the title "The largest rifle, the .950 JDJ, being fired. It kicks like a mule!"

"Doesn't look very fun to shoot!" Render said. "More likely just the end result of gunsmiths who wanted a real engineering challenge, for whatever reason. Or a customer request. In any case, it is a collectible, in some sense, if only for bragging rights." He adds, "But I doubt it sees the range often."

Soon after, he moved in with Carolyn.

• • •

Render was thinking about his career when he moved to the city. He responded to an /r/AskReddit post that asked, "What career path did you choose that you strongly advise against?" One user remarked on their surprise at the lack of what they called "base jobs" in users' responses, giving as examples electricians, plumbers, and welders. "Carpentry is a better example," Render said, having worked as a carpenter himself.

By some accounts, Render enjoyed his work at Atelier 4 as an art handler, packing and crating artwork for shipping. "He informed me he was having a good time in NYC framing artwork and was just looking for the next step in terms of his career," writes Arun in his support letter, confusing packing with framing.

However, it's also entirely possible he'd had grander ambitions for himself. "The best artist in Rhinebeck High School possibly," a village local tells me. Their child went to the school and they sometimes worked there. "He was a good artist; I'm not going to take that away from him. But here you are in the city with a million people that are great artists. What are you doing? You're building packing crates. Certainly, it wasn't what he thought he was going to be doing."

He was forging friendships at work though. His coworker at Atelier 4 Patrick Mangan writes in his letter of support, "We worked side by side for over a year in many high stress, time sensitive situations." They bonded over "an appreciation of the works of David Foster Wallace" and a "love of cinema." He and his wife had Render over to their apartment for movie nights and barbecues, where "he got along great with all our friends." He would always show up with food, drinks, or a new movie to watch.

Render and Finn also grew closer after he moved to the city, and they began collaborating. "He continued to make artwork in a number of ways, usually working on multiple commissions at once," writes Finn in his own letter. Render talked to others on / r / Art and / r / Photoshop and / r / Posters and / r / Illustration and / r / PenmanshipPorn about materials and technique and favorite artists.

Sofia was also artistically focused. In 2013, she had been hired as the Creative Marketing Producer at A24 Films, and she was also the associate director of the Marcie Bloom Fellowship in Film, of which she had been a recent recipient. She was working on the script for her own first film, *Blackout*, inspired by her experience teaching for the Bard Prison Initiative. It would premiere just before Render went to trial. One of Render's commissions that first year he lived in the city was a poster for an independent film called *After the Hurricane*, which she coproduced.

Sofia co-owned her Manhattan apartment with her parents. She was their only child and, one can assume, received their full love, support, and attention, not to mention their influential connections. Her father is an Italian curator and writer, and her mother is an American subculture photographer and filmmaker.

Render got on well with Sofia's family, as did she with his. "Even after they separated he was very caring and they remained in touch as friends," Sofia's mother would write of Render, in her letter of support. Render's mother and aunts continued to comment on Sofia's Facebook photos even after they broke up again.

• • •

In February after moving to the city, Render waded into a Reddit argument beneath a nearly eleven-minute car rant titled "White Privilege Is Dead." Its creator is a Black Republican political hopeful from Alabama, Derrick Grayson. The major talking points of his handful of campaigns all featured in the video, including: America doesn't have a race problem anymore, but we've always had a class problem; the only reason people care about police brutality is because it affects white people as much as Black people; when Black people are brutalized by police, it's because they aren't raised right; he has never personally experienced police brutality because he acts respectful; gun laws are being used to keep firearms out of the hands of white people because they're the ones with something to be mad about; white people are also being denied body armor. Wonder why? Local police forces are being militarized because the US government knows white people are pissed and might take up arms and riot at any moment.

It was on this last point that Render piped up. Another user had commented, disagreeing with Grayson: "Militarization of the police is to prepare for unruly white people who will riot because they can't find jobs?" said the Redditor. "The military-grade equipment is being primarily used for drug raids/arrests, and black people are disproportionately more likely to go to jail for drugs, despite usage rates being the same compared to white people."

Render countered, "The War on Drugs has been the key rationale behind revamping the police force in the United States, but you're kidding yourself if you believe that's what our leaders are truly worried about. Yes, they're putting on a good show, and it's not difficult—systematic impoverishment will always lead to a meteoric rise in drug use among the population in question. But small-time dealers and misdemeanor possession cases in completely disenfranchised, cloistered communities are not posing a threat to national security. The War on Drugs is an excuse for preemptive militarization in anticipation of an effective insurrection."

"Absolutely," said the first user, "the actual rationale behind police militarization has truly nothing to do with the War on Drugs. That does not mean that it is anticipation of an effective insurrection of *angry white people*, as the guy in the video suggests."

.   .   .

In the fall of 2015, Danny Shanahan underwent his "life-threatening aortic dissection, requiring nearly a dozen hours of emergency open-heart surgery," as he writes in his letter of support. According to Mark Lytle, he and Janet had decided to separate before his heart attack and were already planning to sell Render's childhood home. Then they postponed putting it on the market so Danny could heal. "Render traveled home from the city many, many times," to take on the labor of preparing the house for sale, writes Danny. Previously it hadn't been unusual for Render to visit home on weekends, and of course on all holidays, but this was with a new frequency.

Still, Mark doesn't think Render's parents' separation was a stressor for him. "I don't think that there was anything contested," he says. Danny and Janet remained friends. "It happens to couples. They lose the glue."

"They were very close still," Danny's brother-in-law says. "I think they were just going separate ways, going down different paths in life." It was a quiet parting; he wasn't even aware of the separation himself until someone outside the immediate family told him about it.

Render's friend Sean Rucewicz writes in his letter to the court that Render focused on "keeping a calm demeanor for his mother and brother" after his father's surgery. In other words, he buried his feelings about it.

31.

A Place to Call Home

In January 2015, Mali moved out of 1861 Stanhope as planned. Carolyn moved into Mali's old bedroom. It was smaller but adjacent to the unit's common areas; the one that would become Render's was bigger and had the adjacent hallway nook. While Carolyn didn't want to Airbnb out the second bedroom full-time, she began doing so to fill the gap in rent between Mali moving out and Render moving in. Once he did, she continued booking guests, renting out her own bedroom instead. "I think that was a big source of income for her," says Rachel.

Ann was the trustee of her mother's estate and controlled the money Carolyn had inherited from her grandmother. "You know how often kids call home needing money," says Ann. "That's how often she called me." Ann viewed this as normal young adult timing. "I knew that Render was occasionally late giving her the rent. She'd grouse about that. Then again, that could have been, 'I need a little extra money this month.' I wouldn't swear that I knew his name until later."

In addition to needing the stable income from a roommate, Carolyn might have wanted Render around because she felt safer with him there. The first time I talked to Jim on the phone, he said, "The comment I heard was that she perceived him as a protector. I think that Carrie had an issue with somebody at Bard, who was maybe stalking her." Most likely he's referring to Isaac, though his connection to Bard is unclear.

. . .

When subletting her room to Airbnb guests, Carolyn would occasionally sleep on the couch at Wendy's Subway. "Sometimes for days," says Kevin. By his count, ten if not twenty times, admitting that there may be occasions he didn't know about—and that he may be exaggerating. "She needed the money," he says, from Airbnb. Carolyn may also have stayed to read or write when she was in a groove, instead of commuting home. Other people did it, too, on occasion.

Rachel doesn't remember Carolyn sleeping at Wendy's after they moved into the new location in Bushwick, in January 2016. "Never overnight," she says. "Definitely not. No, she stayed at Matt's a couple of times or stayed at my house."

She also stayed at Kevin's and would show up unannounced at Pamela's saying, "I Airbnb'ed my apartment, hope my roommate doesn't hate me."

"She wasn't a landlord, but she was kind of treating it like her business," says Rachel. "There was a degree to which that was her space, and he was just a roommate."

Macgregor knew that Carolyn's Airbnb was a source of conflict between her and Render. "My roommate is crazy," Carolyn would say to him.

"But you hear that from people," he says. "This is not what any of us thought she meant." He remembers her saying that the Airbnb pissed Render off and that they had "ordinary roommate spats" about it. "I don't know if they were ordinary," he says, "but that's how they were described."

Finally, she negotiated taking back the hallway nook from Render, and she put a bed in it, so she wouldn't have to crash with friends or at Wendy's. Render would be paying fifty dollars less, per month, because of this. "I remember her telling me that he had agreed to that arrangement, and she was happy," says Pamela. "It was a relief not to feel like, when she Airbnb'ed, she would be homeless."

Within a month of Render moving in, Carolyn began a course on Shakespeare's *Hamlet* at The New School, with critic and philosopher Simon Critchley. She would also take a class on mysticism with him. "She was immensely likable and had an acute, oblique, and intense intelligence," Critchley says of Carolyn. William James's *The Varieties of Religious Experience*, a book she had first inherited from Callie and read in high school, was a required text for the mysticism class. So was Anne Carson's *Decreation*; several books on Julian of Norwich, Marguerite Porete, Teresa of Ávila, and other medieval female mystics; and selections from Bataille, Cioran, Lacan, Weil, and other contemporaries.

"She was so obsessed with medieval mystics," says Lizzy. "I mean, that has to be the reason she was learning Latin, right?" In her free time, what little of it there was, Carolyn was intently studying the language and had even asked Ann for the funds to take an online class.

"It hadn't occurred to me that I didn't have paperwork from The New School," says Ann. "That must have been when Carrie, unbeknownst to any of the family, turned to student loans."

. . .

Wendy's Subway was a landing pad and sanctuary for Carolyn during this time. She had a chosen family there, a quiet place to do homework, and a dedicated place to turn over ideas with others writing poetry and criticism and pushing into their own relationships with spirituality. "tuesday night work totem," she posted on Instagram, beneath a photo of a vase of white roses, sitting atop the Justice tarot card, on the communal table at Wendy's. A stack of journals sits beside it, and in the background is the bottom of a bookshelf.

"We went through a lot together as a group," says Macgregor. "We became very close and spent many a day and night mostly talking and reading, anything and everything. Talking about our jobs, her talking about school, relationships. Those friendships with the five or six of us that started the place were intense really quick, more than other adult friendships. It was like being in school when you're young. We knew everything about each other."

Then in March, Isaac walked into Wendy's. He had emailed Carolyn the previous afternoon. The entire contents of the email read, "they have taken the cell phone number. the phone is no longer in use. sent: empty." Carolyn was there with a handful of other members when he appeared. Macgregor and Gabe threw him out immediately. Afterward, Macgregor helped Carolyn look into a restraining order. She forwarded him a handful of Isaac's emails, which he shared with the other witnesses, asking them to share what they'd seen with other members who hadn't been present. He attached a photo of Isaac, saying his hair was longer now, and noting that Carolyn seemed "remarkably unfazed."

"I remember Carrie would flippantly say, 'Oh, that's my stalker,' and not give me any more information," says Pamela. "It was someone who would communicate with her often, and she said to me, 'Oh, he's harmless.' I remember being like, 'I don't think that you should be so flippant about this. Don't underestimate somebody's crazy. Why would you call somebody a stalker if you felt like they were harmless?'"

• • •

That April, Jenny emailed her wedding party—the date was suddenly less than four months away. "You guys!" she wrote. "I just love you so much. Thanks for putting out for me. I'd be freaking out except I'm focusing on how much fun we're going to have. Also, if you ever want me to wear a purple burlap bag at your wedding I totally will."

In the replies, Carolyn and Pamela planned a New York dress-shopping date for the week after next. Their color directive was "steel." "I'm down with whatever you guys pick as far as shapes," Jenny had written them. "It'll be August, so no one will wear stockings, and should you have 666 tattooed on the back of your leg (Ashley!) we'll just tell my elderly Southern aunty that you're the actual devil."

. . .

In June, Adjua celebrated her birthday and two friends hosted the party at their apartment in Sunset Park. It was a spacious two-bedroom on the second floor of a brownstone. Adjua calls the occasion "a beautiful rager house party."

"It was the very beginning of summer, one of those perfect evenings," says Rachel Hurn, who had been a fellow bookseller and my cohost of the Essays Book Club at McNally Jackson Books, and like Carolyn, Adjua, Kevin, and me, had since left the store for other ventures. "There was a lot of beer, and they had a little outdoor balcony. People were hanging out there and smoking."

"At some point, Carolyn came through the crowd," says Adjua. "My memory is all of a sudden, she's coming through the crowd and with her elegant, hectic energy was like . . ."

"I was on my way here trying to find a present for you!"

Carolyn told Adjua the saga of her voyage to the party, which had entailed stopping at four different bodegas along the way to find "a yellow, tall glass candle, like Afro-Caribbean. She needed to get a yellow one for me; for some reason that made sense for both of us."

Rachel Hurn was "kind of in this funny place" at the party, as she and her husband, whom she was still just dating at the time, had recently taken a moment to stop and think, *Do we really want to continue this relationship to the point of marriage?* "I remember being at that party and thinking, *This is what it's like to feel single again*, even though I wasn't," she says. Rachel was just about to leave when she saw Carolyn. They had been friends at the bookstore and hadn't seen each other since leaving it.

When Carolyn was first hired, "There was something about her that I distinctly remember was a little edgy," says Rachel. "The way you would think of a classic 'bad boy' or 'bad girl.' That was part of her attraction. There was this special energy I felt around her, and I quickly developed a crush on her. To be honest, I felt like there was some energy between us, like she even had a crush on me too."

Now at Adjua's birthday party, surrounded by people, music blaring, cigarettes turning the air milky, Carolyn hugged her. "I just looked over and I saw this tall pretty girl and I thought, who is that?" she said to Rachel. "And then I realized it was Rachel Hurn."

"Part of me thought, as I was leaving," says Rachel, "because of where I was in my relationship, *If I were single and I stayed at this party, and we got drunk, would something happen with her?*"

• • •

That July, Isaac emailed Carolyn for the first time since being kicked out of Wendy's Subway. His message to her was characteristically cryptic. "ur going to explain what has occurred (optional)," he wrote. Below that was a message that he'd initially written to a Rhinebeck Village Court judge, asking for his restraining order in the town to be lifted because "I think that I have no physically violent intentions toward anyone [in the long run] and never have" (brackets his). He had been evicted from his transitional housing facility, "But I continue to hope that we can all be friends."

Carolyn forwarded the email to Macgregor. She said this was the first time Isaac had contacted her since showing up at Wendy's. She said no action was necessary but that it made her feel better for someone else to have the email, "just in case, whatever that means . . ."

• • •

Later that month, she traveled to Hudson for an extended visit. She wrote to Paula, "I just want to spend some time out of the city to focus on my work and get some perspective before returning to school. I have a few friends up there one in particular who is a good influence on me and has a fantastic book collection and money and travel prospects who I'd like to maybe double with someday." This was likely Tommi, who was living in Hudson at the time.

"She was in love with him," says Kevin of Tommi. Though, "I don't think she'd ever say it quite like that."

She had recently shared some poems with Tommi, to publish in an issue of a literary journal he was curating, and they'd been corresponding about editing them. Before going to Hudson, Carolyn messaged Cameron, who by coincidence was also going to be staying with Tommi while she was in town. "I'm leaving for Hudson tomorrow evening, can't wait to see you Cammielamb!" she wrote him.

"She took a suitcase full of books," says Pamela. "As I think back on it now, that's a bit showy. Maybe she really needed them all for her research, but also maybe she was bringing them to present a certain intellectual . . . situation."

Carolyn posted an Instagram picture from the trip showing Tommi, Cameron, and another Bard friend seated around a circular table. Between them is an ashtray and two half-smoked cigarettes. It's nighttime and the charming white-painted porch in the background is lit by string lights, which spiral around a small evergreen.

"We went to a bar in Catskill," says Cameron. "It was sort of a bar-and-billiards place that was pirate themed."

"Carolyn, aren't you so sick of New York?" Cameron asked.

"No, I love living in New York," she told him. "I just wanted to get away for the summer." She said that she liked her roommate.

"I wanted as much time with her as I could have," says Cameron. He didn't know it then, but it would be the last time he saw her.

"She spent a week or so in a rented room in Catskill," says Tommi of her visit. "She was desirous of finding some new surroundings that would energize her writing." Like Cameron, Carolyn didn't have a car, so Tommi drove her around.

"They had a total falling out," says Kevin.

"Carolyn and I did get into an argument when she was in Catskill," says Tommi. "I recall driving her around and her saying something demeaning to me."

"I knew that she liked him a lot," says Pamela. "I know that in her apartment there was some postcard from him that seemed like an inside joke between the two of them. I didn't know if there was any actual romantic contact."

"Carolyn was always telling friends about romantic relationships she wanted to pursue," says Tommi. "That kind of openness was a charming quality of hers. I don't think she was particularly in love with me."

"She went up there without plans," says Rachel Valinsky. "She was like, 'I'm going to stay up here, and this person is going to be my person.' And then that didn't work. So she was floating around a lot." Her plan was likely to stay with Tommi for part of her time there, but ultimately she didn't. "It was a summer that Matt was the acting director for Language & Thinking," says Rachel—because Thomas Bartscherer had resigned as director. "So he had a house up there. She stayed with Matt for a week or a couple weeks."

. . .

Then in August 2015, Carolyn flew to Portland to be Jenny's maid of honor. On the day of the ceremony, "They were going to do the photos and then the wedding," says Carolyn's aunt Robin. "Susan came late, and the photographer was packing up to go. Then she had to get somebody to help her with her hair."

"My favorite experience in the world was listening to my two girls talking," says Susan, of taking the family photos. "Mike and I said that often we couldn't even tell which voice was whose."

They did the photos with Susan, and then Carolyn and Robin went into the hall to greet people.

Pamela woke up at Jenny and Mike's house with Carolyn, the morning after. "I remember Carolyn climbing into my bed, into Jenny's bed, when Jenny was at her honeymoon suite," she says. "She really wanted Chinese food and was desperately thinking someone was going to give her Chinese food. We were in suburban Portland."

"It's not going to happen, babe," Pamela told her. "We're not in New York anymore."

"She even called some places," she says. "Then I got up and made us burritos."

• • •

Carolyn had three part-time semesters left at The New School and had planned to apply for PhD programs in the spring. "Truly don't know if she actually applied, somewhat doubt it," says Ann. Carolyn had emailed Ann a week before the wedding asking for the last of her tuition money in a lump sum, saying she didn't anticipate having to ask for it ever again. She'd be working, and had a sizable drop in tuition, so she could "reasonably assume" she would be "self-sufficient (-ish), by October."

"Getting her through school was a little difficult," says Ann. "Her problems seemed to center around perfectionism and not finishing courses." Carolyn would call Ann once a month or so and they'd talk for thirty or forty minutes before she would get around to asking for money. "It would take a whole lot of pressure for her to admit how many incompletes, and 'she was going to finish this, and she was going to finish that,' and we talked a lot about accepting that 'it's not going to be absolutely perfect, just get it in on time.'"

She was writing a lot but didn't share much of her work. "I never got to read her papers except for one that she workshopped with me," says Rachel. "She didn't really talk about what she was doing. She was really wrapped up in it, so you'd come in and she'd be deep in thought. She'd lift her head but had been there for hours."

"All of it was imbued with philosophy," says Pamela. "I felt like, if she were to do a doctorate, it would be in something that was very focused on a philosophy-informed understanding of creative writing."

• • •

"Right before I saw her the last time, I'd been trying to get in touch with her for a long time and she wasn't getting back to me," says Paula, whom Carolyn had kept in touch with all these years, thanks to Facebook. "This is when I bitched her out."

"I'm going to be in your neighborhood and that sucks," Paula wrote. "I guess it's really pointless to try and keep in touch."

Finally, Carolyn wrote back, "I'm sorry, babe. I've had a terrible week. When are you in town? Saturday?"

Paula said Sunday. "What's wrong with your week?" she asked. "Say whatever."

"She was talking about anxiety and her period," says Paula. "I guess she was having a really hard time with anxiety."

"I don't have a ton of time, but I'd love to catch up, long lunch or something," Carolyn wrote her. "I won't be able to drink because I'll be hitting the library soon after."

Paula invited her to a Morbid Anatomy flea market she planned to hit up that weekend, in Brooklyn.

"I can't," Carolyn told her. "I'm living off student loans." Instead of going to the market, they met for lunch. Paula told her she was also living on loans. It was their last visit.

• • •

Carolyn turned twenty-five in November and emailed her friends that they would find her at the "dreamy blue Reclamation Bar" where she would be "drinking slowly, reclaiming something, celebrating having made it a quarter-century!"

Wendy's was growing up, too, and would be moving out of its original location soon. "The owner of the building had the last paraffin-umbrella factory in North America and was ninety years old and still going into work every day, on the ground floor," says Macgregor. "He hadn't changed the rents in decades and just loved that artists were there. We knew signing the lease that his family wanted him to sell the space because it was quite valuable at that point."

"That was a moment of, 'Should we fold?'" says Matt. "Carolyn and Rachel were like, 'Nope, let's find a new place.'"

In December, Wendy's hosted one of the last events in the original space, a reading and discussion by Katy Bohinc, Rachel M. Wilson, and Jamieson Webster. The event was part of a series of lectures called "How to Live Together." The description said it was "exploring solitude and the degree of contact necessary for individuals to exist and create at their own pace."

"We had developed something similar at Wendy's, thinking about community and collectivity and care, that had a lot of overlap," says Rachel. "So, we started. Eventually I got the reading list that they were working with. The way it was structured was that different organizations would host a discussion around one book." Wendy's Subway began their reading with Roland Barthes's book *How to Live Together*.

32.

The Most Horrible Thing

You Can Do to Someone

Render's initial parole interview takes place in May 2021. He agrees to it even though he has an appeal pending. In the heavily redacted transcript, he says that he finds drawing and reading very relaxing. He has included several drawings in his packet for the parole commissioners. One of them mentions several letters of support sent on his behalf in advance of his hearing. Names have been redacted. Render says he has a job lined up at a publishing company, upon his release, where he will be doing copyediting and proofreading.

"I was feeling I needed to do horrible things," Render says in response to a series of questions about what transpired in the moments before he killed Carolyn. "There was a person standing in front of me, I had a knife in my hand, and it was almost, you know—this constitutes the most horrible thing you can do to someone."

He appeals his parole denial on the grounds that "the Board failed to consider other factors such as the appellant's institutional accomplishments, programming and lack of disciplinary history," and because "the Board denied release based solely on the seriousness of the offense." His appeal is denied.

• • •

Over the six years of researching and writing this book, I send Render several letters. I finally receive a response in December 2021. In it, he compliments my writing and my taste, tells me I won't be hearing back from his brother, and asks that I not reach out to his mother.

He tells me he must respectfully decline my invitation to speak, because he has already been in touch with a "writer/editor," and it wouldn't be "fair" if he also spoke to me. He claims he has never met this other writer before, and she has never met Carolyn, and that therefore he feels she can be more "objective."

I write back saying that I know he's lying. I tell Render that it was my understanding the writer had met him several times at Bard. I say that the writer had met Carolyn there too. I don't tell him how I know this.

I don't say that I also know she is a Bard graduate in the same year as his brother, whose parents donate money to the school, and whose mother is close friends with a high-up administrator. I only say that, in so many words, he and I should drop any charade of objectivity, since we're both personally invested in this subject. He never responds.

. . .

In September 2022, Render appears in a *Times Union* article about how incarcerated individuals in New York State can now only receive packages from a list of Department of Corrections–approved vendors. The *Union* writes, Render's "mother can no longer bring him care packages during a visit or through the mail." The packages, writes the paper, "felt personalized and often included handwritten notes."

Render tells the paper, "She made the packages lovingly, always trying to add something different and surprising."

This new rule will also negatively impact Render's ability to access certain foods. "Having had the opportunity to browse several of the vendors' catalogs, there is not much offered in the way of health food, organic products, that sort of thing," says Render. "These were the sort of foodstuffs I most looked forward to in packages."

. . .

Render's second opportunity for parole is in May 2023, the month *Stranger Love* premieres for one night only at the Los Angeles Philharmonic and the same month that the *Wall Street Journal* reports on Leon's meetings with Jeffrey Epstein. When the parole board asks Render why he appealed his last denial, he states that he did not know he had filed an appeal.

In the transcript of the hearing, it is clear he has gotten better at telling the story of what happened. His delivery is smoother, details more deliberate than at his first hearing two years earlier. He says, "It was when I was in this Uber, heading back to my apartment, that I started to feel like something was wrong. I started to feel panicky, and I started to feel very anxious, and it felt like a panic attack was coming on.

"By the time I reached my apartment," he says, "it had gotten worse, and I remember going upstairs into my bedroom and starting to get undressed, and telling myself that I was just having a really bad panic attack." He says he thought he needed to sleep it off. There was a "physical discomfort associated with it," he says. "I couldn't sit still." He paced around his apartment.

He continues, "I would say that within ten to fifteen minutes, it sort of reached a point where it no longer felt so much like a panic attack, as it felt like I was most certainly going to die, and there was nothing that I could do to stop that from happening. I remember kind of laying down in bed and closing my eyes, and when I next opened them, I was certain that I was dead. I was certain that somewhere along the line, I had died, and at some point, I had transitioned into some sort of afterlife.

"At this point, I started to become—I suppose my behavior started to become very erratic, and you know, aggressive," he says. "I remember pacing around my room, knocking things over, and you know, at a certain point—I had a knife in my room, and at a certain point, I went to get it, and I remember holding the knife in my hand and looking down at my leg." Render says that he doesn't know why he stabbed himself in the leg, but he speculates it was because he wanted to snap himself out of it, whatever "it" was.

"I remember making a hole in the drywall," he says. He says he went into the kitchen with the knife and broke a blender sitting on the counter. "I believe, during this time, I was saying names, including my roommate's name. I may have also said my brother's name, because I had recently been with him, and then afterwards, texting with him."

Render says he didn't know if Carolyn was home, but she was. He does not tell the board that he had asked Carolyn how to use his phone. He does not mention the contemporaneous conversations with Sofia. "I remember going up to her door," he says of Carolyn. "I remember her opening the door, and I remember her saying 'No.' I just remember sort of lunging forward and stabbing her, almost as if I was watching myself do it. I think, at some point during this, I closed my eyes, because this part of the experience, I remember it happening, but I don't clearly remember what I saw, per the visual."

Render finishes the story, ending when police arrive.

Commissioner Davis thanks Render for sharing what happened from his perspective. "I just want to take a moment and honor the victim," he says. "Because it is quite interesting. You used a number of pronouns to describe your victim, and also label her as the roommate, but you didn't care to address her by her name. What is her name?"

Render's response is redacted.

"We speak her name today," says the commissioner.

"So when you describe that you weren't a big user of marijuana, what do you mean by that?" asks the commissioner.

"I didn't really smoke it more than once or twice a year on any given year since the first time I ever tried it, sir," says Render.

"Okay," says the commissioner. "And just to be clear, you smoked it the night of the instant offense with your brother and his friends because of what?"

"It had been a while since I tried smoking," says Render, "and you know, the last time—or the time before that, when I used it, you know, I had a pleasant experience." This seems different from what Bardey testified, which was that Render told him he'd not smoked weed since a bad experience in December 2015—which, if his last time was the night of the murder, would have been the time before the last time. Then again, Render may be misspeaking; perhaps he means the time-before-the-time-before-the-last-time; the antepenultimate one. "I was with my brother and in a good mood," he says. "It just felt like something that might be fun."

Commissioner Drake asks him if he remembers why he called his brother later that night.

"I—you know, to be honest, I remember wanting to talk to him," says Render. "I remember reaching out to him to say, 'Okay, I'm back at the house, I'm going to bed.' It is a thing in my family we do. When we get back somewhere, 'I got home safely.' A lot of people do this." Finn said something different, under oath. He said it was "extremely out of the normal" for people in his family to call each other late at night. Render does not tell the board that he later told his brother he wasn't going to have a lease anymore.

"And at a certain point," says Render, "I think that it was, you know, that evening, I had been texting with my girlfriend and I had been texting things that were maybe a little unusual because I was intoxicated, and she began to text with my brother." This is the first time in the hearing that he mentions his ongoing conversation with Sofia. "She had texted my brother concerned about, you know, 'What is going on with Render, he seems a little out of it.' My brother told her we used marijuana, and so, I remember, at that point—and what I'm talking about is the point back at my apartment—you know, getting texts from both him and her, and just trying to say to both of them, 'Everything is okay, I'm back at my apartment,' and scared of telling them the truth, which was that I was getting sort of more and more panicked, and more and more freaked out, trying to calm myself down. And at the point where, you know, I suppose it sort of slid into a psychosis, it was beyond—as far as intentions go, as far as me reaching out to them, it goes sort of beyond the logical reason I can give you."

"I have a question," says Commissioner Segarra. "I don't know if it is a question, really. You said you went from a panic attack to a psychosis?"

"I went from a panic attack to a psychosis," he says.

"So you went from a panic attack to psychosis. So I guess I don't know if this is really a question, trust me, I'm going to find the answer—"

"Yes, ma'am."

"—because for someone who went from a panic attack to a psychosis," she says, "your details and recollection before, drawing an accurate picture of this horrific offense, doesn't really jibe for me. I am going to find the answer."

"Yes, ma'am," he says. "You are saying that you think it should be more?"

"No, I didn't say I thought anything," she says. "That whole—I speculate how well your memory is for someone who was having a panic attack to a psychosis, because I have known people to have both, as well—maybe not at the same time, and definitely not going from one to another—that can't remember the color of the shirt that they wore."

"Yes, ma'am."

"And you remember things in detail, and that has taken me aback, man."

"I understand."

"So, that I'm just going to—maybe you think—but you got me thinking. It is nothing to smile about."

"No, I mean, I can—"

"No. No, I saw you smile. I am telling you, it's nothing to smile about."

"I was going to say, I can relate, you know. At first I thought—"

"No. No. No, I'm not asking you for anything. I just made a statement."

"Yes, ma'am."

Commissioner Segarra asks Render what was behind his smile.

"I sort of saw that you were maybe unsure about how a psychosis can manifest in myself."

"No," she says. "No, I think you were being smug about it."

"Definitely not," he says.

"I think you were," she says. "I study body language, sir."

"You are surrounded by enablers who buffer you from your negative experience related to this behavior," says Commissioner Davis. "When you look at your attachment with your family and friends, you look at who shows up in your life as your enabler."

His parole is denied.

33.

How to Live Together

Carolyn emailed Pamela the day after Christmas 2015 about a job listing she'd seen for a provenance documentarian. She signed off in all-caps about her need for money, asking Pamela to keep her "ears peeled."

"She often worked as a waitress," says Pamela. "I think it was for a chicken place under the BQE. She always had multiple different side hustles, and at some point, I remember she got fired from a restaurant job. She didn't like the people there, she didn't like the situation, but she always needed money."

Carolyn was also, as always, taking classes, formal and informal. "SEX-ED is centered on the means by which we give and receive pleasure and the ways in which we understand intimacy," a description of one read. She also signed up for a six-week workshop being taught by poet and prose artist Rachel Levitsky at The Poetry Project, called Prose! Prose! It met once a week for five sessions at a café in the East Village, starting in March 2016. "We'll all come up with our own mongrel formal interventions, then sing them to each other with the help of each other," said the description.

There was a designated notetaker in each class, and the notes became a collaborative text. "In the warm room, seated seminar style around the table, each student took a turn reading a sentence or two, or three, of their own writing," wrote the first notetaker in her emailed report to everyone afterward. The second notetaker tried to transcribe what was said but didn't know everyone's names yet. Rachel, the teacher, suspects the dialogue labeled "Name," in the document sent afterward, is Carolyn's.

"Name: I fetishize the sentence as a perfect way of relating. Primal scene. Language is more related to grammar. Than to a series of sign. I guess my body is language would be absent. A lot of prepositions and not a lot of subjects."

"Name: question of the body. The assumption behind is that there is a mind/ body difference. My problem with prose. It re-affirms the difference."

Before the fourth Prose! Prose! session, Carolyn emailed Rachel that she would be missing that night's class because of "general life precarity." The following week, she would miss it again, as she would be in Los Angeles with Wendy's Subway for AWP, an annual literary conference. She thanked her for the class.

Alongside AWP in 2016, Wendy's Subway was partnering with Los Angeles Contemporary Archive (LACA) to present workshops and readings. Carolyn, Rachel, Matt and his seven-year-old daughter (Malka), Gabe, Macgregor, and Kevin all went. "We had an Airbnb in Silver Lake," says Rachel. "Carolyn and Gabe stayed in the guesthouse."

"It was some actress's Airbnb with her daughter," says Matt. "It was very LA. She had a poster of the one movie she was in that had probably bought the house. It had a kid room. Malka stayed in the kid room."

They spent their days at LACA. "She liked the reading rooms," says Matt. "Thinking about the books, gathering the books, cataloging the books, displaying them. We set up a space that had chairs and tables and interesting books, and people would congregate. She and Gabe would go out every night and every day they'd wake up later. I had Malka, so I was pissed off that they were having fun."

"We had readings every night and a couple of workshops," says Gabe. Wendy's hosted one of them. "We were calling it 'Speedback' instead of feedback, and so, quick impressions on a piece," he says.

"I think she talked to me and Matt on that one," says Rachel. "I remember telling her that there was something about the speed of her writing that was interesting. There's a kind of attunement to rhythm in walking, or in language, or in setting out a space for emotion within the poem. It was very kinetic in that sense—in the poem, she was walking."

Macgregor flew back to New York before the others, and Carolyn and Gabe went to stay at Mac's parents' house in the Pacific Palisades for a few days. There Carolyn passed time in their garden. "It's a beautiful garden," says Macgregor. "There with her own thoughts, reading and writing."

Carolyn and Gabe also connected with some old friends, including Carolyn's friend from Bard, Masha Mitkov. "She was telling me she had the best living situation she'd ever had, roommate-wise," says Masha.

The group went to the marina, where "She went down to the beach and dipped her feet in one last time," says Gabe.

. . .

The folks from Wendy's Subway flew back east, but Carolyn stayed on in California for a few days with her aunt Robin. "We did a lot of talking then," says Robin. "She was at The New School finishing her degree, and talking about waitressing, and really teaching me what the reading room was. It was as if all these parts of who she was had been incubating and then, *boom*, it was all there right in front of me."

"We talked about her, what she was doing and why," says Robin. Carolyn told her she planned on eventually teaching, and that's why she was planning to go back to school to get her PhD. "She framed getting her doctorate as being sort of cowardly and not just 'being a poet,'" says Robin. "I didn't think that was fair. We all know of great poets who are teaching.

"I found her poetry to be really heady," she says. "I like Sharon Olds. I like people who are more about physical sensations and experiences. But I wanted to read more."

Carolyn talked about Render too. "She said he was great because he never missed his rent," says Robin. "On that level, she loved him. She said that he was hardly ever there because he was working or working out. He had his own entrance, the good bedroom. She had the dinky kitchen, the dinky bedroom, and the dinky living room, but she loved all of that because she could spread out and feel homey and leave stuff out and work on stuff."

• • •

Back in New York, it was springtime 2016. "There was some reason why she was staying in my apartment, and I wasn't there," says Pamela. "I had this habit of keeping a white chocolate cookies-and-cream bar, a bottle of vodka, and a pack of emergency cigarettes in my freezer. If you opened my freezer, that's the only thing you would have seen. Then one night I went to go find my candy bar, and it was gone."

"I texted her," she says, "because I knew that she had been in the apartment. I would have thought she'd tell me about it, but maybe she thought I wouldn't notice. I was like, 'Did you eat my candy bar?' She just wrote back a bunch of emojis and was like, 'I have a problem.'

"I remember being kind of annoyed about it," says Pamela. "I did not want to walk to the bodega, and I'm an only child.

"Then I had a birthday, and that year I had a party at Shade Bar," she says. This would have been in April. "I wanted her to come, and I knew at this point in her life she lived at Bobst Library," which was just a few blocks away, part of NYU, near Washington Square Park. "I mean, she was there all the time. She had a very hard time focusing at home, so she'd literally spend days at the library. I remember walking with her to CVS to get a toothbrush, because she'd been at the library for over twenty-four hours. So I knew that it was very convenient for her to come over to Shade, and I texted her, 'Are you not coming to my birthday party?' I really wanted her to come and I was mad because she was telling me that she had a lot of studying to do. I must have said something bratty because she was like, 'Do you have a MacBook charger? I'll come if you don't mind me doing schoolwork in the corner.'"

Sometime later, "I came home, and on my kitchen table was a bottle of prosecco and a bag," says Pamela. "In that bag it was bath salts in a mason jar, with a handwritten note. There was a bag of lavender, some kind of tea, and then the same brand of chocolate bar that she had taken. And a pack of Camel Lights."

The note thanked Pamela from the bottom of Carolyn's "big weird heart," for her endlessly true and loyal friendship. She's glad Pamela was born, that she gets to be a part of her life, and that they can do cool stuff together, and give each other help and support. Two lines were scribbled out. "IT'S GOING TO BE A REALLY FUCKING WONDERFUL YEAR."

Acknowledgments

I owe enormous thanks to Carolyn's family and my own, especially my husband, Patrick Cottrell, who supports me every day. My unending gratitude also goes to Pamela Tinnen, Erin Wicks, Adriann Ranta Zurhellen, Kyla Jones, Rachel Hurn, Genevieve Walker, Lynn Rush, Teresa Carmody, John Reed, Ellen McGarrahan, Emma Copley Eisenberg, Tallulah Woitach, Michael Qualiano, Boemin Park, May Syeda, Ryan Rivas, Chelsea Simmons, Ted Conover, Daniel Connolly, Sarah Schulman, Lindsay Lerman, Elle Nash, Leza Cantoral, Lori Carter, Lauren Wolfe, and Rachel Valinsky and Wendy's Subway. I also want to thank the people of Folio Literary Management, Zando Projects, Ross Investigators PC, The Robison Group, Everything Knowable, Stetson University's MFA of the Americas, the Stetson University Archives, Lighthouse Writers Workshop, the Tuesday Agency, Lambda Literary, the Whiting Foundation, Ucross Foundation, Tin House, and Creative Pinellas, as well as everyone who appears in the book by name, those who are unnamed, and all those who helped with background, research, and writing.

Permissions

About the Author

SARAH GERARD is the author of the novels *Binary Star* and *True Love*; the essay collection *Sunshine State*, an NPR and *New York Times* Critics' Best Book of the Year and a finalist for Southern Book Prize, longlisted for the PEN/Diamonstein-Spielvogel Award for the Art of the Essay; a coauthored art book, *Recycle*; and the chapbook *The Butter House*. She's the recipient of a Creative Pinellas grant, and a winner of the 2021 Lambda Literary Jim Duggins Outstanding Mid-Career Novelists' Prize. Her writing has appeared in the *New York Times*, *Granta*, *Guernica*, *McSweeney's*, *BOMB* magazine, *Hazlitt*, the *Creative Independent*, and in several anthologies. She holds an MFA from The New School. She's a private investigator, and a graduate student in the criminal justice program at CU Denver, focusing on gender-based violence.